AF761711

Innovations in Agri-Business Management

NIPA® GENX ELECTRONIC RESOURCES & SOLUTIONS P. LTD.
New Delhi-110 034

www.nipaers.com
Browse, Search, Read & Buy...
Print Books
eChapters
eBooks
Publishers
Forthcoming
Subject Catalogues
New Titles
Online Resources on:
✓ Current Affairs
✓ Reasoning, Logic & Aptitude
✓ Competitive Examinations
✓ English Language Lab
✓ Writing & Pronunciation Tools
✓ Personality Development
✓ Online Programmes for Professionals
✓ Interview Preparation
Pay Using
PhonePe
Google Pay
paytm
PayPal
UPI
CC Avenue

Innovations in Agri-Business Management

Authors :

Karnam Lokanadhan, Professor & Head
Department of Market Extension

K. Mani, Professor
Department of Agricultural Economics

&

K. Mahendran, Associate Professor
Department of Agricultural and Rural Management
Centre for Agricultural and Rural Development Studies
Tamil Nadu Agricultural University
Coimbatore - 641 003, Tamil Nadu, India

NIPA® GENX ELECTRONIC RESOURCES & SOLUTIONS P. LTD.
New Delhi-110 034

**NIPA® GENX ELECTRONIC
RESOURCES & SOLUTIONS P. LTD.**

101,103, Vikas Surya Plaza, CU Block
L.S.C. Market, Pitam Pura, New Delhi-110 034
Ph : +91 11 27341616, 27341717, 27341718
E-mail: newindiapublishingagency@gmail.com
web: www.nipabooks.com

For customer assistance, please contact
Phone: + 91-11-27 34 17 17
Fax: + 91-11- 27 34 16 16
E-Mail: feedbacks@nipabooks.com

© 2023, Publisher

ISBN: 978-81-19215-63-8

All rights reserved. No part of this publication may be reproduced, stored in a retrieval system or transmitted in any form or by any means, including electronic, mechanical, photocopying recording or otherwise without the prior written permission of the publisher or the copyright holder.

This book contains information obtained from authentic and highly reliable sources. Reasonable efforts have been made to publish reliable data and information, but the author/s, editor/s and publisher cannot assume responsibility for the validity, accuracy or completeness of all materials or information published herein or the consequences of their use. The work is published with the understanding that the publisher and author/s are not attempting to render any professional services. The author/s, editor/s and publisher have attempted to trace and acknowledge the copyright holders of all material reproduced in this publication and apologize to copyright holders if permission and/or acknowledgements to publish in this form have not been taken. If any copyrighted material has not been acknowledged, please write to us and let us know so that we may rectify the error, in subsequent reprints.

Trademark Notice: NIPA®, the NIPA® logos and their presentations (the way they are written/presented) in this book are the trademarks of the publisher and hence may not be used without written permission, if copied or used without authorization, the infringer will be prosecuted as per law.

NIPA® also publishes books in a variety of electronic formats. Some content that appears in print may not be available in electronic books, and vice versa.

Composed and Designed by NIPA®.

Preface

The agribusiness management course has been initiated in Tamil Nadu Agricultural University a decade back for the first time in whole country. Now it has become an identified common course for UG programmes by ICAR Dean's Committee Report on syllabus revision. The agricultural graduates have vast avenues in agribusiness management due to sea change in post production activities. This book has been written in a simple and lucid manner to be understood by UG students even from rural background. The pedagogy involves key terms, chapter summary, chapter highlights, questions, references, websites and further reading materials. The first chapter exposes to the growth in the concept of agribusiness management and its future opportunities and challenges. An introduction is made in the first chapter on entrepreneurship, qualities and characteristics expected from an entrepreneur. In the second chapter, the entrepreneurship initiative programmes by central and state governments, classification of enterprises, their contribution to the national economy and various schemes and promotional programmes by Ministry of Small Scale Industries, Agro based and Rural Industries have been elaborated. From chapter 3 to chapter 12, exposure to management, planning, organizing, controlling directing, staffing, production, materials, marketing, personnel and financial management aspects is dealt with. In chapter 13, Management Information System and application of Information and Communication Technologies in agribusiness are explained. In Chapter 14, Government programmes and regulations to promote agribusiness are narrated. In chapter 15, the importance of agricultural inputs and agro processing are discussed. India's exports and imports of agricultural commodities and their contribution for agribusiness growth are exposed in chapter 16. The retailing and supply chain management are discussed with case studies in chapter 17. At the end of the book, chapter 18 deals with starting an agribusiness enterprise and business plan preparation for marketing the produce and obtaining institutional credit. This book will serve as a text book for agribusiness management course as well as a reference book for entrepreneurial development course. Also, the book will serve the students to prepare for MBA admissions in national institutes. The authors are responsible for errors and omissions. Suggestions for improvement are solicited for further improvement of the book.

Coimbatore
Date : 13.07.2009

Dr.K. Lokanadhan
Dr. K. Mani
Dr. K.Mahendran

Contents

Chapter 1

AGRI-BUSINESS

John H. Davis of Harvard University first used the term agribusiness in 1955. In 1980s it was given three connotations: (1) synonymous with term agriculture, (2) synonymous with agricultural economics and (3) a modified concept of agriculture, excluding farming, or the off-farm aspects of agriculture.

Agribusiness is defined as all business enterprises or sells to farmers/traders/consumers. The transaction may involve either an input or a produce or service and encompasses items such as:

- Productive resources (feed, seed, fertilizer, equipment, energy, pesticides, machinery, etc.)
- Agricultural commodities -(raw and processed commodities of food and fiber)
- Facilitative services (credit, insurance, marketing, storage, processing, transportation, packing, distribution, consultancy, soil testing etc.).

Global Changes in Agribusiness

During the past two decades, the agribusiness sector has undergone overwhelming changes that have affected every phase of the industry. Some of these changes are: the liberalisation of global market, changing technological and regulatory settings, international competition, organised marketing, modern processing and pickier consumer. Agriculture production also is changing from family based, small scale, relatively independent firms to larger firms that are more tightly designed across the production and distribution value chain. In addition to this, there has been a marked change in make-up of inputs used in agriculture, concentration and vertical integration and effective utilization of new production, processing, distribution, and information technologies. The input and production side of modern agriculture is described in Fig.1.1.

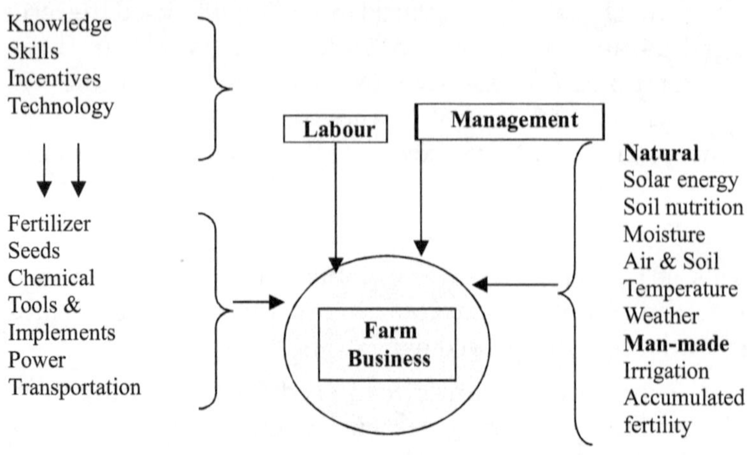

Fig.1.1 : Modern Farming: Changing Use of inputs

Agriculture has evolved into agribusiness and has become a vast and complex system that reaches far beyond the farm gate to include those who are involved in bringing food and fibre to consumers (Fig. 1.2).

Agribusiness includes not only those who farm the land but also the people and firms that provide inputs, process the outputs, manufacture the food products, and transport and sell the food products to consumers. Knowing something about how agribusinesses came about makes it easier to understand how this system operates today and how it is likely to change in the future. Producers, input suppliers, handlers, and processor will have to align with each others to establish an unbroken chain of quality from the generic base to the food table.

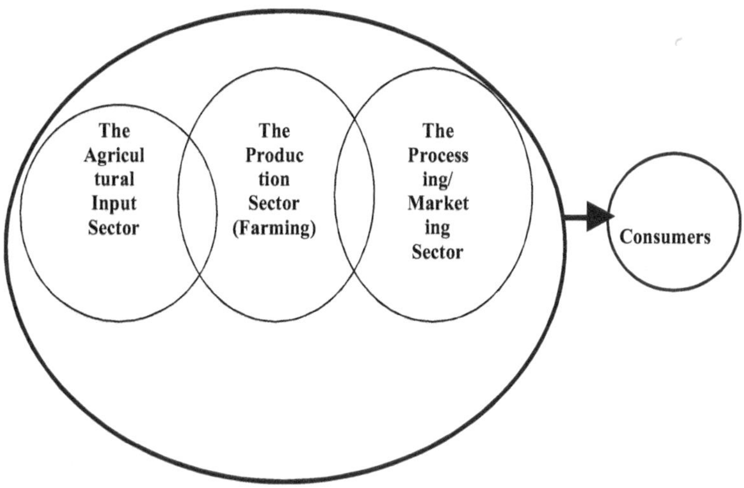

Fig. 1.2 : Agribusiness System

Agriculture undergraduates must be prepared for the management environment they will face in agribusinesses, including management of technology, team building in a contractually integrated food system, and decision making in an information-incentive field. Managers and employees will face unprecedented changes which will be threatening the very sustenance of farm sector. As new firms, new products, and new services emerge, old ones will pass away. Product differentiation and management intensity will demand new talents from agribusinesses.

Changing Environment of the Agribusiness Industry

- The environment/conditions under which the agribusiness industry must operate are changing both on domestic and international fronts.
- Consolidation, concentration, and integration of input supply and product processing sectors take place.
- Consolidation of farms and ranches that are increasingly industrialized with more sophisticated management.
- A new outlook and trend have set in all facets of the economy like
- Social /lifestyle/consumption pattern
- Business /management
- Political /legislative /regulatory
- Workforce/work culture
- Marketing/advertising /media
- New technologies may create totally new industries and destroy traditional ones. For example- Biotechnology holds much promise for revolutionizing both production methods and products.
- The ascendancy of environmental and nutritional awareness among both consumers and producers.
- Ecological and its liability- risk issues- present serious challenges that the agribusiness industry must address and develop strategies to deal with.
- Reconciling farm policies with budget constraints is leading to government policies that return more flexibility to farm managers in choosing " what to" produce. But environmental issues leading to policies that curtail flexibility in choosing "how to" produce.

- On the international front, increasing globalization of agriculture- the loss of U.S. dominance in the international market place.
- Customers to fierce competitors
- Instant communications and new trading techniques have created complex but highly effective international trade relationships.
- *Trade agreements* : Demand side improving incomes in East Asia and former Soviet Block countries will boost world prices of meat and dairy products, fruits and vegetables.
- *Population driving economic trends* : Population growing in size and diversity will place new limits on how, what and variety.
- More disposable income per household increases demand for more income elastic goods as varied diets, and good health have also become more important.
- More Preference for Healthy foods.
- More concern for animals
- Greater convenience.
- Individually packaged fast food meals. Insistence in providing more and more information to consumers.

How to Cope with Changes?

Challenges and Opportunities

- Three areas of agribusiness industry appear to have above-average potential for growth: Aqua-culture, Biotechnology and Pharmaceuticals and Agribusiness Services.
- Global food and fibre markets have significant demand for individuals with international agribusiness

perspectives - attractive and creative job market for graduates specializing in this field.

- Other areas that have above average potential for growth are: agribusiness management, accounting and finance, and ornamental horticulture, cut flowers.
- Stress Differentiation: Start with choosy consumers where there are stronger preferences, there are opportunities for profit through differentiating product.
- Products that stand apart - nutritionally, environmentally, and chemically - will command a premium in the market. Low chemical foods, health-care foods are examples.
- Pioneer's better - Life gains
- Providing assurance of special qualities throughout the food and fiber chain will demand different managerial perspectives from the past. Producers need to look beyond production to marketing, taking an interest in consumer demands and tailoring the production process to meet these demands.
- Input suppliers too must be sensitive to the needs of the ultimate consumers.
- They must understand the impact that each input has on the final quality and characteristics of the products moving to market.

Scope for Agribusiness in India

- India is endowed with varied agro-climate, which facilitates production of temperate, sub-tropical and tropical agricultural commodities.
- There is a growing demand for agricultural inputs like feed and fodder, inorganic fertilizers, bio-fertilizers.

- Biotechnology applications in agriculture have a vast scope in production of seed, bio-control agents, industrial harnessing of microbes for bakery products.
- Export can be harnessed as a source of economic growth. As a signatory of World Trade Organization, India has vast potential to improve its present position in the world trade of agricultural commodities both in raw and processed forms. The products line includes cereals, pulses, oilseeds and oils, oil meal, spices and condiments, fruits and vegetables, flowers, medicinal plants and essential oils, agricultural advisory services, agricultural tools and implements, meat, milk and milk products, fish and fish products, ornamental fish, forest by products etc.
- At present, processing is done at primary level only and the rising standard of living expands opportunities for secondary and tertiary processing of agricultural commodities.
- The vast coastal line and internal water courses provides enormous opportunity for production of marine and inland fish and ornamental fish culture gaining popularity with increase in aesthetic value among the citizens of India.
- The livestock wealth gives enormous scope for production of meat, milk and milk products, poultry products etc
- The forest resources can be utilized for production of by products of forestry.
- Beekeeping and apiary can be taken up on large scale in India.
- Mushroom production for domestic consumption and export can be enhanced with improvement in the state of art of their production.
- Organic farming has highest potential in India as the pesticide and inorganic fertilizer application are less

in India compared to that of industrial nations of the world. The farmers can be encouraged and educated to switch over for organic farming.

- There is wide scope for production and promotion of bio-pesticides and bio-control agents for protection of crops.
- Seeds, hybrid and genetically modified crops, have the highest potential in India in the future, since the productivity of high yielding varieties have reached a plateau.
- Micro-irrigation systems and labor saving farm equipments have good potential in the years to come due to declining groundwater level and labor scarcity for agricultural operations like weeding, transplanting and harvesting.
- Production of vegetables and flowers under green house conditions can be taken up to harness the export market.
- Trained human resources in agriculture and allied sciences will take on agricultural extension system due to dwindling resources of state finance and down sizing the present government agricultural extension system for providing consulting sevices.
- The enhanced agricultural production throws open opportunities for employment in marketing, transport, cold storage and warehousing facilities, credit, insurance and logistic support services.

Types of Small Businesses

With the exception of Government, most of the small businesses can be classified as the following types :

1. Production
2. Retailing

3. Distribution
4. Personal services
5. Professional services
6. Financial
7. Franchising

1. Production: This classification includes all types of production including agricultural production of crops and livestock, as well as forestry.

2. Distribution: This classification refers to those businesses, which bring the goods and services to the consumer or user. This includes such activities as packaging, labeling, transporting, refrigerating, freezing, processing, storing, and performing any service necessary to prepare the goods or to provide the service to eventual consumer.

3. Retailing: Although often included as a phase of distribution, retailing is listed as a separate category because there are a large number of persons employed in retailing. Obviously, it represents one of the best opportunities for the potential entrepreneur. Retailing is that stage of distribution, which deals directly with the consumers. Examples of retailers are grocers, self-service stores, florists, agricultural input retailing and so on.

4. Personal services: The service business is those, which do not primarily supply goods to the public, but instead perform a service. Goods may be used to perform the service but they are of secondary importance. Examples of personal service are hotels, restaurants, agro-service centers, etc.

5. Professional services: Some type of services, in order to protect the public interests, require considerable training on the part of those offering the service. Usually that professional services must have a formal education and rigid examinations before receiving licenses to offer their services to the public. Examples of those offering services are investment brokers, insurance agents etc.

6. *Financial:* Financial businesses are usually service-oriented but since they deal primarily with the loaning or investing of money or the equivalents of money (stocks, bonds, property rights, etc), a separate category describes them best. Examples of financial services are commercial banks, insurance companies, thrift and loan societies etc.

7. *Franchising:* Franchising is a system for selectively distributing goods or services through outlets owned by the franchisee. Basically, a franchise is a patent or trademark, license, entitling the holder to market particular products or services under a brand name or trademark according to prearranged terms and conditions. The franchiser is the owner of his or her own business (the franchisee) and is likely to be more diligent and strive harder for success than the hired manager of a company-owned outlet. Since franchising is a form of selective distribution, the typical franchise agreement prohibits the franchise from setting up competing outlets within the franchise area. Examples of franchise services are diet services, quick-service food-drive inns like fried chicken.

Forms of the Business Organizations

There are three basic forms of business organization methods: the sole proprietorship, the partnership, and the corporation. With only a few limited exceptions, any type of business venture can use any form of business organization. The factors that will affect the business form chosen are:

- Ease of formation
- Exposure to financial risk
- Ability to raise capital
- Tax treatment of income
- Continuity of business upon the death of owner.

A Comparison of the Three forms of Business Organization

Factors	Sole Proprietorship	Partnership	Corporation
Number of owners	One	Two or more	One or more
Ease of formation	Very easy	Easy to very easy	Moderate to easy
Degree of financial risk	Owner is responsible for all debts	Partners share responsibility for debts	Owners have only limited responsibility for debts in name of company
Ability to borrow funds	Limited ability of owner to borrow	Improved ability to borrow due to multiple owners	Can borrow funds directly from public through shares and debentures
Legal requirements	None, except for possible declaration of name	Same as sole proprietorship; written contract between partners recommended	Charter must be secured from state
How taxes are handled	As part of owner's personal tax return	Profits are divided up among owners and are taxed on each partner's tax return	Pays own income tax
Continuity of business	Business is terminated at death of owner	Business may be terminated at death of any partner, unless provisions for continuation are made	Business continues after death of any stockholder

Entrepreneur

Many economic theories emphasize the significant role played by individual entrepreneurs as they combine talents, abilities and drive to transform resources into profitable undertakings. Joseph Schumpeter was the first major writer to highlight the human agent in the process of economic development. He believed that the economy was propelled by the activities of persons who wanted to promote new goods and new methods of productions or to exploit a new source of materials or new market not merely for profit but also for the purpose of creating.

Likewise, Arthur W. Lewis contended that economic growth was bound to be slow unless there was an adequate supply of entrepreneurs looking out for new ideas, and willing to take the risk of introducing them.

The relation between self-sustained growth of an economy and entrepreneurship was further discussed by W.W. Rostow when he claimed that economic growth was the result of an interesting process involving the economic, social and political sectors of society, including emergence of corps of entrepreneurs who are psychologically motivated and technologically prepared regularly to lead the way in introducing new production functions in the economy.

As it is, experts have variously described the entrepreneur as

- A person who innovates
- One who allocates and manages the factors of production and bears risk
- One who has ability to perceive latent economic opportunities and devise their exploitation
- An individual who conceives the ideas of business, design the organization of firms, accumulates capital, recruits labour, establishes relations with input supplier, customers and the government and converts the conception into a functional organization.
- The supplier of resources, supervisor and coordinator and ultimate decision maker.

The Importance of Personality in Business

One of the most important assets of any business owner is a personality, which lends itself to the type of business chosen. There are many different kinds of business and innumerable types of personalities. An objective self-examination is therefore necessary for the discovery of personal strengths and weaknesses, especially as they relate to owning a particular type of business. In assessing one's own personality, the following inventory should prove helpful. Potential business owners should question themselves on each of the following items, noting those areas where improvement is most needed.

A. Physical Qualities

- Appearance
- General health
- Endurance
- Vision
- Hearing

B. Mental Abilities

- General intelligence
- Knowledge of business
- Speed of reaction
- Memory
- Creativeness
- Initiative
- Insight into character

C. Ethics

- Honesty
- Loyalty
- Dependability
- Perseverance

D. Social Qualities

- Courtesy
- Sympathy
- Ability to work with others
- Cheerfulness
- Self-confidence
- Adaptability
- Enthusiasm

E. Executive Qualities

- Ability to direct others
- Ability to organize
- Ability to make decisions
- Ability to take responsibility
- Ability to accept suggestions

Entrepreneurial Competencies

A competency is an underlying characteristic of a person, which results in effective and / or superior performance of a job. Competence is an underlying characteristic of a person, in that it may be motive/traits/ skills or aspect of one's self-image or a body of knowledge which one uses. The existence of these characteristics may or may not be known to the person. In this sense, the characteristic may be unconscious aspect of the person. In simple terms, competence is a combination of a body of knowledge, skills and cluster of appropriate motives / traits that an individual possesses to perform a given task effectively and efficiently. The fifteen identified entrepreneurial competencies are furnished below.

1. Initiative

Takes action that go beyond job requirements or the demand of the situation.

- Does things before being asked or forced to by events
- Acts to extend the business to new areas, products or services.

2. *Seeing and Acting on Opportunities*

Looks for and takes action on opportunities

- Sees and acts on opportunities (Business, educational or personal growth)
- Seizes unusual opportunities to obtain financing, equipment, land work, space, or assistance.

3. *Persistence*

- Takes repeated or different actions to overcome obstacle
- Takes action in the face of a significant obstacle

4. *Information Seeking*

Takes action on own to get information to help reach objectives or clarify problems.

- Does personal research on how to provide a product or service
- Seeks information or asks questions to clarify what is wanted or needed
- Personally undertakes research, analysis or investigation
- Uses contacts or information networks to obtain useful information.

5. *Concern for High Quality of Work*

Acts to do things that meet or beat existing standards of excellence

- States a desire to produce work of high quality
- Compares own work or own company's work favourably to that of others.

6. *Commitment to Work Contract*

Places the highest priority or getting a job completed

- Makes a personal sacrifice or expands extraordinary effort to complete a job
- Accepts full responsibility for problems in completing a job for others
- Pitches in with workers or works in their place to get the job done
- Expresses a concern for satisfying the customer

7. *Efficiency Orientation*

Finds ways to do things faster or with few resources or at a lower cost.

- Looks for or finds ways to do things faster or at less cost
- Uses information or business tools to improve efficiency

8. *Systematic Planning*

Develops and uses the logical, step-by-step plans to reach goals

- Plans by breaking a large task down into sub-tasks
- Develops plans that anticipate obstacles
- Evaluates alternatives
- Takes a logical and systematic approach to activities

9. *Problem Solving*

Identifies new and potentially unique ideas to reach goals

- Identify an alternative strategy to reach a goal
- Generate new ideas or innovative to reach a goal

10. *Self-Confidence*

Has a strong belief in self and own abilities

- ❒ Expresses confidence in self ability to complete a task or meet a challenge
- ❒ Sticks with own judgment in the face of opposition or early lack of success
- ❒ Does something that he says is risky

11. *Assertiveness*

Confronts problems and issues with others directly

- ❒ Tells others what they have to do
- ❒ Reprimands or disciplines those failing to perform as expected

12. *Persuasion*

Successfully persuades others

- ❒ Convinces someone to buy a product or service
- ❒ Convinces someone to provide financing
- ❒ Convinces someone to do something else that would like that person to do
- ❒ Asserts own competence, reliability or other personal or company's qualities
- ❒ Asserts strong confidence in own company's or organization's products or services.

13. *Use of Influence Strategies*

- ❒ Acts to develop business contacts
- ❒ Uses influential people as agents to accomplish own objectives
- ❒ Selectively limits the information given to others
- ❒ Uses a strategy or influence to persuade others.

14. *Monitoring*

- Develops or uses procedures to ensure that work is completed or that work gets standards or quality
- Personally supervises all aspects of a project.

15. *Concern for Relevant Other's Welfare*

- Takes action to improve the welfare of employees
- Takes positive action in response to employees personal concerns
- Expresses concern about the welfare of employees.

Entrepreneur, Enterprises and Environment

For success of any business, three things are important. They are: Enterprises, Entrepreneurs and Environment. Already we discussed on the entrepreneurial personality, abilities, motives and competencies. Also, we have discussed on the enterprises opportunities and their feasibility and viability, only those enterprises meeting the feasibility and viability will be considered for taking. Next important thing is the environment in which the enterprises and entrepreneurs function.

The environment factors or forces which affect the success of business are classified into (1) Economic environment, (2) Demographic environment, (3) Socio-cultural environment, (4) Technological environment (5) Political environment, and (6) Legal environment.

Importance of Environment Analysis

The manager needs to be dynamic to effectively deal with the challenges of environment. The environment of business is not static. Some of the benefits of environment scanning are as follows:

- It creates an increased general awareness of environmental changes on the part of management

- It guides with greater effectiveness in matters relating to Government
- It helps in marketing analysis
- It suggests improvements in diversification and resource allocation
- It helps firms to identify and capitalize upon opportunities rather than losing out to competitors
- It provides a base of objective qualitative information about the business environment that can subsequently be of value in designing the strategies.

Key Terms

Agribusiness, global changes in agribusiness, small business, retailing, personal services, professional services, franchising, sole proprietorship, partnership, corporation, entrepreneur, personality in business, entrepreneurial competences.

Chapter Summary

- In the past two decades, there have been perceptible changes in global markets in terms of regulatory setting, competition, processing techniques and consumption pattern.
- Three areas of agri business industry appear to have above average potential for growth-Aqua culture, bio technology and pharmaceuticals and agri business services.
- In India, there is a vast potential for the production of tropical, sub-tropical and temperate agricultural commodities and therefore, there exists a great scope or agri-business.
- Most of the small businesses can be classified into : 1) production, 2) retailing, 3) distribution, 4) personal

services, 5) professional services, 6) financial and franchising

- The business organizations can be broadly classified into a) sole proprietorship, b) partnership and c) corporation.
- An entrepreneur is an individual who conceives the ideas of business, design the organization of firms, accumulates capital, recruits labour, establishes relations with input supplier, customer and the Government and converts the conception into a functional organization.
- One of the most important assets of any business owner is personality. An entrepreneur must improve his personality in terms of physical qualities, mental abilities, ethical norms, social and executive qualities.
- Competency is another characteristic of a person which results in superior performance in his job.
- For the success of any business, three things are important: a) enterprise, b) entrepreneur, and c) environment.

Chapter Highlights

Global changes in agribusiness, changing environment of the agribusiness industry, challenges and opportunities in the agribusiness, scope for agribusiness specifically in India, different types of small businesses, different forms in the business organizations, characters of an entrepreneur, importance of personality in business, entrepreneurial competences, importance of environment for the success of business have been thoroughly discussed in this chapter.

Review Questions

1. What are the current changes noticed in the agri business sector ?

2. What are the challenges and opportunities of agri business
3. Discuss the scope for agribusiness in India.
4. Explain the different types of small businesses
5. Compare the three different forms of business organizations.
6. How entrepreneurship is vital for the success of a business?
7. What are the functions of an entrepreneur?
8. Explain the significance of personality in business development
9. Discuss the entrepreneurial competences?
10. How environment plays a vital role in the success of a business?

References

Badi R.V. and N.V. Badi.2007. Entrepreneurship, Delhi: Vrinda Publications (P) Ltd.

Madhurima Lall and Shikha Sahai. 2006. Entrepreneurship, New Delhi: Excel Books.

Further Reading Material

Singh.S.P.2005. Agribusiness Industry: Challenges & Opportunities in the 21st Century An overview of Agricultural Education, Paper Presented at the Department of Agricultural Management, Tamil Nadu Agricultural University, Coimbatore on July, 2005.

Rawlins.N.O.1980.Introduction to Agribusiness, New Jersey: Prentice Hall, Inc.

Chapter **2**

SMALL BUSINESS

The Committee on Economic Development has defined small business as one which satisfies two or more of the following criteria.

- Management is independent (usually the managers are owners).
- Capital is supplied and ownership is held by an individual or small group.
- The area of operation is mainly local. Workers and owners are in one home community. Markets need not be local.
- Relative size within the industry – the business is small when compared to the biggest in its field. The size of the top bracket varies greatly so that what might seem large in field would be definitely small in another.

Overall View of SSIs in 2005-06

Small Scale Industries (SSIs) form the backbone of the Indian manufacturing sector. The SSIs account for about 95 per cent of the industrial units and is contributing about 40 per cent of the value addition in the manufacturing sector, nearly 80 per cent of the manufacturing employment and about 35 per cent of the exports (directly and indirectly). More than 123.40 lakh units are spread over the country producing 7,500 items and providing employment for more than 294 lakh persons (Uma Rani.N. 2007).

Percentage share to GDP	6.75
Estimated number of units (lakhs)	123.40
Percentage share in Industrial Value	39
No. of items produced	Over 7,500
Reserved items for the sector	326
Employment in persons (Lakhs)	294.90
Export Value of products from SSIs	Rs. 1,24,476 crores
Direct share in Total Exports (%)	35
Indirect share in Total Exports (%)	1

Objectives of a Small Business

Objectives are the ends towards which all the activities of the organization are directed. One or more of the following could be the objective(s) of a small business.

- Service
- Profit
- Community participation
- Growth
- Functioning as a subsidiary

Characteristics

The characteristics associated with small business and small scale units are:

- High diversification with a wide range of products
- Mostly one man venture
- Involvement of less capital
- Geographically wide dispersal

Importance

There are a number of reasons why small firms are of importance to our country.

- They are the important sources of competition and challenge to the economic power of larger firms.
- They broaden the distribution of economic and political power and do not result in concentration of power.
- They are the sources of innovation and creativity.
- They offer career opportunities to those who are more productive in the unstructured environment of a small company.
- They provide dynamism, innovation and effectiveness that lead to the productive economic system.
- There exists vast agribusiness opportunities in developing economy of India.
- They generate employment with less investment
- They promote exports
- They have control over production which is widely distributed.
- They develop risk takers.

Advantages

- Less capital outlay but more employment generation
- Do not require sophisticated technology.
- Facilitate decentralization and dispersal of business units.
- They offer a wide range of choices to consumers.
- Can serve specialized needs.
- Utilize resources in full without wastage.

Disadvantages

- Inadequate management ability
- Inadequate finance
- Poor competitive position
- Uncertainty in business continuity.

Growth Stages

Following are the various growth stages of any small business units :

1. *First stage :* One operation where one person does all the activities.

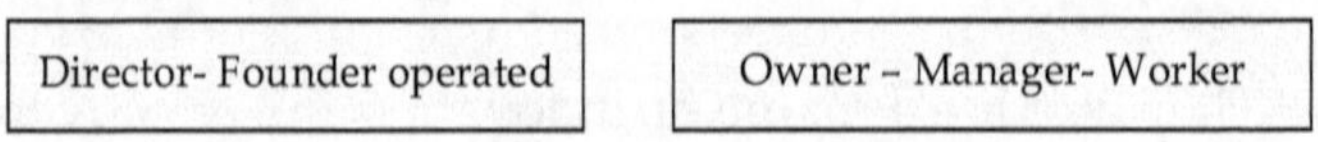

2. *Second stage :* Separation of management and non-management functions. Hired subordinates do some of the manual and or mental activities while owner manages.

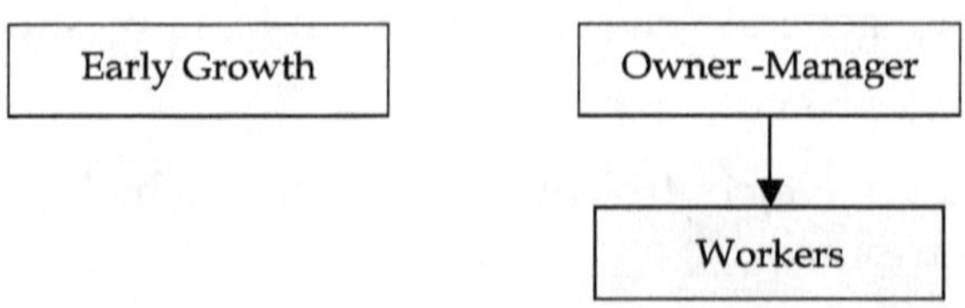

3. *Third stage :* Separation of ownership and management functions. Owner begins to relinquish the responsibilities for the day to day running of the business activities to a professional manager.

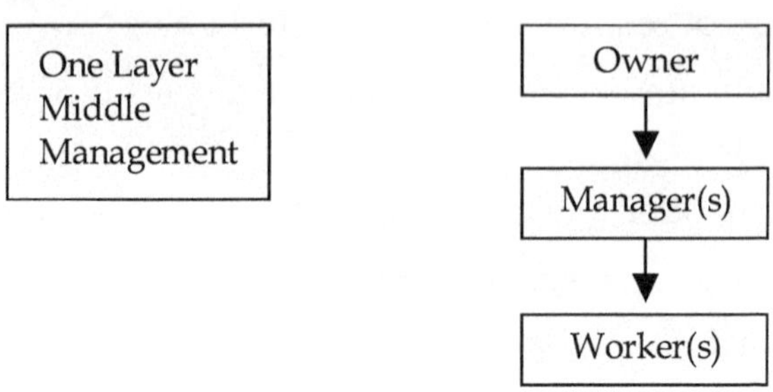

Multi-Layer Management

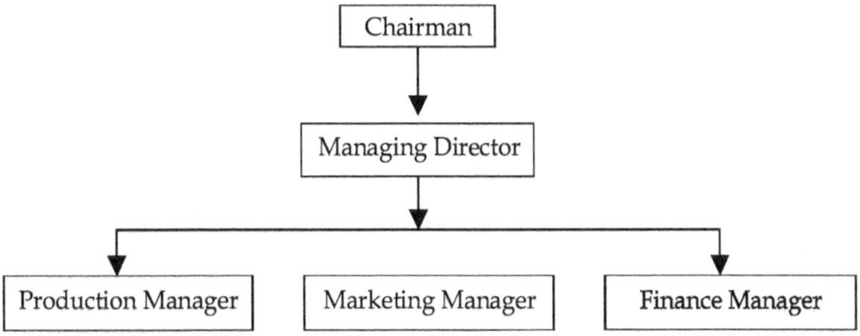

The Small Scale Industries (SSIs) constitute an important segment of the Indian economy in terms of their contribution to the country's industrial production, exports, employment and creation of an entrepreneurial base. The Government established the Ministry of Small Scale Industries and Agro and Rural Industries (SSI & ARI) in October, 1999 as the nodal Ministry for formulation of policies and Central sector programmes/schemes, their implementation and related co-ordination, to supplement the efforts of the States for promotion and development of these industries in India. The Ministry of SSI & ARI was bifurcated into two separate Ministries, namely, Ministry of Small Scale Industries and Ministry of Agro and Rural Industries in September, 2001.

There was a longstanding demand from entrepreneurs, small industry associations and related stakeholders for a single comprehensive legislation. Therefore, the "Micro, Small and Medium Enterprises Development (MSMED) Act, 2006" is the first Act enacted for micro, small and medium enterprises which, *inter alia*, provides for establishment of a statutory National Board for Micro, Small and Medium Enterprises, filing of memoranda, measures for promotion, development and enhancement of competitiveness of micro, small and medium enterprises, credit facilities, procurement preference and provisions related to delayed payments to micro and small enterprises. The micro and medium enterprises have been defined for the first time in this Act.

The President under Notification dated 9th May 2007 has amended the Government of India (Allocation of Business) Rules, 1961. Pursuant to this amendment, Ministry of Agro and Rural Industries and Ministry of Small Scale Industries have been merged into a single Ministry, namely, *"Ministry of Micro, Small & Medium Enterprises"*.

Worldwide, the micro and small enterprises (MSEs) have been accepted as the engine of economic growth and for promoting equitable development. The MSEs constitute over 90% of total enterprises in most of the economies and are credited with generating the highest rates of employment growth and account for a major share of industrial production and exports. In India too, the MSEs play a pivotal role in the overall industrial economy of the country. It is estimated that in terms of value, the sector accounts for about 39% of the manufacturing output and around 35% of the total export of the country. Further, in recent years the MSE sector has consistently registered higher growth rate compared to the overall industrial sector. The major advantage of the sector is its employment potential at low capital cost. As per available statistics, this sector employs an estimated 29 million persons spread over 12.3 million enterprises and the labour intensity in the MSE sector is estimated to be almost 4 times higher than that of the large enterprises.

Classification of Industries (New Enterprises)

Under the MSMED Act 2006, the earlier, rather limited concept of 'Industries' has been widened to that of 'Enterprises'. Enterprises have been classified broadly into two categories, namely enterprises engaged in the manufacture/production of goods pertaining to any industry; and enterprises engaged in providing/rendering of services. Enterprises have been defined in terms of investment in plant and machinery/ equipment (excluding land and building) as below (Table 2.1).

Table 2.1 : Classification of an Enterprises

Classification of Enterprises	Investment in Plant and Machinery Equipment (excluding) Land and Building)	
	Manufacturing Enterprises	**Service Enterprises**
Micro	Up to Rs. 25 lakh	Up to Rs. 10 lakh
Small	More than Rs.25 lakhs and up to Rs. 5 crores	More than Rs. 10 lakhs and up to Rs. 2 crores
Medium	More than Rs. 5 crore and up to Rs. 10 crore	More than Rs. 2 crore and up to Rs. 5 crore

The specific schemes/programmes undertaken by the organizations of the Ministry seek to facilitate/provide one or more of the following:

- Adequate credit from financial institutions/banks
- Funds for technology up gradation and modernization
- Integrated infrastructural facilities
- Modern testing facilities and quality certification laboratories
- Access to modern management practices, entrepreneurship development and skill up gradation through appropriate training facilities
- Assistance for better access to domestic and export markets and
- Cluster-wide measures to promote capacity-building and empowerment of the units and their collectives, in addition to all or some of the above-mentioned supports. The formulation and implementation of the policies and programmes/projects/schemes are undertaken by the Ministry with the assistance of its attached office and public sector enterprise, namely, the Small Industry Development Corporation (SIDCO) and the National Small Industries Corporation Ltd (NSIC).

Government has also set up the National Commission on Enterprises in the Unorganized Sector (NCEUS) to suggest policies and programmes for addressing the wide range of issues affecting the productive potential of the large segment of unorganized micro and small productive units.

Small Industries Development Organization (SIDO)

The Office of the Development Commissioner (Small Scale Industries) (DC SSI) is also known as the Small Industry Development Organization (SIDO). Established in 1954, it is the apex body for assisting the Government in formulating and overseeing the implementation of its policies and programmes/projects/ schemes. The SIDO is headed by the Additional Secretary & Development Commissioner (SSI).

SIDO provides a comprehensive range of common facilities, technology support services, marketing assistance, entrepreneurial development support, etc., through its network of 30 Small Industries Service Institutes (SISIs) with 28 branch as 4 Regional Testing Centres (RTCs), 7 Field Testing Stations (FTSs), 2 Small Entrepreneur Promotion and Training Institutes (SEPTIs) and 1 Hand Tool Design Development and Training Centre.

The SIDO also has a network of Tool Rooms and Process-cum-Product Development Centres (PPDCs) to provide technology and training support. These institutions are run as autonomous bodies, registered as societies under the Societies Act.

Over the last 52 years, the SIDO has served a very useful purpose as a catalyst of growth of the micro, small and medium enterprises (MSMES)through its vast network of field organizations spread all over the country.

The major activities of SIDO include the following:

- Advising the Government in formulation of policies and programmes/projects/schemes for the promotion and development of the MSME.
- Providing techno-economic and managerial consultancy, common facility and extension services to the MSME.
- Providing support for technology up-gradation, modernization, quality improvement and infra-structure facilities.
- Assisting the MSME in human resource development through training and skill up gradation.
- Providing economic information services to the MSME.
- Maintaining a close liaison with the Central Ministries, Planning Commission, State Governments, Financial Institutions and other organisations concerned with the development of the MSME.
- Evolving, implementing and coordinating policies and programmes for development of the MSME as ancillaries to large and medium industries.
- Providing testing and calibration services to the MSME.

SIDO Schemes/ Measures for Promotion of Small Scale Industries

- Advertising and Publicity
- Laghu Udyog Samachar and Other Publications
- Information and Facilitation Counter (IFC)
- Small Enterprise Information and Resource Centre Network (SENET)

- Modernization of SIDO Libraries, Science and Technology, Research and Development
- Training and Manpower Development.

The Training Programmes Conducted are

- Industrial Motivation Campaigns (IMCs)
- Entrepreneurship Development Programmes (EDPs)
- Skill Development Programmes (SDPs)
- Management Development Programmes (MDPs)
- Industrial Motivation Campaigns (IMCs)

National Small Industries Corporation Ltd. (NSIC)

The National Small Industries Corporation Ltd. (NSIC), was established by the Government in 1955 as a Public Sector Company, with a view to promoting, aiding and fostering the growth of micro, small and medium enterprises (MSMEs) in the country, with a focus on commercial aspects of their operations. NSIC implements several schemes to help the MSMEs in the areas of raw material procurement, product marketing, credit rating, acquisition of technologies, adoption of improved management practices, etc. through its 7 Zonal Offices, 26 Branch Offices, 15 Sub Offices, 5 National Technical Services Centres, 2 Software Technology Parks and 3 Technical Services Extension Centres, spread practically all over the country. The Corporation, an ISO: 9001-2000 Company has also set up a number of turnkey projects in many developing countries.

National Entrepreneurship Development Institutes (NEDIs)

Entrepreneurship development and training is one of the key elements for the promotion of Micro, Small and Medium Enterprises (MSMEs), particularly, to the first generation entrepreneurs. To undertake this task on regular basis, the Ministry has set up 3 national-level Entrepreneurship Development Institutes, viz., National Institute of Small Industry Extension Training (NISIET) at Hyderabad, National Institute of Entrepreneurship and Small Business Development (NIESBUD) at Noida and Indian Institute of Entrepreneurship (IIE) at Guwahati, as autonomous societies. These institutes are engaged in the development of training modules, undertaking research and training and providing consultancy services for entrepreneurship development and promotion of MSMEs.

National Commission for Enterprises in the Unorganized Sector (NCEUS)

The National Commission for Enterprises in the Unorganized Sector has been constituted in September, 2004 for a period of three years. The Commission has been given the mandate to examine the problems of enterprises in the unorganized sector and suggest measures to overcome them. It consisted of a Chairman, three full time members, three part-time members and an Advisory Board consisting of eminent experts from fields related to the unorganized sector.

Apex Consultative Body with wide Representation of Stakeholders

Under the new Act, action has been initiated for constitution of the National Board for Micro, Small and Medium Enterprises, which will be headed by the Central Minister in charge of MSMEs and will consist of members from (i) MPs, (ii) Representatives of Central Ministries, (iii) State Governments, (iv) UT Administration, RBI, SIDBI, NABARD (v) Associations of MSMEs including women, (vi) Persons of eminence and (vii) Central Trade Union Organizations.

Functions of the National Board for MSMEs will be to (i) examine the factors affecting the promotion and development of MSMEs and review the policies and programmes of the Central Government in this regard, (ii) make recommendations on matters reference to the above or any other matter referred to it by the Central Government and (iii) advise the Central Government on the use of Fund or Funds constituted under section 12 of the MSMEs Act.

Advisory Committee

As per the provisions of MSMEs Act, 2006, the Central Government has already constituted an Advisory Committee, for a period of two years with effect from 27th September, 2006, which is headed by Union Secretary in-charge of MSMEs.

WTO Cell

A separate WTO Cell in the Office of Development Commissioner (Small Scale Industries) was set up during 1999 to coordinate the latest developments in regard to World Trade Organization. The objectives of the Cell inter-alia include (a) to keep abreast with the recent developments in the WTO, (b) to disseminate information to SSI Associations and other stakeholders about the various aspects of WTO and its likely implications for the small enterprises, (c) to coordinate with other Ministries and Departments of the Govt. of India, (d) to assist policy formulation for MSMEs in conforming with the provisions of WTO Agreements and (e) to organize WTO Sensitization Workshops/Seminars for creating awareness, capacity building and sectoral study.

With a view to create awareness among the MSMEs units, SSI Associations and other stakeholders on WTO Agreement and its implications for them, this Ministry is organizing workshops/seminars all over the country. As part of this process, three awareness programmes on various aspects of WTO are organized. Also one-day workshops on Intellectual Property Rights (IPRs) are conducted.

The Cell is maintaining close liaison with other concerned Ministries and Departments like Ministry of Commerce and Industry, Directorate General of Foreign Trade, Directorate General of Anti-Dumping and Allied Duties, and DG (Safeguard), so as to keep updated with regard to WTO Agreements and to protect the interests of small scale industries.

Intellectual Property Rights (IPRs)

With the onset of the trade related aspects of Intellectual Property Rights (TRIPS) agreement under WTO and the consequent changes made by various countries in their IPR laws including India, the issues of IPR have gained special importance in the Small Scale Industry sector. It was noticed that changes of far reaching consequences were being effected in the business land scape without the MSME sector being aware of it. It was also felt that IPRs require understanding and attention by the industry. To meet this objective, the IPR Cell was created in the office of DC (SSI) in the year 2001-02 for generating awareness amongst the MSMEs on IPR related issues. The small scale entrepreneurs are being sensitised on the need for protection and methodology to be adopted for IPR management through not only diffusion and up gradation of technology, but also employing existing IPR resources for the purpose.

By protecting their intellectual property, small scale units can increase their competitiveness. IP protection will help in -

- Preventing competitors from copying or closely imitating a company's product or services.
- Avoiding wasteful investment in research and development and marketing.

- Creating a corporate identity through a trademark and branding strategy.
- Increasing the market value of the company and enhancing access to new market.
- Intellectual Property Rights consist of Patent, Trade Marks, Industrial Designs, Copy Rights, Trade Secrets and Geographical Indications etc.

Biotechnology

A Biotechnology Cell was created in the office of the Development Commissioner (Small Scale Industries) on 16.08.2002 to deal with the matter for the development and promotion of biotechnology industry in the small scale sector. A Task Force has also been created in the Office of the Development Commissioner (SSI) to suggest new initiatives for the development and growth of small enterprises in this sector wherein Department of Biotechnology, Govt. of India and Biotech Consortium India Limited (BCIL) are members. The objective of the Biotechnology Cell is also to identify the potential areas of biotechnology for exploitation and concerted efforts for promoting the MSME industrial activities in this area. The areas of tissue culture, bio -fertilizers, bio-pesticides, mushroom cultivation, solid waste management are in focus. To disseminate information on the use of biotechnology, a number of sensitization programmes on biotechnology in various parts of the country have been organized during the recent years and more such programmes will be organized in near future. These sensitization programmes are being organized in collaboration with the Department of Biotechnology and Biotech Consortium India Ltd.(BCIL), New Delhi and various State Government agencies.

To assist MSME entrepreneurs in getting basic understanding of the technologies, products and processes, a set of project profiles have been prepared in coordination with the Department of Biotechnology and Biotech Consortium India Limited covering the following areas:

- Plant tissue culture
- Bio fertilizers
- Bio pesticides
- Fresh water prawn culture/Hatchery
- Vermi composting
- Micro propagation technology
- Medicinal plant extractions
- Organic farming

Performance of SSIs

Based on the data received from the sampled units, the quarterly index of Industrial Production with the base year 2001-02 for the period April 2002 to March 2006 has been compiled. The growth rates of SSI sector for the year 2002-03, 2003- 04, 2004-05 and 2005-06 estimated on the basis of the new series of Index Industrial Production (IIP) vis-à-vis old series of IIP and with total manufacturing sector are given below (Table 2.2).

Table.2.2 : Growth Rates of SSI Sector.

Year	Growth Rates of 1970 IIP (%)	Growth Rates of 2001-02 Base IIP (%)	Growth Rates of Manufacturing Sector with Base Year 1993-94
2002-03	7.68	8.68	6.0
2003-04	8.59	9.64	7.4
2004-05	9.96	10.88	9.2
2005-06	10.40	12.32	5.1

Source: Annual Report 2006-07, Ministry of SSIs

It may be seen that the overall industrial growth rate of the Small Scale Industries sector in terms of Index of

Industrial Production (IIP) (Base: 2001-02=100) rose to 12.32% during the year 2005-06 as compared to 10.88% during the year 2004-05.

The SSI sector has also consistently registered a higher growth rate as compared to the overall manufacturing sector. The SSI units' production at current and at 2000-01 prices and exports are furnished in (Table 2.3). The total number of SSIs, Production (at current prices and at 2000-01 prices), fixed investments made, employment and exports increased from 2002-03 to 2005-06.

Table. 2.3 : Growth Parameters of SSI Units in India since 2002-03 to 2005-06.

Year	SSI Units (lakh numbers)			Fixed Investment (Rs.Crore)	Production (Rs.Crore)		Employ-ment (lakh persons)	Exports (Rs.Crore)
	Registered	Unregistered	Total		Current prices	At 2000-01 prices		
2002-03	16.03	93.46	109.49	1,62,317	3,14,850	3,06,771	260.21	86,103
	-	-	(4.07)	(5.16)	(11.54)	(8.68)	(4.36)	(20.73)
2003-04	17.12	96.83	113.95	1,70,219	3,64,547	3,36,344	271.42	97,644
	-	-	(4.07)	(4.87)	(15.78)	(9.64)	(4.31)	(13.52)
2004-05	18.24	100.35	118.59	1,78,699	4,29,796	3,72,938	282.57	1,24,417
	-	-	(4.07)	(4.98)	(17.90)	(10.88)	(4.11)	(27.42)
2005-06	19.30	104.12	123.42	1,88,113	4,97,842	4,18,884	294.91	NA
	-	-	(4.07)	(5.27)	(15.83)	(12.32)	(4.37)	

Source: Annual Report 2006-07, Ministry of SSIs
Figures in parentheses indicate percentage changes over the pervious year. NA - Not available.

The Office of the DC (SSI) provides estimates in respect of various performance parameters relating to the growth of SSI Sector. The table showing the time series data on various economic parameters is given below.

Comparison of The SSIs Sector with the overall Industrial Sector

The small-scale sector has maintained a higher rate of growth vis-à-vis the overall industrial sector. The comparative growth rates of production for both the sectors during last five years are given below (Table 2.4). The SSis have shown more growth rates as compared to overall industrial growth.

Table. 2.4 : Growth Rates of Production

Year	Growth Rate of SSI Sector (%)	Overall Industrial Sector (%)
2002-03	8.58	5.70
2003-04	9.64	6.90
2004-05	10.88	8.40
2005-06	12.32	8.10

Source: Annual Report 2006-07, Ministry of SSIs

The contribution of SSI to the Gross Domestic Product (GDP) is given in (Table 2.5). The SSIs contributed at about 5.9 per cent of Gross Domestic Product in 1999-2000 and slightly declined to 5.82 percent in 2003-04.

Table.2.5 : Contribution of SSIs

Year	Contribution of SSI (%) at 1999-2000 Prices	
	Total Industrial Production	Domestic Product Gross (GDP)
1999-2000	39.74	5.86
2000-01	39.71	6.04
2001-02	39.12	5.77
2002-03	38.89	5.91
2003-04	38.80	5.82

Source: Annual Report 2006-07, Ministry of SSIs

Credit Linked Capital Subsidy Scheme (CLCSS)

The Ministry of Small Scale Industries (SSIs) is operating a scheme for technology up gradation of Small Scale Industries (SSIs) called the Credit Linked Capital Subsidy Scheme (CLCSS) for the The SSI units, including tiny, khadi, village and coir industrial units, in taking up technology up gradation on a larger scale. The specific features of the scheme are ; (a) the ceiling on loans under the Scheme was raised from Rs. 40 lakh to Rs. 1 crore; (b) the rate of subsidy was enhanced from 12 per cent to 15 per cent; (c) the admissible capital subsidy is to be calculated with reference to the purchase price of plant and machinery, instead of the term loan disbursed to the beneficiary unit; (d) the practice of categorization of SSI units in different slabs on the basis of their present investment for determining the eligible subsidy has been done away with ; and (e) the operation of the Scheme was extended up to 31st March, 2007.

National Small Industries Corporation Ltd.
Schemes of the Corporation
Marketing Assistance

- Raw material Distribution
- Consortia and tender marketing
- Single point registration for Government purchase
- Exhibitions and technology fairs
- Buyer's - seller's meet
- Export of products and projects
- Meeting credit needs of Small Enterprises through tie-up arrangements with Banks
- Performance and Credit Rating Scheme for Small Enterprises.

Support Services

- Supplier database
- Market intelligence
- Technology providers
- Information providers

- Linkages with relevant Institutions
- Business to Business services
- Business to Consumer services
- Value additions like directories on who makes machines, who makes components, spare capacity bulletin boards, discussion forums, virtual exhibitions, etc.

Training and Entrepreneurship Development

- Entrepreneurship Development Institutions (EDI) Scheme
- National Entrepreneurship Development Board (NEDB) Scheme
- National Institute of Small Industry Extension Training (NISIET), Hyderabad.
- Indian Institute of Entrepreneurship (IIE), Guwahati.
- National Institute for Entrepreneurship and Small Business Development (NIESBUD), Noida.

The Ministry of Agro and Rural Industries (ARI) was set up in September, 2001

The strategy of the Government has been to improve the economic and social conditions of the underprivileged sections of the rural population with emphasis on agricultural production and also the non-farm sector to promote productive employment opportunities, by integrating traditional production infrastructure, skills and locally available raw material.

Khadi and Village Industries

It is a statutory organization engaged in promoting and developing khadi and village industries for providing employment opportunities in the rural areas, there by strengthening the rural economy.

While the khadi programme comprises hand spun and hand woven cotton, woollen, muslin and silk varieties, the village industries programmes have been classified into seven broad groups. These are:

- Mineral Based Industry
- Forest Based Industry
- Agro and Rural Industry
- Polymer and Chemical Based Industry
- Rural Engineering and Bio Technology
- Hand Made Paper and Fibre Industry
- Service Industry.

The khadi and village industries sector makes a significant contribution to the Indian economy. As per the data available, KVIC was able to sustain and help generate a total of 82.77 lakh employment opportunities up to 2005-06 compared to the preceding year's level of 76.78 lakh, registering a growth of 7.80 per cent. In village industries, employment increased significantly by 8.73 per cent while in khadi, the increase was marginal.

During 2005-06, khadi cloth worth Rs.468.30 crore was produced, generating employment for 8.68 lakh persons. In the Village Industries sector, the achievement during 2005-06 in respect of production and cumulative employment was Rs.11915.54 crore and 74.09 lakh persons respectively (Table 2.6). The production of Khadi and Village Industries production value increased from Rs.8,568.37 crore in 2002-03 to 12,383.84 crore in 2005.06 while the employment increased from 66.45 lakh persons to 82.77 lakh persons during the period under report.

Table 2.6 : Performance of Production and Employment of Khadi and Village Industries

Year	Production (Value in Rs crore.)			Employment (lakh persons)		
	Khadi	Village Industries	Total	Khadi	Village Industries	Total
2002-03	443.07	8,126.30	8,569.37	8.58	57.87	66.45
2003-04	451.93	9,228.27	9,680.20	8.61	62.57	71.18
2004-05	461.54	10,458.89	10,920.43	8.64	68.14	76.78
2005-06	468.30	11,915.54	12,383.84	8.68	74.09	82.77

Source: Annual Report 2006-07, Ministry of Agro-based and Rural Industries

Coir Sector

The coir industry is a labour-intensive and export-oriented industry which uses coir husk, a by-product of coconut. The Coir Board, a statutory body established under the Coir Industry Act 1953, looks after the promotion, growth and development of the coir industry, including export promotion and expansion of the domestic market. The Coir Board implements a number of schemes, which include assistance for participation in exhibitions, training for skill development and assistance under Mahila Coir Yojana, training, financial assistance for modernization of existing units, undertaking R&D activities, etc. The coir industry has deep roots in the State of Kerala and it is spreading to other coconut growing states like Tamil Nadu, Karnataka, Andhra Pradesh, Orissa, Tripura, Goa and so on.

The coir products consist of coir fiber, yarn, rope and other products like curled coir and rubberized coir. Their quantity of production varied over years depending upon the availability of coir sheath. During 2005-2006, a total quantity of 6,37 lakh MT of various coir products were produced (Table 2.7).The domestic consumption of coir and coir products also varied over years and it was from 6.34 lakh MT in 2005-06 (Table 2.8). The export of coir and coir products worth Rs. 508.45 crore has recorded a growth of

6.2 per cent in value terms during 2005-06 as compared to that of 2004-05 (Table 2.9). This is the highest ever export for the coir industry.

Table 2.7 : Production of Coir and Coir products
(Qty. in metric tonnes)

Items	2002-03	2003-04	2004-05	2005-06
Coir Fiber	3,53,700	3,64,000	3,85,500	3,15,500
Coir Yarn	2,26,800	2,32,500	2,45,500	1,90,000
Coir Products	75,750	77,900	98,000	1,05,000
Coir Rope	50,000	50,000	50,000	40,000
Curled Coir	28,000	29,500	36,500	25,000
Rubberised Coir	50,250	51,000	60,000	62,000

Source: Annual Report 2006-07, Ministry of Agro-based and Rural Industries.

Table 2.8 : Consumption of Coir and Coir Products
(Qty. in metric tonnes)

Items	2002-03	2003-04	2004-05	2005-06
Coir Fiber	89,200	38,400	3,65,750	4,05,000
Coir Yarn	1,25,300	1,96,959	2,22,500	2,35,000
Coir Products	26,500	19,469	22,500	38,000
Coir Rope	49,700	49,692	49,500	49,500
Curled Coir	27,500	29,424	35,700	37,000
Rubberised Coir	49,700	50,538	54,000	60,000

Source: Annual Report 2006-07, Ministry of Agro-based and Rural Industries.

Table 2.9 : Export of Coir and Coir Products

Year	Quantity (Metric tonnes)	Value (Rs. Crore)
2002-03	84,183	352.71
2003-04	1,02,253	407.50
2004-05	1,22,927	473.40
2005-06	1,30,627	508.45

Source: Annual Report 2006-07, Ministry of Agro-based and Rural Industries

Thrust Areas for Development of Coir Industry

The thrust areas for development of coir sector in the country are as follows:

- Modernization of production infrastructure by means of appropriate technology without displacement of labour.
- Expansion of domestic market through publicity and propaganda.
- Promotion of export of coir and new products by undertaking market promotion abroad.
- Promotion of research and development activities like process improvement, product development and diversification and elimination of drudgery and pollution abatement.
- Development of manpower through training.
- Extension of Research and Development findings through field demonstration.

Scheme of Fund for Regeneration of Traditional Industries (SFURTI)

The main objective of SFURTI is to establish a regenerated, holistic, sustainable and replicable model of integrated cluster based development of traditional industries. This will primarily mean:

- More competitive traditional industries with more market driven, productive, profitable and sustained employment for the participants;
- Strengthened local socio-economic governance system of the industry clusters, with the active participation by the local stakeholders that can help them to continue and undertake development initiatives by themselves; and

- Building up innovative and traditional skills, improved technologies, advanced processes, market intelligence and new models of public-private partnerships, so as to gradually replicate similar models of cluster-based regenerated traditional industries.

Beginning of Sickness

As per RBI "*a small scale industrial unit should be considered as sick, if it has at the end of an accounting year, accumulated losses equal to or exceeding 50 % of its peak net worth in the immediately preceding 5 accounting years*".

As per SBI "*a sick small scale is one which fails to generate internal surplus on continual basis and depends for its survival upon frequent infusion of external funds*".

Symptoms of Industrial Sickness

- Frequent or continuous closure of units due to problems of work load, power supply or natural causes.
- Frequent break down of machinery and facilities.
- Heavy rejection of goods due to quality problems.
- Continuous decline of capacity utilization
- Dearth of Funds problems and inability to pay statutory obligations.
- Persistent cash problems
- Distorting financial ratios.
- Low morale of the employees and poor team work amongst employees and partners.

The number of sick SSIs and amount of loan outstanding are furnished in (Table 2.10). The number of sick SSIs decreased from 2002 to 2007 and upto 2007, there were 1.14 lakh sick units. The amount of loan outstanding of the sick SSIs has been varying during the above period and upto 2007, the amount outstanding of sick units was Rs. 5,267 crores.

Table 2.10 : Number of Sick SSIs and Amount of Loan Outstanding.

Year	Number of Sick SSIs (in lakh units)	Amount of Loan Outstanding of Sick SSIs in Rs. Crore Financed by Scheduled Commercial banks
2002	1.77	4,819
2003	1.68	5,706
2994	1.39	5,285
2005	1.38	5,380
2006	1.27	4,981
2007	1.14	5,267

Source : Hand Book of Statistics of Indian Economy 2007- 08, RBI.

Causes of Industrial Sickness

Internal Causes and External Causes

External causes of industrial sickness are beyond the control of the industry, and usually affect the industry group as a whole.

- Planning and implementation
- Management
- Labour and industrial relations

Internal causes are within the control of the industry. It may be due to some internal deficiencies or short comings in its various functional areas.

- Inadequacy or non availability of Raw materials
- Infrastructure bottlenecks
- Market constraints
- Government controls and policies
- Work culture
- Other extraneous factors.

Assessment of Viability of Sick Industries and their Rehabilitation

Viability study

It should cover on

- Historical Background and Present Position.
- Management
- Production
- Infrastructural Facilities
- Labour
- Marketing
- Government Policy
- Finance
- External Factors.

Rehabilitation of Small-Scale Industries

- Marketing Facilities Available under one Roof of SSI
- Right of Decision Making
- Punishment and Rewards
- Advertisement Facility
- Setting up of A Small-Scale Units Judicial Cell
- Coordinated Contribution by Various Agencies
- Equal Attention on Various Factors
- Declaration of a Year of Reviving Small-Scale Sick Unit
- Government Policy- An Effort to Strengthen the Small-Scale Industries in India
- Taxation Benefits: Boon for the Growth of SSI
- Tax holidays

- Depreciation Allowance
- Rehabilitation Allowance
- Investment Allowance
- Expenditure on Scientific Research
- Greater Attention on Total Quality Management (TQM)
- Liberal Credit Policies
- Infrastructure
- Technology
- Export Promotion of Products.

Key Terms and Concepts to Remember

Small Business, Growth of Small Business, Entrepreneurship Development Programmes, Small Scale Industry (SSI), Micro, Small and Medium Enterprises (MSME), Industrial sickness.

Chapter Summary

Small Business

- Small firms are the important sources of competition and challenge the economic power of larger firms. They generate greater employment potential with lesser investment.
- Small Industries Development Organization (SIDO) has been established to advise the government in formulation of policies and programmes/projects/schemes for the production and development of the MSMEs.
- National Small Industries Corporation (NSIC) was established by the Government as a public sector company with a view to promote the growth of Micro Small and Medium Enterprises (MSMEs) in the country.

- A separate WTO cell in the office of Development Commissioner (Small Scale Industries) was set up in 1999 to coordinate the latest developments in regard to World Trade Organization.
- The SSI sector has consistently registered a higher growth rate as compared to that of overall manufacturing sector.
- The external causes for the industrial sickness were the deficiencies in the planning and implementation of various strategies relating the concerned industries, while the internal causes were non - availability of inputs and market constraints.

Chapter Highlights

The importance of small firms in the natural economy has been highlighted in this chapter. The definitions of micro, small and medium enterprises are given. The specific schemes/ programmes undertaken by the Ministry of Micro, Small and Medium Enterprises have been explained. WTO cell has been set up to co-ordinate the latest developments in regard to World Trade Organization. The symptoms, causes and rehabilitation of small scale sick units have been highlighted.

Review Questions

1. How small business firms are important to the development of Indian economy.
2. Explain the different growth stages of small business units.
3. Define Micro, Small and Medium enterprises.
4. Explain the various programmes/schemes undertaken by Ministry of MSMEs.
5. What are the limitations of Small Industries Development Organization ?

6. Explain the functioning of different training Institutes in the country, which are involved in the development of small industries.
7. Write short notes on WTO cell and Biotechnology cell engaged in the development of small scale industries.
8. Write short notes on i) Khadi and Village Industries and ii) Coir industries.
9. What are the symptoms and causes of industrial sickness? Explain the rehabilitation methodes of small scale Industries.

References

Annual Report 2006-07, Ministry of SSIs, Govt. of India.

Annual Report 2006-07. Ministry of Agro-based and Rural Industries, Govt. of India.

Badi R.V. and N.V.Badi, 2007. *Entrepreneurship*, Delhi: Vrinda Publishers (P) LTD.

CED, Committee for Economic Development,1947. *Meeting the Special Problems of Small Business*. New York, 14

Hamilton, William. H., Donald. F. Connelly, D.H Oward Doster, 1992. *Agribusiness: An Entrepreneurial Approach*, New York: Delma Publishers Inc.

Hand Book of Statistics of Indian Economy, 2007-08, RBI, 80.

Madhurima, Lall. and Shikha, Shai.2006.*Entrepreneurship*, New Delhi: Excel Books.

Further Reading Material

Baumack.C.M. and K. Lawyer. 1979. How to Organize and Operate A Small Business. New Jersey: Prentice Hall Inc.

Halles W.D. R.TP. Hindle. 1977. Small Business Management: Planning and Operation, New York: Van Nostrand Reinhold Company.

Justis R.T. 1981. Managing Your Small Business, New Jersey: Prentice Hall Inc http://msme.gov.in

Laveesh Bhandari, (Ed)2005.*Small Scale Industry-Large Scale Exit Problems,* New Delhi: Academic Foundation.

Picle, Hal.B. and Royce L. Abrahamson, 1990.*Small Business Management (Fifth Edition),* USA: John Wiley & Sons.

Ryan.J.D., Lee A. Eckert and Robert J. Ray, 1996. *Small Business. An entrepreneur's Approach (4th Edition),* Florida: Harcourt Brace College Publishers.

Chapter 3

MANAGEMENT

Management can be viewed as a group effort towards a common goal in which team behaviour plays the important role. According to this view, the material resources and external environment are common to all management; what makes for effectiveness and success of one group relative others is management - that is, the human element - behaving in group and leading the business to its determined goal.

Management may in short be called a science of decision-making or a science of choice. A farmer has to make judicious decisions on the use of scarce resources, having alternative uses to obtain the maximum profit and family satisfaction on a continuous basis from the farm as a whole. In other words, management seeks to help the producer in deciding problems like what to produce, how much to produce and when to buy and sell and organization and managerial problems relating to these decisions.

Management - Definition

According to *Lawrence A. Appley*, management is an art of getting things done through the efforts of other people.

Henri Fayol defined management as the conduct of affairs of a business, moving its objective through a continuous process of improvement and optimization of resources via the essential management functions. The manager has to forecast and plan, to organize, to command, to co-ordinate, and to control the business for attaining its goals.

According to *William Spriegel*, management is that function of an enterprise, which concerns itself with the direction, and control of the various activities to attain business objectives. Management embraces all functions that relate to the initiation of an enterprise - its financing, the establishment of all major policies, the provision of all necessary equipment, the outlining of the general form of organization under which the enterprise is to operate and the selection of the principal officers.

Management is also a mechanism by which a defined human group pursues a determined set of objectives through systematic group efforts for their implementation most effectively and economically. This definition recognizes the role of the human element and of group efforts, places due emphasis on the pre -determination of objectives, wants the management process to be systematic and draws attention to the effective and economic implementation.

Importance of Management

- The very success or failure, even the very survival of an enterprise depends on its management. The economy and effectiveness with which managerial functions are performed are an index of its successful operations. It is the management, which provides effectiveness to human efforts.

- Management plays an impressive role on the performance of four key tasks, namely, achieving economic performance, creating productive work, managing the social impact and responsibility of a business and managing the time dimension.

- Joseph Schumpeter, the great economist viewed management and entrepreneurs as the 'engine of growth'.
- Management is the driving force and shows how best man could make effective utilization of world's scarce resources and make a substantial contribution to the progress and well being of a given society.
- Management while taking cognizance of the changing conditions and providing foresight and imagination is constantly on the run for improvement.
- Orderliness is the keynote of management and this is the guiding star for the effective and successful performance of difficult endeavours and tasks of managers.

Elements of Management

The basic elements, which are to be necessarily present in all forms of management, are discussed below.

- There has to be a horizon - a universe, an ambit, within which the management must perform. This ambit may be large or small bit, but it ought to be properly defined.
- There must be an organization, which gives the institutional structure to management. The human team and material inputs used are constituted in the organizational structure. The organization may be elaborate and complex, or it may be simple.
- There is a need for planning which is a decision making process. Planning is a system, a programme and a way of implementation and its monitoring. Planning is a way of organizing and utilizing resources to attain maximum benefit from an economic activity.

- Any management must have better staffing which involves both qualitative and quantitative aspects.
- Management needs leadership and direction, as it involves teamwork. Without proper leadership and direction, the goals cannot be reached.
- There is a need for co - ordination in the management process. Staff have to be coordinated toward achieving the goal of the firm.
- There must be proper evaluation, monitoring and control. The execution of the project has to be evaluated with a very strict time frame and its performance has to be properly monitored and controlled.

Management as a Decision Making Process

A successful manager requires the ability and capacity to make correct decision. The following model indicates the functions of a manager.

- Formulation of goals or objectives of the firm.
- Recognition and definition of a problem or opportunity.
- Obtaining information - observation of relevant facts
- Specification and analysis of alternatives.
- Decision - making - choosing an alternative.
- Taking action or implementation.
- Bearing responsibility for the decision or action taken.
- Evaluating the outcome.

Decisions can be classified on the basis of characteristics like:

- Importance
- Frequency

- Imminence
- Revocability, and
- Alternatives

For the purpose of obtaining proper sequence in production process, the various typical farming decisions are furnished under three major heads (Fig.2.1), namely :

- Production and organizing problem decisions
- Administrative problem decisions
- Marketing problem decisions

Management Approaches

There are many approaches to study management. Among them, management by objectives (MBO), quality circles, profit centered approach and SWOT analysis are the important ones.

Management by Objectives

Management by objectives (MBO) is defined as a comprehensive managerial system that integrates many key managerial activities in a systematic manner and that is consciously directed towards the effective and efficient achievement of organizational and individual objectives.

Emphasis on Performance Appraisal

In the traditional approach, managers are required to pass judgment on the personal worth of subordinates. In MBO approach, subordinates assume the responsibility of setting short-term objectives. Primarily, subordinates then evaluate performance against the set objectives themselves. This approach encourages self-appraisal and self-development and the emphasis is where it ought to be on performance rather than on personality. The active involvement of subordinates in the appraisal process leads to commitment and creates an environment for motivation.

Inclusion of Long - Range Planning in the MBO Process

In the MBO programs that emphasis performance appraisal and motivation, the focus tends to be on short-term objectives. This orientation, unfortunately may result in undesirable managerial behaviour. For example, a production manager, in an effort to reduce maintenance costs, may neglect the necessary expenses for keeping the machines in good working order. The break down of machinery may not be evident at first, but it can result in costly repairs much later. In an effort to show a good return on investment in a given year, the nurturing of good customer relations may be neglected. Similarly a manager may not invest in new products that would take several years before contributing to profit. Recognizing these shortcomings, many organizations now include long-range and strategic planning in MBO programmes.

The System Approach to MBO

Management by objectives has undergone many changes; it has been used in performance appraisal as an instrument for motivating individuals, and, more recently in strategic planning. But there are other managerial subsystems that can be integrated into the MBO process. They include design of organizational structures, portfolio management, management development, compensation programmes and budgeting. These various managerial activities need to be integrated into a system. For MBO, to be effective, it has to be viewed as a comprehensive system. In short, it must be considered as a way of managing, and not as an addition to the managerial job.

The Process of Managing by Objectives

It includes setting preliminary objectives at the top, clarifying organizational roles, setting subordinates towards objectives.

Benefits and Weakness of MBO

One can learn management from experience and research by taking a realistic view and analyzing some of the benefits and weaknesses of MBO.

Benefits of MBO

Saying that it results in greatly improved management can summarize all the advantages of MBO. Other benefits of MBO approach are classification of organization's roles and structures, encouragement of personal commitment and development of effective controls.

Weaknesses of MBO

With all its advantages, a system of management by objectives has a number of weaknesses. Most of them are due to shortcomings in applying the MBO concepts. Some of the specific shortcomings are :

- failure to reach the philosophy of MBO
- failure to give guidelines to goal setters
- difficulty of setting goals
- emphasis on short-run goals and
- danger of inflexibility

Quality Circles

Quality control circles or simply quality circles (QC) are groups of people from the same organizational area, who meet regularly to solve problems they experience at work. Members are trained in solving problems, applying statistical quality control and working in groups. Usually a facilitator works with each group, which normally consists of six to twelve members. Although QC members may receive recognition, they usually do not receive monetary rewards. Quality circles evolved from suggestion programmes. In both approaches, workers participate in solving work related problems. Although in suggestion programmes, the problems usually are quite specific, those deal with by quality circles are often more complex and require involvement of several team members. The team consists of primarily of rank- and -file workers and sometimes includes supervisors. So-called efficiency experts are usually excluded from the team. The concept of quality control originated in the USA, but the Japanese have perfected it. In a world market, faced with a competitive situation that demands quality products, quality circles are used and implemented by many organizations.

Management by Profit Centered Approach

The emphasis on productivity and by extension, profitability led to scientific management from classical theory of management. The profit centered management approach fostered a rational approach to solving organizational problems. More importantly, it laid the groundwork for professionalism of management. The profit-centered approach to management was limited by underlying assumptions about human beings. The assumptions were that people were 'rational' and motivated by 'economic' and 'physical' needs of workers as a group failing to consider the tensions created when these needs are frustrated.

SWOT Analysis

Most of the firms adopt a very casual and haphazard approach to the generation of project ideas. To stimulate the flow of ideas, 'SWOT' analysis approach will be useful. SWOT is an acronym for strengths, weaknesses, opportunities and threats. SWOT analysis represents conscious, deliberate, and systematic effort by an organization to identify opportunities that can be profitably exploited by it. Periodic SWOT analysis facilitates the generation of ideas.

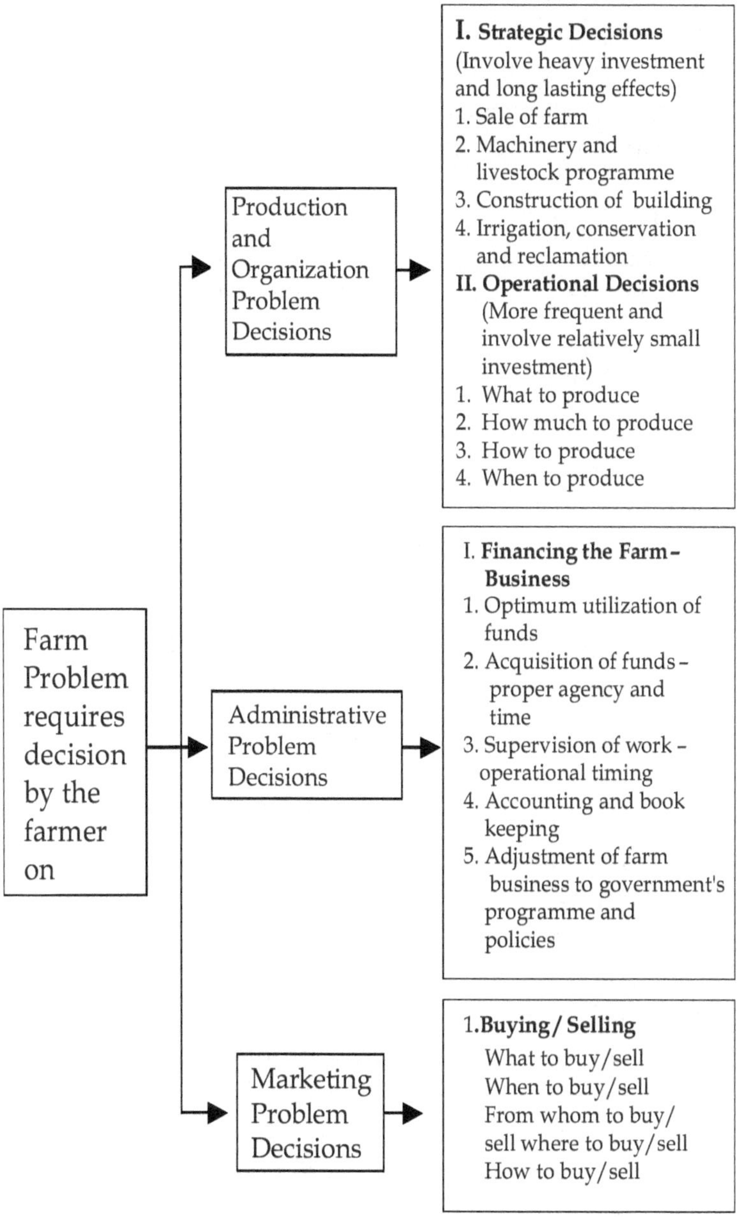

Fig. 3.1: Farm-Business Decision Making

Importance of Management

- Success or failure or survival of enterprise depends on management
- Management plays an impressive role for achieving economic performance, creative productive work, managing the social impact of business and time dimension.
- Management effectively utilizes world's scarce resources for progress and well being of the society.
- Management through its foresight and imagination strives for improvement.

Elements of Management

The basic elements present in all forms of management are organization, planning, staffing, leadership and direction, coordination, evaluation, monitoring and control.

Approaches to Study Management

Management by objectives, quality circles, profit centered approach and SWOT analysis.

Key Terms and Concepts to Remember

- Management
- Management by objectives
- Performance appraisal
- Planning
- Quality circles
- Profit centered Approach
- SWOT Analysis
- Production and organization problems
- Strategic decision
- Operational decisions
- Administrative Problem Decision
- Farming the farm business
- Marketing problem decision.

Chapter Highlights

Management is a science of decision making or a science of choice. Management seeks to help the producer to decide on what to produce? when to buy and sell ? and organization and management problems relating to these decisions.

Management as a human group pursues determination of objectives through systematic group efforts for effective and economic implementation.

Review Questions

1. Define management as you understand
2. Write on the importance of management
3. Briefly write on the elements of management
4. Describe the approaches to study management
5. Mention the benefits and weakness of MBO
6. Differentiate quality circle approach and profit centered approach of management study
7. Write short notes on SWOT analysis.

References

Singh N. 2000. Principles of Management: Theory, Practices and Techniques, New Delhi: Deep and Deep Publications Pvt Ltd.

Further Reading Material

Heller.R. and T.Hindle.2000. Essential Manager's Manual, London: Color Library Direct Ltd.

Dinakar Pagare. 1995. Business Management (Fifth Edition), New Delhi: Sultan Chand & Sons.

Koontz.H., H. Weihrich and A.Ramachandra Aryasri. 2004. Principles of Management, New Delhi: Tata McGraw-Hill Publishing Company Ltd.

Chapter 4

PLANNING

Planning is the beginning of all the other processes of management, namely, organizing, staffing, directing, communicating and controlling.

Planning is deciding in advance what to do, how to do, when to do and who is to do it. Planning bridges the gap from 'where we are' to 'where we want to go' (Koontz and O'Donnell).

In the words of Theo Haimann, "Planning is the function that determines in advance what should be done". It consists of selecting the objectives, policies, programmes and procedures of the enterprise and also the means of achieving their objectives.

As a part of planning process, the manager has to ensure that his team members understand the purposes and objectives of his enterprise and also methods to achieve them.

Importance of Planning

1. Selection of "Optimum" Goals

Planning involves rational thinking in setting goals and decision - making concerning a proposed course of action.

The goals should be set such that maximum efficiency is attained regarding the usage of men and materials.

2. *Tackling Increased Complexities*

An organization is an heterogeneous group of human beings who differ from one another in many respects. It is unlikely that they will work effectively and harmoniously in the interest of the organization, unless they have a plan.

3. *Meeting Environmental Changes*

Business environment changes more rapidly in terms of social values, competition, new product discoveries and consumer's tastes and preferences - and these changes will pose challenges for the growth of any organization. Only proper and effective planning can help the management by adjusting and adapting the inputs and transformation process to suit the environmental changes.

4. *Safeguard against Business Failure*

Business failures are blamed on cut-throat competition, unpredictability of consumer tastes and preferences, rapid technological changes and abrupt economic and political developments. However, in many cases, failure is caused due to rash and unscientific decision - making. Planning cannot avert all business failures. But it forces the management to assess and evaluate each emerging business opportunity and problem, and examine the various courses of action to meet them effectively.

5. *Effective Co-Ordination and Control*

Planning makes it easy to exercise control and co-ordination. The work to be done, the persons and the departments which have to do it, time limit within which it is to be completed and the cost to be incurred, are all determined in advance.

Characteristics

1. *Planning*

Planning is an intellectual exercise. It is concerned with thinking in a creative way as to how the existing combination of resources may be adjusted and adapted to match the emerging opportunities.

Planning enables the management to make decisions regarding a) what is to be done; b) how it is to be done; c) when it is to be done; and d) by whom it is to be done.

2. *Planning and Forecasting*

Forecasting describes what one *expects* to happen if no changes are made to escape from that happening. Planning describes what one *wants* to happen.

3. *Accomplishment of Group Activity*

Planning is essential to any goal directed activity. It enables people with divergent perceptions and motivations to work together to achieve common goals of the enterprise.

4. *Choice between Alternatives*

Planning seeks to adjust and adapt the existing mix of resources to meet the emerging opportunities.The first choice to be made by management is with regard to objectives of the business, i.e., profitability, growth, consumer satisfaction, man power development, prestige, and so on. The next choice is in respect of the strategy to be adopted to accomplish the objectives. Then comes the operational part, i.e. determining the time frame, assignment of tasks and other resources for the accomplishment of the objectives.

5. *Pervasiveness of Planning*

Active involvement of managers at different levels is essential to the success of planning.

6. Flexibility

Successful running of an organization involves matching of its resources with the emerging opportunities in the business environment.

7. Integrated Process

Planning involves selection of achievable objectives, and formulation of simple and realistic policies, programmes, procedures etc., for the accomplishment of that objective. Effective planning takes care of the conflicting views and settles for a course of action that is in the maximum interest of the organization, besides satisfying the personnel involved.

Limitations of Planning

1. Uncertainty

Assessment of future can only be in terms of guess work, probabilities, speculations and assumptions. The goals may be based on scientific analysis of relevant facts, and yet such analysis cannot be cent percent correct.

2. Action Packed Routine

Managers are ever preoccupied with day-to-day problems. This leaves them little time to think and plan about the problems of tomorrow.

3. Rigidity

Planning involves setting of objectives, and determination of the ideal course of action for their implementation. It implies that there will be little scope for deviation from the chosen path.

4. Costly

Planning is not only an expensive exercise, but also a time consuming process.

Steps in Planning

A step-by-step procedure has to be followed in the planning process in order to reach the set goals of the organization.

1. Identification of the Opportunity or Problem

Planning must facilitate the organization to suit it to its environment. The constraints and opportunities provided by the environment may be in the form of government regulations, existing cultural norms, limited financial resources in the capital market, changing technology, production of goods and services as per customer preferences, etc. Hence, correct identification of opportunity or problem to be addressed is the first step of planning.

2. Collection and Analysis of Relevant Information

Effective planning depends on the quality, relevance and validity of the information on which it is based. The sources of information may be classified as external and internal. External source will include suppliers, customers, professional people, trade publications, newspapers, magazines, conferences, etc. Internal sources will comprise of meetings, reports, and contacts with superiors, same ranks and subordinates.

3. Establishment of Objectives

Establishment of objectives points out the desired outcome that an organization may aim at stability of operations, growth, a higher rate of return, market leadership and so on.

4. Determination of Planning Premises or Limitations

Planning has to take into account numerous uncertainties in its environment. Important components of the internal environmental limitations are a) technology,

b) structural relationship and organizational design, c) employee attitude and morale; and d) managerial decision-making process. Internal environment is within the control of management, which can appropriately adjust and adapt it to the requirements of the external environment.

Uncertainties relating to the external environment are beyond the control of management. These may be in respect of a) fiscal policies of the government, b) economic condition; c) population trends; d) consumer tastes and preferences; e) competitor's plans and activities; and f) personal practices.

Only those factors which critically affect the enterprise plans should be identified and evaluated.

5. Examining Alternative Courses of Action

Often, there will be more than one action plan to achieve a desired objective. For example, if the objective is to maximize profits and there are no limits to increasing production, the objective can be achieved through, either tapping unexpected markets, or intensifying sale efforts in the existing markets, or increasing the price, or diversifying production. The number of alternative plans prepared by a manager would depend on his imagination, skill and experience.

6. Weighing Alternative Courses of Action

Evaluation of each alternative action-plan will have to be from different points of view, namely, a) its effectiveness in contributing to the accomplishment of organizational objectives; b) its ability to withstand the effects of environmental changes; and c) its integration with on-going action plans.

7. Selecting the Best Course of Action

Whether the evaluation of various alternatives is directed by individual preferences and prejudices, or it is based on mathematical and statistical techniques, the course of action is to be optimum, or the best under the given circumstances. Selection of the best course of action depends on resource availability, objectives, efficiency and economy.

8. Determining Secondary Plans

Secondary plans flow from the basic plan. These are meant to support and expedite the achievement of the basic plans. For example, once the basic plan is decided upon, a number of secondary plans dealing with purchase of raw materials and machines, hiring and training of workers and so on would have to be prepared to facilitate execution of the basic plan.

9. Providing for Future Evaluation

In order to ascertain if plans selected for the purposes are proceeding along right lines, it is necessary to devise a system for continuous evaluation of plan.

In order to achieve greater results, the planning process needs to be proceeded in a sequential manner. The steps involved in the planning process are depicted in (Fig. 4.1).

Classification of Planning

Planning is often classified on the basis of the length of the period covered by it. Accordingly, there may be long range and short range planning. However, the length of the planning period will depend on the organizational level at which planning is being done-the type of business, the production cycle, managerial practices, etc.

Identification of the opportunity or problem

↓

Collection and analysis of relevant information

↓

Establishment of objectives

↓

Determination of planning premises or limitations

↓

Identifying alternatives

↓

Comparing alternatives in light of goals sought

↓

Choosing an alternative

↓

Determining secondary plans

↓

Providing for future evaluation

Fig.4.1 : Steps in Planning

1. Long-Range Planning

Long-Range planning covers a long period in future, e.g., five or ten years, and, sometimes even longer. It is concerned with the functional areas of business such as production, sales, finance and personnel. It also considers long-term economic, social and technological factors which affect the long-range objectives of the enterprises. All enterprise activities are directed to achieve the targets set by long-range planning. Long-range planning is also called *strategic planning*, because it is concerned with preparing the enterprise to face the effects of long-term changes in business environment, such as entry of new products, new competitors, and new production techniques and so on.

2. *Short-Range Planning*

Short-range planning, also called *tactical planning*, covers a short period, usually less than one year. It deals with specific activities to be undertaken to accomplish the objectives set by long-range planning. Thus, it relates to current functions of production, sales, finance and personnel.

3. *Planning to Accomplish Specific Goals*

While long range and short-range planning encompass all the major functional areas of the enterprise, planning also requires to accomplish certain specific goals covering one or a few of these areas. But such planning is only supplementary to long-range or short range planning of the enterprise and, in a sense, it can be called intermediate planning. Planning can also be explained in terms of i) Production Planning and ii) Project Planning and these two are explained below.

i. Production Planning

It concerns with the planning of size of production and sales. That is,

- Determining the extent to which a particular product is acceptable to consumers.
- Estimating the amount of anticipated sales.
- Determining the period up to which a product would be in demand.
- Developing a new product to replace the old one, or improving the existing product.
- Intensifying sales in the existing markets and developing new markets.

ii. Project Planning

It concerns with a specific project or plan, such as setting up a new factory or plant, or scheme relating to modernization, amalgamation, or absorption of existing enterprises.

Projects are large, discrete and well defined tasks. A long-time lag is inevitable between the beginning of a project and its completion.

Types of Plans

On the basis of the length of the planning horizon, plans may be long-term, medium-term and short-term in nature.

Depending on their nature and scope, plans can be broadly classified as follows:

i) Standing or repeated use plans

a) Objectives
b) Policies
c) Procedures
d) Rules
e) Strategies

ii) Single - use plans

a) Programmes
b) Budgets

i. Standing or Repeated Use Plans

Standing or repeated use plans are developed by the organization to serve as guidelines with respect to activities which will occur frequently over time.

a. Objectives

Objectives may be defined as the future results or a desired state of affairs which the organization seeks and strives to achieve.

According to Charles Perrow, objectives are categorized into:

- *Societal* objectives which are concerned with creation and maintenance of cultural values through the production of goods and services.
- *Output* objectives are concerned with the kind of output i.e., durable goods, etc.
- *System* objectives are concerned with quality, innovativeness of the goods and services, etc.
- *Derived* objectives are concerned with secondary areas, e.g., community development.

b) Policies

Policies may be defined as guide, thinking and action of those who have to make decisions in the course of accomplishment of the enterprise objectives.

The following points must be borne in mind while formulating a policy:

- Broad outlines, leaving it to the managers to decide within its frame work.
- Consistent (Policies should not be contradictory to each other)
- Adequate number (without duplication)
- Sound and practicable
- Flexible

c) Procedures

Objectives and policies do not lay down ways and means through which objectives are achieved. So this drawback is eliminated by procedures which determine

- The specific tasks to be performed
- The time when these tasks will be performed
- The persons who will perform them

d) Rules

A rule means a decision made by the management regarding what is to be done and what is not to be done in a given situation. Rules do not leave any scope for decision making. Nor do they permit any deviation.

e) Strategies

Strategies concern with how the organization plans to meet the uncertain and competitive world outside, and makes different assumptions as regards the tactics and strength of the competitors. Formulation of a strategy is influenced by the external and internal environments of the organization. The external environmental forces consist of opportunities, threats and constraints, while the internal environment reflects the strength and weakness of the organization.

ii. Single - Use Plans

a) Programmes

Programmes refer to a set of clear instructions in a definite and logical sequence to perform a particular task. They explain how to carry out a given course of action. They are ordinarily supported by budgets.

b) Budget

A budget is a plan relating to a period of time, expressed in numerical terms. A budget may cover projected activities of a firm for a definite period of time, providing pre determined standards of performance in the fields of sales, purchases, production, income, expenditure, investment and profit. The standards are set considering the objectives and resource position of the enterprise. They also serve as a basis of evaluating the performance in various fields, and for correcting the deviations and deficiencies, if any.

Objectives of Budgeting

- Planning the action to be pursued within a specific period.

- Coordinating the activities in different fields of enterprises.
- Controlling: Deviations and deficiencies can be corrected.
- Motivation: Budgeting provides specific goals-which can be accomplished through motivation.

Key Terms and Concepts to Remember

Goals, forecasting, alternatives, strategic and tactical planning, objectives, policies, procedures, rules, strategies, programme, project and budget.

Chapter Summary

- Planning determines the objectives and policies in advance and means of achieving the objectives.
- Planning describes what one wants to happen to his enterprise.
- Planning requires rational thinking in setting realistic goals for the growth of an enterprise.
- Planning safeguards against business failure.
- There are wide gaps between the set goals through planning and actual realization. This is because of difficulties in assessing future events of both internal and external business environments.
- In order achieve greater results in any enterprise, a step - by - step procedure needs to be followed in the planning process.
- Planning can be classified into long-range planning or strategic planning, short term planning or tactical planning and intermediate planning. Short-range plans must be coordinated with long-range plans.

Chapter Highlights

This chapter highlights on different components of planning like meaning, characteristics, importance, limitations, step wise procedures and classification of planning.

Review Questions

A. Define the following

1. Planning
2. Strategic planning
3. Tactical planning
4. Objectives
5. Policies
6. Rules
7. Strategies
8. Programmes
9. Project
10. Budget

B. Answer the following

1. How planning process is important for the growth of an enterprise ?
2. Explain the major characteristics of planning.
3. What are the major limitations of planning ?
4. Discuss the steps involved in the planning process with a flow chart.

References

Harold Koontz and Heinz Weihrich, 1990 "Essentials of Management". (New York: Mc.Graw - Hill Publishing Company).

Harold Koontz, Heinz Weirich and Ramachandra Aryasri,A. 2004 "Principles of Management" (New Delhi: Tata Mc Graw. Hill Publishing Company Limited).

Further Reading Material

Heller.R. and T.Hindle.2000. Essential Manager's Manual, London: Color Library Direct Ltd.

Dinakar Pagare. 1995. Business Management (Fifth Edition), New Delhi: Sultan Chand & Sons.

Chapter 5

ORGANIZING

Organization means a system with parts which work together, or system with parts dependent upon each other. According to Louis Allen, organization is a process of identifying and grouping the works to be performed, defining and delegating responsibility and authority, and establishing relationships for the purpose of enabling people to work most effectively together in accomplishing objectives.

There is a difference between the words "Organizing" and "organization". Organizing refers to i) the identification and classification of required activities, ii) the grouping of activities necessary to attain objectives, iii) the assignment of each grouping to a manager with the authority (delegation) necessary to sepervise it, and iv) the provision for co-ordination, horizontally and vertically, in the oganization structure.

Organization implies a formalized intentional structure of roles or positions. The "intentional structure of roles" would refer to the roles people are asked to fill should be intentionally designed to ensure that required activities are done and that activities fit together so that people can work smoothly, effectively and efficiently in groups.

Importance of Organization

1. Efficiency in Management

Planning, direction and control can have meaning only when these functions are undertaken within the frame work of a properly designed and balanced organization. Organization is an effective instrument for realizing the objectives of an enterprise.

2. Instrument of All Round Development

A balanced organization helps an enterprise to grow and enter new lines of business. It can achieve the necessary momentum and adaptability to meet the various challenges posed by the environmental forces.

3. Adoption of New Technology

In a rapidly advancing world, changes are bound to take place in the techniques of production, distribution and man-power management. An effective management can foresee such changes in environment, which will involve rescheduling of activities as a new approach to delegation of authority and responsibility.

4. Aid to Initiative

For an organization to continue to remain effective, it is necessary that it encourages initiative among its staff. Then alone, it can discover talents and creativity among its employees.

Nature or Characteristics of an Organization

1. Division of Labour

It is the root of any organization structure. In order to improve the efficiency of any organization, the total efforts of persons who joined together for a common purpose have to be divided into different functions. These functions are further divided into sub-functions each to be performed by different persons. After the division of the total effort into functions and sub-functions, the next step is to group the activities on the basis of similarity of work. For example, in a manufacturing enterprise, its total activities may be divided and grouped under a) Production, b) Marketing, c) Finance and d) Personnel.

Even within each of these groups or departments, one or more sub-departments or sections may be created to look after particular activities so as to enhance the overall efficiency of the firm.

2. *Co-ordination*

An organization has to adopt suitable methods to ensure proper co-ordination of the different activities to be performed at various work spots. This implies that there must be a proper relationship between: a) an employee and his work, b) one employee and another and c) one department or sub-department and another.

3. *Objectives*

Objectives of a business cannot be accomplished without an organization; similarly an organization cannot exist for long without any objective and goal.

4. *Authority - Responsibility Structure*

For successful management, positions of personnel are so ranked that each of them is a subordinate to the one above it, and superior to the one below it. Management authority may be defined as the right to act, or to direct the actions of others.

5. *Communication*

For successful management, effective communication is vital because management is concerned with working with others, and unless there is proper understanding between people, it cannot be effective. The channels of communication may be formal, informal, downward, upward and horizontal.

Process of Organization

The important steps in an organizational process are :

1. *Determining the Activities to be Performed*

The first step in this process is to divide the total effort into a number of functions and sub-functions each to be performed, preferably, by a single individual or a group of individuals. Thus, specialization is a guiding principle in the division of activities.

2. *Assignment of Responsibilities*

It involves selection of suitable persons to take charge of activities to be performed at each work point. Also, the tasks to be performed by each member or group should be clearly defined.

3. *Delegation of Authority*

Along with the assignment of duties, there should be proper delegation of authority. It would be unrealistic to expect an individual to perform his job well if he lacks the authority to secure performance from his subordinates.

4. *Selecting Right Men for Right Jobs*

Before assigning a particular task to an individual, his technical competence, interests, and aptitude for the job should be tested. If the individual concerned lacks the technical ability to do his job, he can not perform it to the best of his ability.

5. *Providing Right Environment*

It involves provision of physical means like machines, furniture, stationery etc. and generation of right atmosphere in which employees can perform their respective tasks.

Key Elements of Organization Process

The following are the key elements in the process of organization.

1) Departmentation, 2) Delegation and 3) Decentralization.

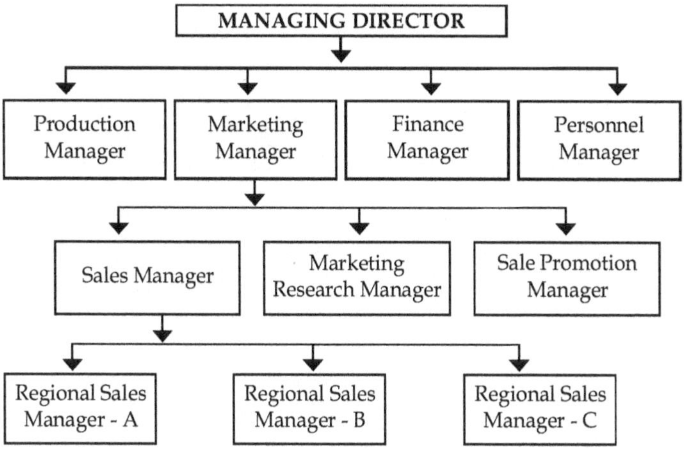

Fig. 5.1 : Organization Structure and Design

1. Departmentation

Departmentation implies the grouping of various activities on the basis of their similarity, into separate units. Departmentation of the enterprise activities can be done by:

- *Functions:* Production, sales, finance and personnel departments can be created.
- *Production:* For each product or group of products, a separate department is created.
- *Territory:* For each geographical division or territory, a separate department is created.
- *Customer:* Departmentation by customer is followed to look after the sales function where, in the interest of efficiency and economy, special attention needs to be given to different customers.
- *Number:* In case of departmentation by numbers, activities are grouped on the basis of their performance by a certain number of persons, whereas under departmentation by time, activities are grouped on the basis of the time of their performance.

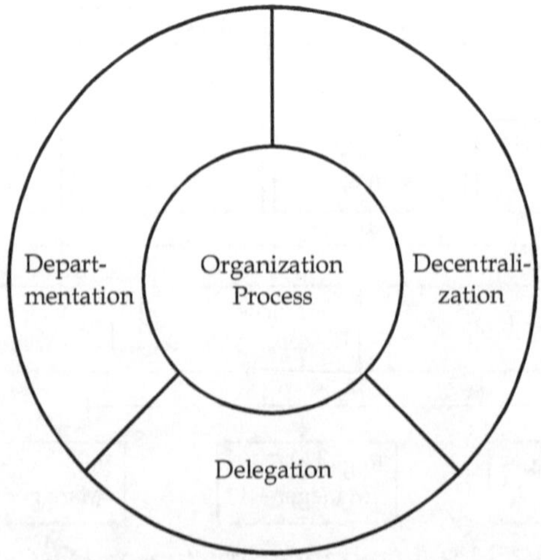

Fig. 5.2 : Key Elements of Organization Process

2. *Delegation*

The delegation has three important features, namely,

- Assignment of duties and responsibilities.
- Delegation of authority to perform the assigned duties and responsibilities.
- Accountability.

3. *Decentralization*

Decentralization is the opposite of centralization. Under centralization, the decision-making authority is vested in the hands of one or a few individuals.

Decentralization refers to dispersal of decision-making authority. It means that decisions are to be made by persons and at places away from the centre.

Decentralization may take the form of: a) departmentation or divisionalisation of enterprise activities; and b) dispersal of decision-making powers among executives at various levels.

Principles of Organization

The structure of the organization should be designed such that it achieves the stated goals. The basic principles of an organization are:

1. *Objectives*

The objectives of an organization are decisive in the determination of its structure. Does it plan to produce a single product to begin with, and then go on adding to its product-line as the financial resources permit? Does it want to produce quality product? Does it plan to retain customer goodwill by providing after sales services? All these questions will influence the organization structure.

2. *Unity of Command*

The unity of command stipulates that each is responsible to only one superior. If a subordinate is made to follow the orders from more than one boss, he will be in a perpetual dilemma and not knowing whose orders should be carried out first, how to allocate his time between different bosses, so as to satisfy them all and displease none, and what to do in case of conflicting orders.

3. *Span of Control*

The span of control refers to the number of subordinate managers reporting to a single senior manager stationed above them in the management pyramid. The span of control should be legitimate (neither too wide nor too narrow) without split in the line of control.

The optimum span must be determined for each enterprise taking into account of all the variables - organizational and human - the nature of enterprise, its traditions, tasks and ambitions. The span of control will differ from level to level; the optimum span should be determined individually for the different levels of management.

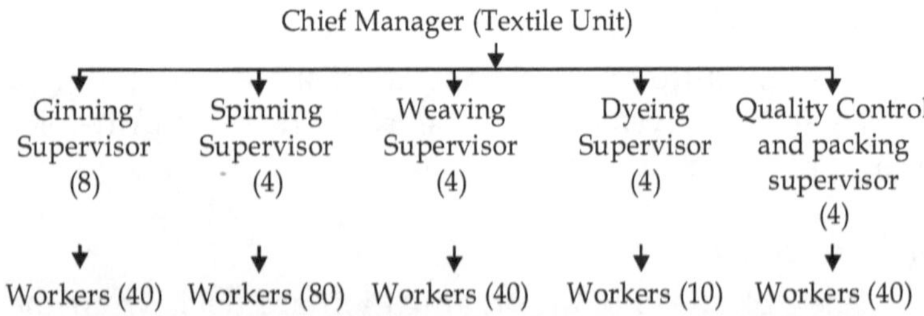

Fig. 5.3 : Span of Control and Different Levels of Management

However, there is no consensus on how many reporting subordinates is the best number for next senior who takes the report. According to Gillmore, in the case of most organizations, there should be no more than six levels of management, including that of the chief executive.

4. Scalar Pattern

This principle is sometimes, known as the chain of command. The line of authority from the chief executive at the top to the first line supervisor at the bottom must be clearly defined. The authority chain travels down the scalar line. Each position or level in the chain of command (authority) reports to the next superior and the process is repeated till the top is reached. Each such position enjoys formal authority depending upon the

- Position in the scalar chain and
- Status of centralization or decentralization in the organization.

5. Clear Definition of Authority and Responsibility

Authority may be defined as the power to make decisions which guide the actions of another. Responsibility is the obligation of a subordinate to whom a superior has assigned a task, to perform the service as required. Duty or responsibility may be in terms of functions, or in terms of targets or goals.

The authority and responsibility of each manager should be clearly defined in writing such that he knows what is expected of him and the limits of his authority to get it done.

6. *Balance between Authority and Responsibility*

If any responsibility assigned to a manager is not matched by the authority delegated to him, he will not be able to get the desired performance from his subordinates.

7. *Absolute Responsibility of Managers for Acts of Subordinates*

While authority can be delegated, responsibility is not. The manager continues to be as responsible as the subordinate concerned for what the latter has done, or failed to do.

8. *Power*

It is the ability of a person to influence another person to perform an act. There are five types of power: reward, coercion, reference, expertise, and legitimacy.

The difference between authority and power are given below:

Authority	**Power**
1. It rests on the chain (or position). With the change in the position, the authority of individual also changes.	It rests on the individual. Even if his position has changed, his power remains unchanged.
2. It is delegated to an individual by his supervisor.	It is earned by an individual through his own efforts. The individual gets it from people below him or from his peers.

contd...

3. It is mostly well defined, conspicuous (shown on the organization chart) and finite in commensurate with responsibility.	It is undefined, inconspicuous and infinite. Its location cannot be known from the formal organization chart.
4. It is what exists in the eye of the law.	It is what exists in fact.
5.It serves as a basis of formal organization	It serves as basis of informal organization.

9. Accountability

The subordinate is accountable for his actions and omissions. The accountability improves his responsibility and there by his performance. Every position in the organization structure should be assigned specific tasks, as also individuals or groups who are accountable for the accomplishment of those tasks. Care should be taken to see that people who are accountable for the performance of the given tasks have the required ability and information to carry out those tasks.

10. Delegation

The three elements, i.e., assignments of duties, delegation of authority and accountability for the performance of duties and responsibilities and exercise of authority are together termed as delegation.

The entire process of delegation involves the determination of results expected, the assignment of tasks, the delegation of authority for accomplishment of these tasks, and the assuming of responsibility of their accomplishment.

Decentralization is a pattern of responsibility arising from delegation.

Distinction between Delegation and Decentralization

Delegation	Decentralization
1. It is an act or a process	It is the end-result of delegation and dispersal of authority at various levels.
2. If refers to relationship between two individuals i.e., a superior and his immediate subordinate.	It refers to relationship between the top management and various departments and divisions in the enterprise.

11. Job Range and Depth

The job range refers to the manageable size of the work while the depth refers to the extent of the job rectification or perfection.

Job Range: A weaving master can manage, for example, 10 weaving units.

Job Depth: Day to day rectification of mechanical failure, major trouble in weaving machine has to be attended by the mechanical/textile manager.

12. Specialization

Specialization is acquired when a person (or a department or division) devotes his time to the performance of single leading operation. It is the key to efficiency and effectiveness. Specialization is concerned with delegation of authority horizontally rather than vertically.

13. Distinction between Line and Staff Functions

Line functions are concerned with the accomplishment of the main objectives of the organization. In a manufacturing unit, for example, production and sales are the line functions which are basic to the organization. As against this, staff functions are those which are of an advisory in nature and auxiliary to the line functions.

Departments concerned with purchases, advertising, public relations, legal services etc. only provide advice and aid to the line departments.

Staff personnel do not generally have authority to implement any change. They only offer advice or recommendation which need not be accepted by the line personnel.

14. Flexibility

Flexibility in the organization structure is necessary to enable it to adjust and adapt itself to any change in its environment, e.g., conditions of booms, depression, political instability, etc.

15. Simplicity

The organization structure should be simple i.e., with as few levels of authority as possible, such that there is free communication between persons operating at different levels, thus making for effective co-ordination.

Patterns in Organization Structure

The organization structure is determined by the nature and size of an enterprise. The pattern of organization structures commonly to be found is:

i) Line organization
ii) Functional organization
iii) Line and Staff organization
iv) Project organization
v) Committee organization
vi) Free-form organization

i) Line Organization

Under this, the persons having the greater decision-making authority are placed at the top, and those having the least decision-making authority are at the bottom. In between, there are other levels of management, such as intermediate and supervisory. The superior at each level makes decisions within the scope of the authority delegated to him by his boss. He communicates his decisions and orders to his subordinates.

ii) Functional Organization

A functional organization is one where the work is organized on the basis of specialization. Each specialist conveys his instruction direct to the line personnel, rather than through a formal chain of command. Functional organization improves specialization and thereby the efficiency.

iii) Line and Staff Organization

A line and staff organization is one where specialist advisers, in the role of functional managers, assist the line managers in the performance of their duties. In a firm engaged in the production of textiles, the production manager (in-charge of production), the marketing manager (in-charge of sales) and the finance manager (in-charge of financial matters) may be treated as line executives, and their departments are called Line Departments.

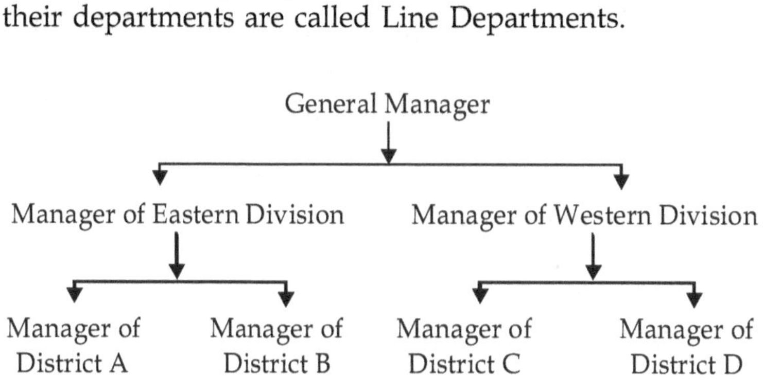

Fig. 5.4 : Line Organization

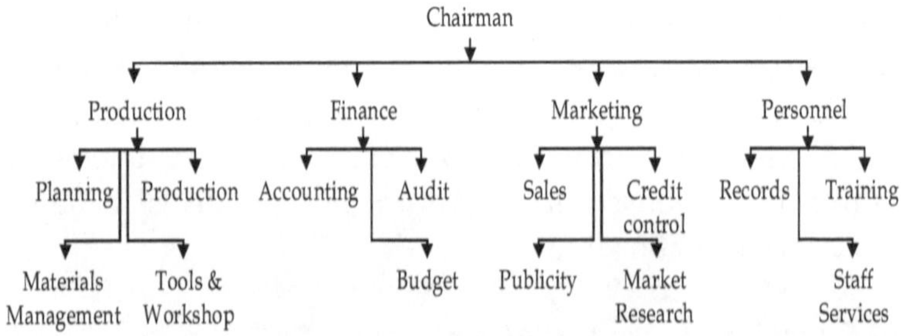

Fig. 5.5 : Functional Organization

Line executives have direct control over the subordinates under them. Staff executives have no such authority. They are only meant to aid and advise the line managers at the same level.

iv) Project Organization

It is set up with the objective of overcoming the major weaknesses of the functional organization, namely, absence of unity of command, delay in decision-making, and lack of co-ordination.

In a project organization, a division or department charged with completion of a specific programme may exist for a relatively long time. A project organization can also be the beginning of an organization. The project may become a long-term or permanent effort that eventually becomes a programme (or branch) organization. The latter may in turn become separated from the parent organization and be established as a full-fledged product division functionally organized.

v) Committee Organization

A committee means a group of persons formed for a special purpose. Committees are of the following types.

a) Standing and ad-hoc Committee: Standing Committee is a permanent one which is routinely chaired by the incumbent.

Ad-hoc committee is a temporary special purpose committee which is appointed to deal with specific problems.

b) Executive and Advisory Committee: An executive committee has the responsibility of making and executing its decisions. An advisory committee only examines a specific problem and gives its recommendations.

vi) Free-Form Organization

A free-form organization is similar to project organization and it is ad hoc-in nature.

The job in free form organization cannot be defined with certainty. Specific tasks are assigned to persons considering their expertise and competence.

Horizontal Integration of Firms

The firms producing similar or identical products come together so that their collective bargaining power increases.

Milk producers, vegetable growers, oil seed growers and so on can form union to have more bargaining powers. In this type, the middlemen are avoided, consumers are not exploited and the marketing cost is reduced so that the producers can get a major share in the consumer's rupee.

Vertical Integration of Firms

The various firms which are engaged in processing the products at different levels can be merged. A single firm may be engaged in more than one process. The marketing channel can be shortened by eliminating or reducing the number of middlemen. Both producers and consumers can be benefited as the marketing cost is reduced (A firm combines activities of different levels in the marketing channel).

Co-operative Milk Producers' Union.

Tamil Nadu Co-operative Oil Seed Growers' Federation (TANCOF).

Conglomeration of Business

The different firms join together (conglomerate) and try to fix the price and output for their own benefit. In this, horizontal or vertical integration or both may take place.

Key Terms and Concepts to Remember

Unity of command, span of control, scalar pattern, authority, responsibility, power, accountability, delegation, decentralization, departmentalization, line and staff functions.

Chapter Summary

- Organizing is a process of identifying and grouping of works to be performed, defining and delegating responsibility and authority and establishing relationships for enabling people to work together efficiently in order to accomplish the objectives of the enterprise.
- Division of labour enhances the efficiency of an organization.
- Delegation of authority and assignment of responsibility ensure smooth functioning of an organization.
- Departmentalization, delegation and decentralization are the three key elements in the process of organizing.
- Organization is essential for realizing the objectives of an enterprise. Planning, directing and controlling can be done only within the frame work of a properly designed organization.
- There are different patterns of organization such as i) line organization, ii) Functional organization, iii) Line and staff organizations, iv) project organization and so on.

Chapter Highlights

In this chapter namely, Organizing, meaning, importance, characteristics, process, key elements principles and patterns of organization are elaborately discussed.

Review Questions

1. *Distinguish Between the Following Concepts*

1. Organizing and organization
2. Departmentation and decentralization
3. Authority and power
4. Unity of command and chain of command
5. Job range and job depth
6. Line and staff functions
7. Horizontal and vertical integration.

2. *Answer the Following*

1. Discuss the importance of organization
2. What are the principles of organization ?
3. Explain the characteristics of organization
4. What are the important steps involved in an organizational process?
5. Briefly explain the key elements of organizational process.
6. Explain the patterns in an organization structure.

References

Koontz.H., H. Weihrich and A.Ramachandra Aryasri. 2004. Principles of Management, New Delhi: Tata McGraw-Hill Publishing Company Ltd.

Koontz. H., and H. Weihrich. 1990. Essential's of Management, (Fifth Edition), New York : McGraw-Hill International Edition.

Further Reading Material

Heller. R. and T. Hindle. 2000. Essential Manager's Manual, London: Color Library Direct Ltd.

Dinakar Pagare. 1995. Business Management (Fifth Edition), New Delhi: Sultan Chand & Sons.

Chapter 6

DIRECTING

Directing is concerned with telling subordinates what to do and ensuring that they do it as best as they can. It includes assigning tasks and duties, explaining procedures, issuing orders, providing on-the-job instructions, monitoring performance, and correcting deviations.

Directing must have two dimensions, namely, i) magnitude and ii) aim or direction.

The directing function includes the following:

i) Supervising
ii) Guiding
iii) Leading
iv) Motivating, and
v) Communicating

i) Supervision

The aim of supervision is to ensure that sub-ordinates work efficiently to accomplish the tasks assigned to them. Directing and supervising are similar in the sense that both seek to motivate the subordinate staff and provide leadership so that the predetermined goals are effectively accomplished. However, only the lowest level managers are designated as supervisors. One reason for this is that while all other levels of management have sub-ordinates who are managers themselves, the supervisory staff deals with workers who are engaged in basic operations.

Qualities of a Good Supervisor

1. Knowledge about the organization
2. Technical competency
3. Ability to instruct and explain
4. Ability to listen to others to gather information, to solve problems, to share experiences, etc.
5. Ability to secure co-operation
6. Ability for orderly thinking
7. Ability to judge people
8. Patience
9. Ability to improve workers' morale
10. Ability to enforce discipline
11. Ability to delegate the work among his sub-ordinates according to their capabilities.

ii) Guiding

This refers to a specialized task of leading the sub-ordinates to accomplish the result by overcoming the hurdles. Direction and purpose are very important for a manager to guide his sub-ordinate.

iii) Leadership

The following definitions refer to different aspects of leadership.

According to *Chester Barnard,* leadership is the ability of a superior to influence the behaviour of his subordinates and persuade them to follow a particular course of action.

Allen defined leader as one who guides and directs other people. He must give effective direction and purpose.

George R. Terry defined leadership as the activity of influencing people to strive willingly for mutual objectives.

According to *Robert C. Appleby,* leadership is a means of direction, and it is the ability of management to induce sub-ordinates work towards group ideas with confidence and keenness.

The following are the primary functions of a leader. He acts as:

1) Executive, 2) Planner, 3) Policy maker, 4) Expert, 5) External group representative, 6) Controller of internal relations, 7) Conveyor of rewards and punishments and 8) Arbitrator and mediator.

Types of Leaders

- *Autocratic* wants to run the show all by himself.
- *Laissez Faire* or Free rein leader permits his followers to do whatever they want to do.
- *Democratic* leadership is based on the assumption that the leader derives his power by consent of the followers. Participation, consultation and agreement of the group members are important features of democratic leadership.
- *Expert or Functional* leader does not have any formal authority. He stands out because of his special qualifications for the job handled by him, which is also the main reason why followers look up to him for guidance and control.
- *Institutional* leader is one who wields power over his followers due to the position or office occupied by him in the organizational hierarchy.

Qualities of Leadership

According to Henry Fayol, the qualities that a leader must possess are:

- Health and physical fitness
- Mental vigour and energy
- Courage to accept responsibility
- Steady, persistent and thoughtful determination
- Sound general education,
- Management ability, embracing foresight and the art of handling men
- Sense of judgement
- Understanding or empathy
- Motivation
- Communicating skill

Exercising Leadership

Effective leadership involves democratic directing rather than autocratic commanding. Leadership depends upon the interpersonal influence possessed by the leader. In order to exercise effective leadership, the leader should create a good working environment that contributes materially for the motivation of better work performance. The leader should be skilful in communicating his order down the chain of command, using formal and informal channels.

Once the sub-ordinates are chosen, the leader should try to build effective supervisory relationship with them. The following factors are significant in doing this.

- Attitude towards sub-ordinates
- Choice of sub-ordinates
- Training given to them

- Opportunities for attaining their job satisfaction
- Rewards for work well done
- Motivation

Motivation

Variation in individual effort and performance is attributable to the extent to which a person feels motivated. Motivation also refers to expansion of his mental and physical effort to accomplish the given task.

Motivation refers to goal-directed behaviour. It means what a person will choose to do when several alternatives are available to him. It also refers to the strength of his behaviour after he has exercised the choice, and the persistence with which he will engage in such behaviour.

Characteristics of Motivation

i) A Psychological Concept

Even workers with extraordinary abilities will not be able to perform as desired until they are effectively (psychologically) motivated.

ii) Motivation is Total, not Piece meal

Workers cannot be motivated in piece meal or parts.

iii) Motivation is Determined by Human Needs

Once a particular need is satisfied, he may lose interest in the activity that provides him satisfaction of the said need. In such a case, he will have to be provided awareness of satisfaction of his other needs so that he continues to be inclined to pursue the said activity.

iv) Motivation may be Financial or Non-Financial

Financial rewards: They include salary or wage increase, overtime and holiday payments, bonus, payment made under profit sharing plans, fringe benefits like amenities and facilities at concession rates.

Non-financial rewards: Free conveyance facility to residential areas and place of work, free lunch, provision of own secretary, servants at home, furnished rent free accommodation etc.

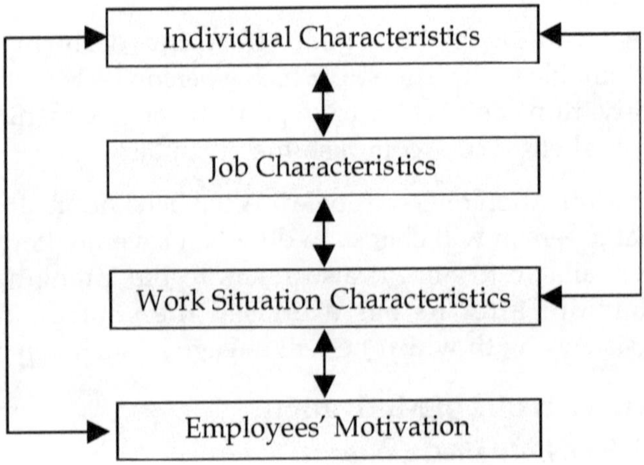

Fig. 6.1 : Characteristics of Motivation

Motivation is a constant process: Human needs are infinite. No sooner a person has satisfied one need, then he seeks to satisfy another.

Motivation is the result of interactions among three groups of factors, namely, i) influences operating within the individual, ii) influences operating within the organization and iii) influences operating in the external environment.

v) Communicating

Communication means sharing ideas in common. It means a verbal or written message, an exchange of information, a system of communicating, and a process by which meanings are exchanged between individuals through a common system of symbols. It also means a technique for expressing ideas effectively.

Nature of Communication

i) It takes Who to Complete Communication

Communication is a two-way traffic. There should be a sender and receiver of a message communicated.

ii) Message to be understood in the Same Sense

If the receiver does not understand it, the communication will not be complete.

iii) Message to have Substance

The transmitted message should give out ideas, information or facts which should be of interest to the receiver.

iv) Communication may be Oral, Written or Gesture

v) Communication may be Formal or Informal

Formal communication follows the formal channels provided in the organization structure. E.g., Sales manager will communicate with the deputy sales manager.

Informal communication is through personal contacts and it is faster in communicating messages than the formal channels.

Elements of Communication Process

- A communicator who sends message
- Message or information be communicated
- Encoding i.e., putting the message in suitable words
- Transmission
- Receiver or respondent or audience
- Decoding (understanding the message exactly as it has been sent)
- Response i.e., reaction of the respondent by way of reply, action or use of message

Types of Communication

On the basis of relationship between the parties concerned, communication may be a) formal and b) informal

On the basis of its flow of direction, communication may be a) oral, b) written and c) gesture.

Key Terms and Concepts to Remember

Directing, supervising, guiding, leading, motivating and communicating.

Chapter Summary

- Directing is a process of telling the subordinates what to do and ensuring that they do it as efficiently as they can.
- Directing function includes i) supervising, ii) guiding, iii) leasing, iv) motivating and v) communicating.
- Supervision ensures that sub ordinates work efficiently to accomplish the tasks assigned to them.
- Guiding is a task of leading the sub ordinates to accomplish the results by overcoming the hurdles.
- Leadership is the ability of a supervisor to influence the behaviour of his subordinates and persuade them to follow a particular course of action. There are different types of leaders, viz., i) autocratic, ii) laissez fair, iii) democratic, iv) expert and v) institutional leader.
- Motivation refers to expansion of mental and physical effort by an individual or group of persons to accomplish the given tasks.
- Communication means sharing ideas in common and it may be oral, written or gesture.

Chapter Highlights

This chapter comprises of meaning of directing, different types of directing functions like supervising, guiding, leading, motivating and communicating.

Review Questions

1. *Define the following*

1. Directing
2. Supervising
3. Guiding
4. Leading
5. Motivating
6. Communicating.

2. *Answer in brief*

1. What are the qualities of a good supervisor?
2. What are the primary functions of a leader?
3. Explain the different types of leaders.
4. What are the qualities of leadership?
5. Discuss the characteristics of motivation.
6. Explain the nature of communication.
7. What are elements of communication process?

References

Koontz.H., H. Weihrich and A.Ramachandra Aryasri. 2004.. Principles of Management, New Delhi: Tata McGraw-Hill' Publishing Company Ltd.

Koontz.H., and H. Weihrich . 1990. Essential's of Management, (Fifth Edition), New York : McGraw-Hill International Edition.

Further Reading Material

Heller.R. and T.Hindle.2000. Essential Manager's Manual, London: Color Library Direct Ltd.

Dinakar Pagare. 1995. Business Management (Fifth Edition), New Delhi: Sultan Chand & Sons.

Chapter 7

CONTROLLING

Control means the power or authority to direct and order or restrain. In the context of an entrepreneurial function, control may be defined as "comparing operating results with the plans, and taking corrective action when results deviate from the plans".

Control requires two things: first, there is a clear - cut and specific plan according to which any work is to proceed and second, it is possible to measure the results of operations with a view to detecting deviations.

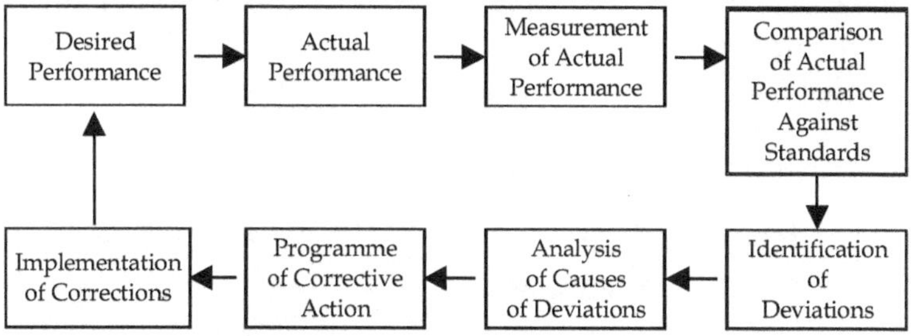

Fig. 7.1 : Management Control Process.

Need for Control

A control system is needed for three purposes namely, to

- Measure progress
- Uncover deviation and
- Taking corrective action.

To Measure Progress

The control process measures progress towards those goals. In an undertaking, control consists of variety of tools to measure whether everything occurs in conformity with plan adopted, the instructions issued and principles established.

To Uncover Deviations

Once a business organization is set into motion towards its specific objectives, events occur that tend to pull it 'off target'. Major events which tend to pull an organization 'off target' are as follows:

- Changes
- Complexity
- Mistakes
- Delegation

To Indicate Corrective Action

Controls are needed to indicate corrective actions. They may reveal that plans need to be redrawn or goals need to be modified or their is a need for reassignment or clarification of duties or additional staffing.

Steps in a Control Process

There are three basic steps in control process:

- Establishing standards
- Measuring and comparing actual against standards
- Taking corrective action

Establishing Standards

First, establishing standards against which results are to be measured may be done. Key areas for establishing standards like profitability, market position, productivity, etc. are to be identified. The different standards that can be used for control process are given below :

i) Physical Standards

- Labour hours per unit of output
- Level of production per machine hour

ii) Cost Standards

Direct and indirect costs per unit produced, material cost per unit, selling cost per unit of the product, etc.

Revenue Standards

Average sales per customer, sales per capita in a given market area, etc.

Capital Standards

Rate of return on capital invested, Current asset/ current liabilities = current ratio, etc.

Intangible Standards

Competence of manager and employees. Standards should emphasis the achievement of result more than in conformity to rules or methods.

Measuring and Comparing Actual Results Against Standards

Measurement of performance can be done by personal observation while they are engaged in work and by a study of summaries of figures, reports, charts and statements.

Desirable Variations

Output above the standard or expenses below the standard are the desirable variations.

Undesirable Variations

A delay in the delivery schedule agreed upon with the customer, or higher diesel consumption by vehicles are undesirable variations.

When to Introduce a Control System

Measurement and comparison may be done at stages in the total process or at the end. It depends upon the purpose. If the purpose of control is to catch trouble while it is forming, then this should be done at various strategic points before the end of the process.

Taking Corrective Action

Compare actual performance with prescribed standards and find deviations. Corrective action should be taken without wasting of time so that normal position can be restored quickly. Identify the causes for deviations like inadequate and poor equipment and machinery, inadequate communication system, lack of motivation of subordinates, defective system of training and selection of personnel, defective system of remuneration, etc.

Important Devices or Tools of Control

1. Traditional Devices

- Budgeting or budgetary control
- Cost control
- Production control
- Inventory control
- Break-even point analysis
- Profit or loss control
- Statistical Data Analysis
- Audit

2. *Modern Devices*

- Return on Investment Control
- Programme Evaluation and Review Technique (PERT)
- Management Information System (MIS)
- Cybernetics
- Management Audit

Traditional Devices

1. *Budgetary Control*

A budget is a financial plan for a definite period of time. Budgetary control evolves a course of action that would make the realization of the budgeted targets possible. *Zero-based budgeting* as a method of budgeting under which all activities are reevaluated each time a budget is formulated.

2. *Cost Control*

It refers to control of all the costs of an undertaking, both direct and indirect, in order to achieve cost effectiveness in business operations.

3. *Production Control*

Production control is the process of planning production in advance of operations, establishing the exact *route* of each individual item, part or assembly, setting starting and finishing dates for each important item, assembly and the finished product; and realizing the necessary orders as well as initiating the required follow up to effect the smooth functioning of the enterprise.

4. *Inventory Control*

It refers to controlling the kind, amount, location, movement, and timing of the various commodities used in and produced by the industrial enterprises.

5. *Break - even Point Analysis*

The break even point may be defined as the point when sales revenue is equal to total cost (fixed and variable). In other words, it represents the level of activity when there is neither any profit nor loss.

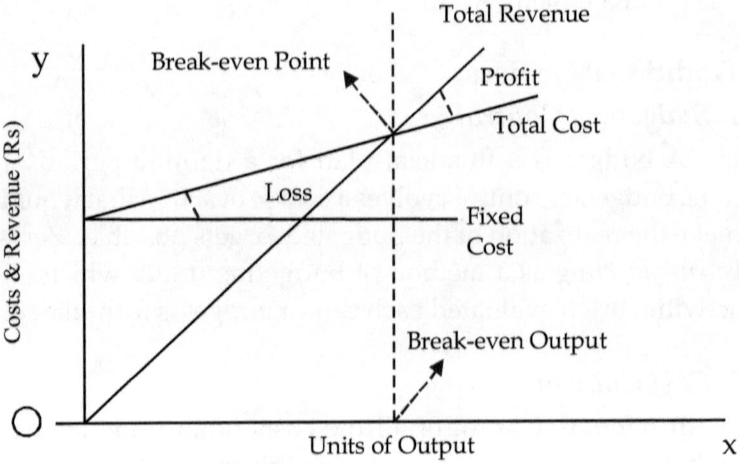

Fig. 7.2 : Break-even point analysis

Table 7.1 : Estimation of Break-even Output.

$$\text{Break-even output} = \frac{\text{Fixed overhead}}{\text{Contribution}}$$

Contribution = Sales revenue - Variable cost

Selling Price	:	Rs. 200.00
Variable Cost		Rs. 300.00
Contribution	:	Rs. 300 - Rs. 200 =
Per unit		Rs. 100
Fixed Cost	:	Rs. 1,50,000
Break-even Output	:	1,50,000 / 100
		= 1500 units

6. *Profit and Loss Control*

Profit and Loss Control refers to a control system under which sales, expenses, and profits of each branch or "product division" are compared with those of other branches and product divisions, as well as with historical trends, with a view to measuring deviations and taking necessary corrective action.

7. *Statistical Analysis*

Comparison of ratios, percentages, averages, etc. of different periods can be done to monitor - deviations and their causes.

8. *External and Internal Audit*

External audit is enforced by law in respect of all joint stock companies, co-operatives, etc. Its objective is to safeguard the interest of the share holders against the malpractices of management.

Firms may also have internal audit under which staff members of the company may verify financial transactions and financial records for analyzing the overall control system of the organization.

Key Terms and Concepts to Remember

Budgeting, cost control, production control, inventory control, break-even analysis and profit and loss control.

Chapter Summary

- Controlling means exercising power or authority to direct and order or restrain.
- Controlling system is required to measure progress, uncover deviation and taking corrective action.
- The three steps involved in the controlling process are: i) establishing standards, ii) measuring and comparing actual against standards and, iii) taking corrective action.

- As regards standards, there are i) physical, ii) cost, iii) revenue, iv) capital and, v) intangible standards.
- There are traditional tools of control like budgeting, cost control, production control, inventory control, break even output estimation, etc. and modern devices like return on investment control, PERT, MIS management, audit, and so on.

Chapter Highlights

In this chapter, a brief discussion on definition of control, need for control, steps involved in the control process and important tools of control has been made.

Review Questions

1. What is controlling and explain the need for controlling in any business enterprise.
2. Discuss the steps involved in the control process with a flow chart.
3. Explain the different tools used in the control process.
4. Explain the Break-even analysis with illustration.

References

Koontz.H., H. Weihrich and A.Ramachandra Aryasri. 2004. Principles of Management, New Delhi: Tata McGraw-Hill Publishing Company Ltd.

Koontz.H., and H. Weihrich . 1990. Essential's of Management, (Fifth Edition), New York : McGraw-Hill International Edition.

Further Reading Material

Heller.R. and T.Hindle.2000. Essential Manager's Manual, London: Color Library Direct Ltd.

Dinakar Pagare. 1995. Business Management (Fifth Edition), New Delhi: Sultan Chand & Sons.

Chapter **8**

PRODUCTION MANAGEMENT

Functional Areas

In any business organization, the commonly identified functional areas are production, marketing and finance. In recent years, the personnel and materials that go into the production process, packing process and marketing process have gained importance and given due importance by treating them separately as personnel and materials management.

Organization functional areas are

- Production Management
- Marketing Management
- Financial Management
- Personnel Management
- Materials Management

The above functional areas are not watertight compartments. The decisions/actions taken in one functional area affect the other functional area. The decisions in production and marketing are influenced by the actions on such matters as volume, terms and conditions of loan. The quantity, quality and timely availability of materials also has a bearing on production and marketing decisions. The labour motivation towards work and supervising ability/skill of supervising personnel also affects production and marketing.

Production/Operations Management

In general, operations management refers to management of all operations of a production unit. So it may be interchanged with production management. Production is a system for converting inputs into finished products. The production often refers to manufacturing industries. Yet, in reality, production can be defined as the creation of value or wealth by producing goods and services. Production management refers to planning, organization, direction, co-ordination and control of the production functions carried out in such a way that the desired goods or services could be produced at the right time, in right quantity and at the optimum cost.

The production management involves the following activities:

- Developing the product/service
- Establishment of proper organization structure
- Selection of personnel
- Establishment and maintenance of factory building, plant and equipment
- Management of purchases, storage and transportation of raw materials
- Ensuring effective control

In production management, decisions to be taken consist of

a) What to produce ?
b) When to produce ?

c) How much to produce ? and

d) How to produce ?

Production includes a) manufacturing of commodity (physical output) and b) creation of services.

Deciding whether to Buy or Make

The process of changing raw materials into finished products that is delivered to customer is a long process, usually involving many companies performing different productive functions. One company may refine the raw materials, several may perform manufacturing processes, and another may assemble the parts into the finished product and so on. A given company may perform a large or small part of this process. Fixing the place and size of the segment is an important decision.

Deciding to Specialize or Generalize

A food (fruit) processor may

- Grow or buy his fruit requirements
- Sell his output to a wholesaler, retailer or directly to consumer

The advantages of specializing and concentrating in a small segment are:

- Less capital investment is needed
- Management can concentrate better on small segment
- Planning, directing and controlling are less complex

The advantages of a larger segment are

- More control of the process
- Less idling (time) of men and machinery
- Greater potential of growth

Economics of Decision to Set up a Production Unit

The decision on what segment of the total transformation process depends on the economics of situation. Having decided on the segment of the transformation process, one can begin to plan, obtain and install the producing unit.

Physical Facilities

The physical facilities of the firm would include building, machineries and equipments, furniture and fixtures and others. They must be designed to aid employees in producing the desired product or service at a low cost. The design function includes lay out, selection of machines and equipments and determination of features desired in the planning.

Steps in Planning the Physical Facilities

Good selection and arrangement of physical facilities can pay dividends. Planning the physical facilities require the following steps.

- Determine the goods and services to be produced and performed.
- Break the product or services into parts, operations and activities. Parts are the divisions of the product that, when assembled form output. Some outputs have only one part while others may have many. Operations are the steps or segments of work performed to accomplish the conversion of inputs into outputs. Activities such as moving raw materials are necessary for the performance of operations. Non-activities including delays are caused by imbalance of times of the operation. Activities and non-activities may not be identified fully until the final lay out planning is done. The number and extent of non-activities should be minimized.

- Determine the time to perform different operations. Each operation required to produce a good or perform service consumes the time of work of machines and personnel. The total time includes the time to perform the operation plus time for unavoidable delays and personnel needs. The time of work determines the number of machines and the number of people needed to perform the work and speed of conveyors.

- Estimate the number of machines and workers needed

  Knowing the time that a machine takes to perform an operation on a product, and knowing the planned production, the number of machines needed can be determined.

- Decide the best arrangement for the sequence of operations

  The operations management has to ensure the least movement of product and people. However, people and machines should not be idle and space available should not be wasted. The plant can be planned according to either or a combination of both of the following two types of layout.

a. Product or Service layout.
b. Processor or Function lay out

a) The product layout places machines or serving units in such a way that the product moves along a line as it passes through the sequence of operations. Materials and people move forward from operation to operation with little back tracking.

Advantages

- Specialization of workers and machines
- Less inventory

- Fewer instructions and control
- Faster movement
- Less space for storage

b) The process layout is based on keeping machines and workers busy so that idle time is reduced to a minimum. Machines performing the same type of work and workers with similar skill are grouped together.

Advantages

- It has flexibility to take care of change
- It uses general-purpose machines and equipment
- Efficient use of machines and personnel

Some specific matters that the manager should include in the final layout planning are:

- Space for movement
- Utilities
- Supply of equipments
- Safety
- Working conditions
- Cleanliness and maintenance
- Product quality

Few layouts are combination of both product and process layouts to take advantage of the situation. Further, decreasing inventory compensates idle time created by differing production. To sum up, the general layout has to be determined and also the detailed layout has to be planned for achieving efficiency and effectiveness.

Implementing the Plan

The first step in implementing the plan is to test whether it is sound (working well). There are many ways to do this. One method is to have employees or other persons who can give some experienced opinions - review of the plans and suggestions. Another method is to stimulate the process by moving templates or models of the goods or people through the process so that their movements can be analyzed. Some mishaps can be deliberately included to see what happens. The actual implementation of the plan will depend on whether it is a brand new venture, a layout for an existing building or rearrangement of the present layout.

Designing and Controlling Work

The planning and control process is a communication system designed to convey to employees what, how, where, who, when and why the work is to be done.

1. Work Design

After the layout of the plant, plan for the movement of materials. Steps involved in work design and improvement are:

- State the problem
- State the functions
- Collect the information
- List alternatives
- Formulate, review and test the selected changes
- Install and follow up changes

2. Work Measurement

Physical work can be measured more precisely than mental work but it still requires judgment. The time to perform can be divided into i) time to perform the work and ii) time for personal needs and irregular activities.

The methods used to determine time to perform the work are:

- Estimates by people experienced in the work
- Time study, using a watch or timing device

Adding Time for Personal Needs

Personal and irregular time allowances are added to normal time to obtain the total time in which operation should be performed under normal conditions. Time for use of rest rooms, poor working conditions and fatigue are some allowances of personal needs.

3. Planning

The optimum plan from a production stand point is to maintain a constant level of production to its capacity for both machine and person of one product, with inputs needed arriving and outputs taken by customers as and when they are finished.

4. Scheduling the Time for Work to be Done

Orders are scheduled into production

- On a preplanned schedule
- When inventory is reduced to a certain low level
- When orders are received and inventory is not available.

Schedules set the times to produce specified goods. The scheduling can be done by one of the following methods:

- Sending orders into the shop in sequence. The shop processes the job through operation on a first come first served basis.
- Setting priorities and processing orders accordingly. Rush orders which have top priority.
- Using either (1) or (2) for each operation.
- Setting a specific time for each operation and for each job.

Controlling Production: Quantity and Quality

If no control is expressed over operations, the process will fail. Then, the principle of exception should be followed. Controlling by exceptions involves comparing the plans with the plant's performance. In simple systems, this comparison can be made informally by personally observing performance. Orders may be filed by due date, work to be completed in each department may be recorded each day or bar charts may be used. The record is obtained through feedback or by having forms returned with information on work performed. Changes may not be done when performance equals or exceeds the plans. An exception arises when performance does not reach the level desired. Then the operations manager has to decide what to do to improve future performance.

The methods used in quality control have been developed further than those for other control systems and are used in many other systems, including cost control. The system begins with setting the level of quality desired. The quality level is based on:

- The value of quality to the customer
- The cost of the quality.

Then controls should be established to obtain that quality. The cost will increase, if an attempt is made to exceed that level of quality. At the same time, if quality is allowed to go below the level, then the firm will lose its customers.

Steps needed in any system of control are:

- Set standards for your quality range.
- Measure your actual performance.
- Compare performance with standards.
- Make corrections when needed.

Standards of quality may be set for dimension, colour, odour/flavour, strength, content weight, service and other characteristics.

ISO Standards

The World Trade Organization's agreement on technical barriers to trade emphasizes the vital role laid by International Standards in providing the technical foundation for global markets.

When this is done, conflicts are minimized and agreements are more. On this occasion, it may be worthwhile to review the development of the new version of ISO 9000 Standards for Quality Management Systems, which have now become so essential for acceptance of products and services at the International level.

The ISO 9000 Standards originally evolved for Quality Management Systems for manufacturing units. The same formulation was then extended to service and software fields. There has been a need felt over the years for a generic system which is all comprehensive and at the same time easily applicable to the business of the user, whether it be in manufacturing or service or software fields. Also, in the meantime the environment management standards have come in. Taking into account all these and the fact that the ISO 9000 Standards were last revised in 1994, ISO's Technical Committee TC 176 had taken up the task of bringing out "Year 2000" revision. This is expected to be announced at the end of year 2000, though by now the finalized draft has been circulated which contains all the essential features.

The Changes

The current ISO 9000 family of Standards contains over 20 Standards and documents. The year 2000 ISO 9000 Quality Management Standards (QMS) on the other hand will have only three primary standards, which are

1. ISO 9000 - Quality Management Systems - *Fundamentals and Vocabulary*
2. ISO 9001 - Quality Management Systems- *Requirements*
3. ISO 9004 - Quality Management Systems - *Guidance for Performance Improvement*

The current ISO 9001, ISO 9002 and ISO 9003 Standards will be consolidated into a single ISO 9001 Standards. A reduction of scope of the ISO 9001 requirements will be permitted to omit clauses that do not apply to a particular organization. In addition to the three core standards, ISO 10011, the auditing standard will be consolidated with the ISO 14010, ISO 14011 and ISO 14012 environmental auditing standards.

Principles of Revision

The principles driving the revision process are:

- Applicability to all product and service sectors and to all sizes of organizations,
- Simplicity to use, clear in language, readily translatable and easily understandable,
- Ability to connect Quality Management Systems to organizational processes,
- Provision of a natural stepping-stone towards performance improvement,
- Greater orientation toward continual improvement and customer satisfaction,
- Compatibility with other management systems, such as ISO 14000, for Environmental Management,
- Need to provide a consistent basis and address the primary needs and interests of organizations in specific sectors such as aerospace, automotive, medical devices, telecommunications and others.

Process Model: The revision of the ISO 9000 QMS makes a radical change and repositions the 20 elements of the current ISO 9001 into four parts.

- Management responsibility
- Resource Management
- Product and/or Service realization
- Measurement, analysis and improvement

The process model is similar to the well-known Deming's PDCA (Plan, Do, Check and Act) cycle of quality improvement. This kind of a structuring permits the applicability of this model to any business or service. The concept of continuous improvement is intended to stimulate the efficiency of the organization, to increase its competitive advantage in the market and to better respond to customers' needs and expectations.

Another new item that has been addressed is the measurements to evaluate customer satisfaction, which provide for key information for continuous improvement.

In terms of resources, attention has been given for the need to provide and make available all necessary resources, which will now include elements such as information, communication, infrastructure and work environment protection.

Changes have also occurred in terminology. Now the more natural term "organization" is used instead of "supplier" in the old standard. The expression "product and service" is used instead of only "product" as was in the old standard. These changes are friendlier with the normal use and meaning of the words. Also, compatibility with ISO 14001 environmental standards is sought to be achieved through informative annexes correlating the clauses.

Transition

There is an ISO document on Transition Planning Guidance to help the change over. Further, authentic information regarding revision can be obtained from the Bureau of Indian Standards (BIS), which has played a leading role in the deliberations of the ISO's Technical Committee. Since the new standards are integration and simplification of the older one, transition should be easy and also there is sufficient time given for the process.

The process model is well suited to really focus on the needs of customers and if genuinely implemented should help the growth of business. In fact, this is the real essence of the change over. While the past standard no doubt implied this, there was no explicit requirement to measure customer satisfaction and initiate continuous improvements. On the other hand, in the new standard these are explicit and essential part of the elements. Also, they include other interested parties (suppliers, owners, employees and society) under management responsibility.

Over 5,000 firms in India are estimated to have obtained ISO 9000 Certification so far. It is no more a luxury but has been considered common place for achieving standards of product or service. There has also been the unfortunate side, namely the creeping in of the "certificate culture". Once the certification is obtained, organizations tend to be complacent and do not effect continuous improvement. What the customer needs is not a certificate to be shown to him but provision of an improved product and service, which is by itself the best certificate that any organization can get. This has been the secret of the Japanese and Korean success. The new standards will help simplify the procedural part and invigorate the commitments of organizations to continuously provide better products and services to their customers.

Quality Management

Hazard Analysis Critical Control Point (HACCP)

Since its introduction in the early 1970's, HACCP system is a cost effective management tool for food safety assurance that can be applied to all sections of the food chain from primary production to processing, manufacturing, distribution and retails to the point of consumption. The WTO and Sanitary and Phytosanitary Measures (SPS) agreements emphasize that food safety standards be based on scientific principles as they relate to risk assessment. Currently, the emphasis by organizations like Bureau of Indian Standards is to issue certification on HACCP, which will enhance the marketability of Indian food products, like meat, poultry, vegetables, sea foods and processed foods in the global market. Training programmes need to be conducted to increase the awareness of HACCP among the food managers, which could also help in achieving certification.

Food safety is a social responsibility and its achievement can only be possible with the active participation of all segments, *viz,* the producer, the processor, the consumer and the government.

Farm Operations

The greatest amount of attention that needs to be paid is to the observance of hygienic and sanitary practices in various farm operations. Inadequate consideration given to potential hazards at the farm level is often responsible for making subsequent correction of the problems unnecessarily expensive or in some cases rendering them insoluble. Some of the typical problems and the foods in which they are encountered are pesticide residues in fruits, vegetables, egg and milk; pathogens in fruits, vegetables, spices, poultry and sea food; insects in fruits, vegetables, spices; high microbial load in most fresh produce, milk, meat and poultry; mycotoxins in cereals, oilseeds and milk.

Almost all these problems can be effectively overcome by adherence to farm practices.

Total Quality Management (TQM)

ISO 9000 deals with the process. Total Quality management is about people. TQM links quality to customer satisfaction by acting on four aspects - customer requirements, management commitment, total company wide participation and systematic analysis of quality problems. TQM provides the overall concept that fosters continuous improvement. TQM philosophy stresses a systematic, integrated, consistent, organization wide perspective, involving every one and every thing in an organization. ISO is a milestone in TQM journey.

Core Concepts for TQM are

- Customer satisfaction - Be customer focused.
- Internal customers are real.
- All work is process. Make it a good place to work, create a work culture, which will lead to satisfied customers.
- Measurement - measure the work.
- Teamwork - Top management must be involved.
- People make quality - Do it right first time, quality is an attitude, empowering.
- Continuous improvement cycle.
- Prevention of poor quality production.

Key Terms and Concepts to Remember

Functional areas, production/operations management, specialization or generalization, physical facilities, product layout, process layout, designing and controlling of work, work measurement, scheduling the time for work, controlling quantity and quality of product, ISO standards, total quality management.

Chapter Summary

Functional areas of an organization are

- Production management, b) materials management, c) marketing management, d) financial management, e) personnel management.
- Production management refers to planning, control of the production functions carried out in such a way that the desired goods or services could be produced at the right time, in right quantity and at the optimum cost.
- In production management, design functions include layout and selection of machines and equipments. There are two types of layouts : product layout and process layout.
- After the layout of the plant, planning for the movement of materials has to be done. Then measurement of works carried out, scheduling of time for work and finally evolving control measures for ensuring quality have to be done.
- ISO standards have been prescribed for ensuring high quality of product or services as per international standards.
- The greatest amount of attention that needs to be paid is to the observance of hygienic and sanitary practices in various farm operations.
- Total Quality Management (TQM) links quality to customer satisfaction by acting on four aspects – customer requirements, management commitment, total company wide participation and systematic analyses of quality problems.

Chapter Highlights

In this chapter, definition of operations / production management, activities involved in production management, production management decisions, decision making on specialization or generalization their advantages and disadvantages, physical facilities – steps involved in planning the physical facilities, product and process layout their advantages and disadvantages designing and controlling of work, features of International and Standards Organization (ISO) standard, quality management – HACCP, farm operations and total quality management have also been discussed.

Review Questions

1. What are different functional areas of an organization?
2. Define production / operations management.
3. What are the activities involved in production management ?
4. What management decisions are taken under production management ?
5. What are the advantages of i) specialization and ii) generalization in the business process.
6. What are the general physical facilities required for a firm ?
7. Explain the different steps involved in planning the physical facilities
8. What are two types of layout ? Explain their advantages ?
9. How designing of work helps in improving the production efficiency ?
10. Explain the control function to be performed by a production manager in order to ensure desired quantity and quality of the product.

11. Write a brief note on the features of ISO standards.
12. Explain the concept of Total Quality Management (TQM).

References

Koontz.H., H. Weihrich and A.Ramachandra Aryasri. 2004. Principles of Management, New Delhi: Tata McGraw-Hill Publishing Company Ltd.

Koontz.H., and H. Weihrich . 1990. Essential's of Management, (Fifth Edition), New York : McGraw-Hill International Edition.

Russell.R.S. and B.W. Taylor III.2006. Operations Management, New Delhi: Prentice Hall of India Pvt. Ltd.

Further Reading Material

Heller.R. and T.Hindle.2000. Essential Manager's Manual, London: Color Library Direct Ltd.

Dinakar Pagare. 1995. Business Management (Fifth Edition), New Delhi: Sultan Chand & Sons.

Chapter 9

MATERIALS MANAGEMENT

Materials Management deals with purchasing and controlling of the materials used in the production process.

Materials (Goods) Planning and Control

Decisions to be taken in this are:

- Amount of materials needed for output desired
- Amount of inventory and its storage and reordering
- Vendor relations
- Quality materials and price per unit
- Quantity and time of order
- Methods of receiving and transporting
- Handling of defective materials and stock

Policies and procedures should be established so that most of these decisions become routine in nature. When exceptions occur, the concerned authority should correct them.

Materials are a form of investment and until they are sold and produce revenue, the money cannot be used for other income producing purposes. Consequently, the manager wants to buy (the materials) in small quantities and sell the output rapidly in order to obtain income. But, if quantities are too small, the income producing opportunities may be lost and customers may be missed. Also, purchasing in small quantities usually results in higher prices. The losses due to theft should be kept minimum. While increasing controls may reduce cost from losses, it also increases, the controlling cost. The problem is to find the balance between these two costs.

Inventory Control of Raw Materials

The use of inventory is to take care of seasonal variations in demand. The inventory of materials, parts, goods and supplies represent a high investment in all business. Many companies failed because their inventories locked up too much money or the items in inventory become obsolete, impaired or lost. The purpose of inventory is to disconnect one segment of a process from another, so that each segment can operate at its optimum level of performance.

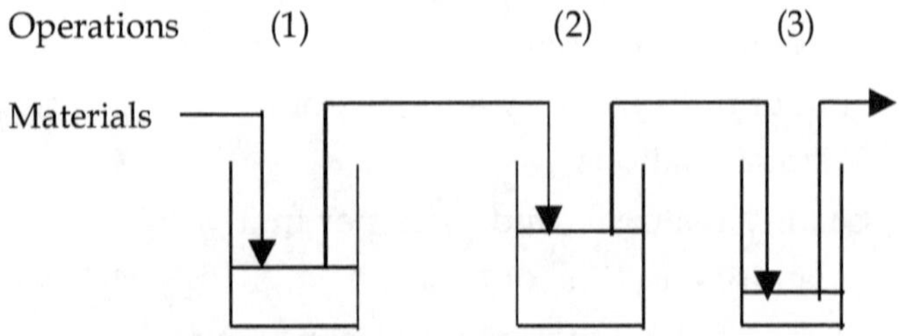

Fig. 9.1 : Inventory between Different Operations

Types of Inventories

- Purchased materials, parts, products
- Goods in process or between operations
- Finished goods at the factory, warehouse or store
- Repair parts for machines
- Supplies for the office, shop or factory
- Tools

Each of these types of inventory is performing basically the same function and can be studied in the same way. Some of the inventories represent a much greater investment, cause more serious trouble if the items are not in stock and are more costly to restock than others.

Determining Economic Inventory Level

The detailed analysis made to determine economical inventory level must consider total inventory which should not be so great such that it makes it difficult to pay current bills in cash. The (Fig. 9.2) shows how the number of units of a purchased item varies over a period of time. When a purchased item is received, the inventory increases instantly. The units are removed from inventory, as they are demanded. At certain levels or when inventory falls to a specific level, a purchase order is sent to the vendor. The order will be received sometime later. In the meantime, more units may be drawn from inventory. This cycle is repeated for each item purchased.

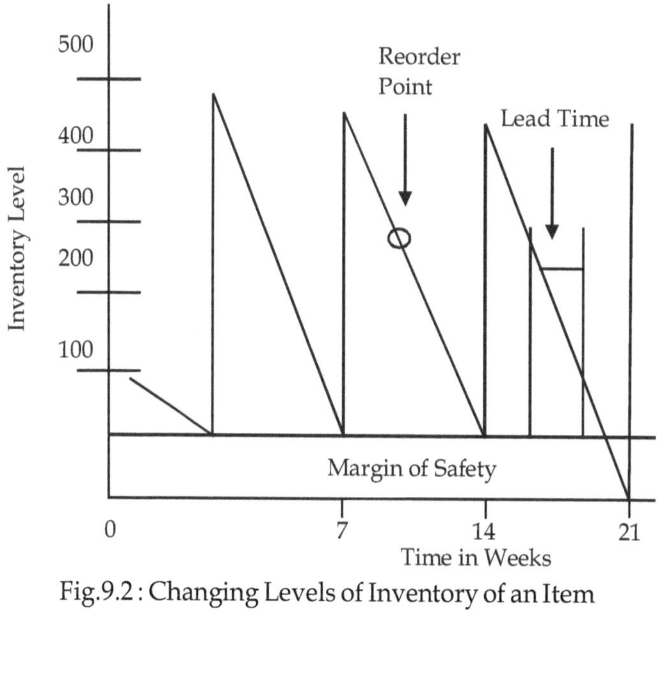

Fig.9.2 : Changing Levels of Inventory of an Item

For items in process and in finished goods, the inventory builds up over a period of time as goods are produced so that the vertical line in the figure will be sloping upwards to the right. The inventory builds up because production is greater than demand. Too little inventory may cause stock- -outs (shortage of the material or product when it is required for production or sale). The problem is to strike the optimum inventory to carry converted in terms of Economic Order Quantity (EOQ) for consumption of materials and economic lot size for each batch production.

The variables are :

- Annual requirement of the item (c)
- Ordering cost (s)
- Inventory carrying cost per unit (I)

The model is given by the equation,

$$EOQ = \sqrt{\frac{2CS}{I}}$$

Uses of the Model

The model is an excellent guide in scientific inventory management. This compels the manager to analyze the requirements and cost of inventory holding. It is useful in the inventory management by fixing.

- Maximum and minimum levels of stock holding.
- Ordering level I (that is, the stock point when reordering is required, and
- The most economic quantity to order.

The above is a simple and deterministic model, which assumes constant rate of consumption, constant cost of ordering and holding inventory and uniform lead - time (that is, the time lag between replenishment, action and actual supply or availability of the items).

Determining When to Order

The level of inventory at which an order should be issued is based on:

- The quantity to be used between times, an order is issued and items are received.
- A quantity needed to provide a margin of safety.

The time to be allowed in (1) is determined by the time taken for

- Order to be processed by the firm
- Order to be transported to the vendor
- Vendor to make and pack the items
- Items to be transported to the firm

Estimates of cost of carrying inventory ranges from 15% to over 100% of the average inventory investment for a year. Values of 20% to 25 % are often used. The reordering point quantity can be estimated by computing various levels and reordering points and adding the cost of carrying the inventory and cost of running out of goods multiplied by the probability of running out. The lowest cost is the best order point.

Quantity per Order

The quantity per order affects the level of inventory and the time between orders. Orders may be placed :

- At certain intervals such as once in a week, a month or quarter, when the amount ordered can bring the level of inventory up to a predetermined standard amount.
- When the inventory reaches a certain quantity.

Ordering Procedure

Many items can be ordered on a routine basis. The procedure starts with need as reflected by the reorder points and requires keeping a

- Perpetual inventory which records when the inventory has reached the reorder point.
- Quantities set aside that will not be used without making out a purchase order.

Items Requiring Special Analysis

- *Expected changes in price* : Short delays in buying for expected decrease in price or increased quantities for expected increase in price result in savings. However, stock - outs or too heavy inventory costs should be guarded against.
- *Expected changes in demand*: Seasonal products fall into this category.
- *Orders for a demand for special goods*: Quantity ordered is equal to amount demanded so that no material is left over.
- *Short supply of materials* : Speculative buying should be avoided, unless the manager is well versed in that business.

Placing Responsibility of Ordering

One person should have the responsibility for ordering all materials but that person should obtain the help of those knowledgeable people in the area where the goods are needed. By having a single person responsible, duplicate orders for the same material are avoided, the specialized skills needed for purchasing can be used and the responsibility for improvements in buying - process is established.

Sources of Supply

This is important because,

- Price of purchased goods is a major cost in the production

- Reliability in delivery and quality affects the operations
- Vendor can be valuable source of information
- Vendor can provide valuable service

Raw Prices of Materials

The prices of raw materials from different vendors are not the same. Higher prices may be charged for :

- Higher quality
- More reliable and faster service
- Better terms for returning goods
- More services such as packaging and information
- Better or delayed payment plan
    - The purchase manager can purchase an item at a lower price, but the total cost of processing the item may be higher.
    - Price and transport cost from a distance place may be less than from a local source but faster service from local source may allow the purchasing firm to have less inventory.
    - One source may supply a wide range of goods needed so that the expenses of ordering from many sources can be reduced.

The sources of supply may be brokers, wholesalers, manufacturer or others. Each of these sources provides a valuable service. *Wholesaler* stocks many items and makes quick delivery of wide varieties of items. *Manufacturer* does not involve intermediate handler, but it is restricted to a product it can supply. Manufacturer may have sales representatives or agents who can help small business. Regional and National Trade Fairs and Trade Association provide valuable information on sources and their products and services.

Using Few or Many Sources

Arguments for a single source

- A closer and more individual relationship can be established
- Better services during shortages
- Discounts for large purchase

Multiple sources provide a greater variety of goods and often on better terms. Care should be exercised on ethics of supplier and should be guarded against including gifts, entertainment, misrepresentation and reciprocity. A small company should try to maintain a good image in its dealings with vendors in order to obtain good services.

Receiving Materials

The receipt and forwarding of materials to inventory constitute the last step in acquiring inputs.

- Checking whether the material is in conformity with order, proper condition and quality.
- Materials are checked for damage in transport, for specified characters such as colour, size and items specified and for proper quantity and price.

Materials can be stored in same the containers in which they are received or in separate containers or by individual item. The receiving agent prepares material for storing.

Key Terms and Concepts to Remember

Materials, inventory, time of order, economic inventory control, margin of safety, reorder point, lead time, inventory carrying cost, and Economic Order Quantity (EOQ).

Chapter Summary

- Materials management deals with purchasing and controlling of materials used in the production process.

- Decisions to be taken under materials management are : amount of materials needed for output desired, amount of inventory, vender relations, quantity and time of order and so on.
- Too large inventory would lock up too much money. Too small inventory would result in losing customers and income generating opportunities.
- The most economic quantity to order can be estimated considering the requirements and cost of inventory holding.
- The level of inventory at which an order should be issued is based on the quantity to be used in between, an order is issued and items are received.
- Sources of supply of raw materials are important because price of such purchased goods is a major cost in the production. There are certain advantages in placing orders to single as well as multiple sources of suppliers.

Chapter Highlights

Definition of materials management and inventory, determining the economic inventory level, quantity per order, ordering procedure, placing responsibility of ordering, sources of supply of raw materials, prices of raw materials and receipt of materials have been elaborately discussed in this chapter.

Review Questions

1. Define materials management.
2. What decisions are taken up under materials management?
3. What are the different types of inventories?
4. Explain Economic Order Quantity (EOQ) and its advantages.

5. When and how an order for the supply of materials is to be placed?
6. How sources of supply and prices of raw materials are important?
7. What are the advantages of single as well as multiple sources of supply?

References

Koontz.H., H. Weihrich and A.Ramachandra Aryasri. 2004. Principles of Management, New Delhi: Tata McGraw-Hill Publishing Company Ltd.

Koontz.H., and H. Weihrich . 1990. Essential's of Management, (Fifth Edition), New York : McGraw-Hill International Edition.

Chandra Bose.D.2006. Inventory Management, New Delhi: Prentice -Hall of India Pvt. Ltd.

Further Reading Material

Heller.R. and T.Hindle.2000. Essential Manager's Manual, London: Color Library Direct Ltd.

Dinakar Pagare. 1995. Business Management (Fifth Edition), New Delhi: Sultan Chand & Sons.

Russell.R.S. and B.W. Taylor III.2006. Operations Management, New Delhi: Prentice - Hall of India Pvt. Ltd.

Chapter **10**

MARKETING MANAGEMENT

Marketing management refers to distribution of the firm's product or service to the customers in order to satisfy their needs and to accomplish the firm's objectives.

Marketing includes developing the product or service, pricing, distribution, advertisement, merchandising, doing personal selling, promoting and directing sales and service to customers.

Marketing is an essential function because unless the firm has a market, or can develop a market for its product or service, other functions of staffing, producing and financing are futile. Marketing functions are schematically given below :

Marketing Concept

↓

Marketing Policies

↓

Marketing Strategies (What to do ? and How to do ?)

↓

Marketing Strategies (How to do ?)

Fig. 10.1 : Schematic View of Marketing Functions

Marketing Concept

The marketing concept is based on the importance of customers to a firm.

- Determine what are the customer's needs and how those needs can be satisfied.
- Select the market that would be served.
- Decide what advantage that will give a competitive edge over other firms.
    - Meeting customer's needs
    - Learning customer's needs
    - Conscious about the firm's image
    - Looking for danger signals

Market Segmentation

A market should be defined in terms of various characteristics such as economic status, age, education, occupation and location. The best opportunity is to identify a market segment that is not well served by other firms. In determining the firm's market segment, the fundamental aspects to be considered are:

- What is the place of the firm in the industry and how it can compete with others?
- Whether the firm is known for its quality or price.
- Image of the firm among the customers.
- If the firm has limited number of customers, the reasons for it.

A common error found in many retailing firms is 'straddling the market' or attempting to sell both high quality and low quality goods. As a result, the retailer has a limited inventory of everything but does not have a good selection of anything. In sum, the firm should assess its share in the market. This perception is possible only when the firm stresses quality, reliability, integrity and service rather than low prices.

Marketing Policies

Formulation of strategic marketing policies for certain areas would consider:

a) Morality and public service
b) Product
c) Market
d) Profit
e) Personal selling
f) Customer relations
g) Promotion
h) Credit policies
i) Use of Credit card

a) Morality and Public Service

Policies on morality and public service consist of general statements expressing the firm's desire to be honest in its dealings with public and its customers.

b) Product

The small firm often finds its most effective competitive weapon in the field of product strategy. It may concentrate on narrow product line, develop a highly specialized product/service or provide a product service - 'package' containing an unusual amount of service. Competitor's products, prices and services should be examined to determine whether the firm can build a better product.

c) Market

Market policies are designed to clarify with geographic areas the firm wishes to serve and other marketing characteristics appropriate for the firm.

d) Profit

Profit policies may require that sales goals be specified that will provide the firm a sufficiently large sales volume or profit as percentage of sales may be specified, which calls for low marketing costs.

e) Personal Selling

Personal selling policies may range from those guiding the structure of the firm's sales organization to those covering the sales representative's behaviour.

f) Customer Relations

The firm's relationship with its customers may be indicated with a question. Should the firm have a policy that customer is always right?

g) Promotion

The pattern of the firm's advertisement may reveal the firm's promotion policies. The firm should follow a policy of tasteful advertising at all times. Sales promotion may be restricted to trade shows or to industrial publications or to some other advertising media.

h) Credit Policies

In order to stimulate sales, customer should be provided with credit. However, an appropriate credit policy is essential to be successful in granting credit.

i) Use of Credit Cards

Now a days, plastic credit cards are being used by many of the people. Hence, the sales against credit cards will attract middle income to high-income customers as customers in retail stores.

Approaches to Marketing Strategies – What to do?

Marketing strategy refers to how firm meets the needs of the market better than its competitors. There are really two problems involved, namely, determining available strategies and choosing the one to be used by the firm.

Available Marketing Strategies

- Analyze present and future market situations
- Shape the product to suit the market
- Evaluate the company's resources
- Keep informed about the competitors

Marketing Strategies (How to do ?)

This is also called 'Means of Strategies' and it includes:

1. Market research and sales forecasting
2. Pricing the product or service
3. Determining the channels of distribution
4. Conducting advertising, merchandising and sales promotion.

1. Market Research and Sales Forecasting

Areas to be considered are:

- Identification of customers for the product or service of the firm
- Determination of customers' needs
- Evaluation of sales potential for the firm
- Indexing of sales potential in the firm's trading area

Steps in Market Research

- Recognition of a problem
- Preliminary investigation and planning
- Gathering factual information
- Classifying and interpreting the information
- Reaching a conclusion

Sources of Marketing Information

Secondary Sources of Published Data: Secondary sources contain data originally compiled and published elsewhere e.g. Business India.

Primary Source of Published Data: A primary source of published data consists of compilation and initial publication of data e.g. Census report.

Primary Source of Unpublished Data: Firm's records, external data collected from dealers, customers and competitors.

2. *Pricing the Product or Service*

One half of the failures in small business can be traced to a product or service that was being sold at the wrong price.

Relating Price to Costs: All items should be priced at a level to provide an adequate profit margin.

Setting a Price Strategy

The firm's goal should be to find the price - volume combination that will maximize profits. The product, price, delivery, service and fulfillment of psychological needs form the total package that the customer buys. The price should indicate the product image.

Price cutting: It should be considered as a form of sales promotion. Price cutting will be useful wherever the added sales resulting from price-cutting offsets the added cost. However, in case of inelastic demand, price - cut will not increase sales.

Other Aspects of Pricing

- *Mark - up Pricing:* An initial mark- up price should cover operating, particularly selling expenses, operating profit, and subsequent price reduction. An initial mark- up may be expressed as a percentage of sales price or product cost. Mark - up price is needed to meet competitor's prices and promotional activities.

- *Price Lining* refers to offering of merchandise at distinct price levels. Shirts sold at Rs.150, Rs.750, and Rs.350 etc. Income level and buyer's desires of a store's customers are important factors that determine price lining. Advantages of price lining are the simplification of customer's choice and reduction of the store's minimum inventory.
- *Odd Pricing:* Small business managers believe customers will react more favourably to prices ending in odd numbers. E.g. Rs.13, Rs.15, Bata prices-Rs. 179.95, Rs. 499.95, etc.

3. Determining Channels of Distribution

A marketing channel is the pipeline through which a product flows on its way to its ultimate consumer.

- *Design own channel of distribution:* Channels should be tailor- -made to meet the needs of firm. New products commonly require different distribution channels from those needed for products, which are well established and widely accepted.
- *Avoid multiple channels:* Multiple distribution channels sometimes create conflicts. Distribution will be adversely affected unless these conflicts are resolved.
- *When to change the channel:* Change in buyer's location may dictate a change in marketing channels. Changes in concentration of buyers may also require a change in marketing channels.

4. Advertising, Merchandising and Sales Promotion

Advertising is used to inform the customers of the availability of the firm's products or service and the uses they can make of them, and to convince customers that the firm's products are superior to its competitor's products. In order to be successful, advertising should be based on the firm's capability to provide quality workmanship and efficient service. It should be closely related to changes in customer's needs and desires.

Merchandising and Sales Promotion

Merchandising denotes the promotional efforts made for a product or service in retailing firms, especially at the point of purchase. It includes window displays, banners, shelf stickers, the label and package of the product, product demonstration, giving free samples and special price offer.

Sales promotion consists of activities that have the purpose of making other sales efforts (e.g. advertisement) more effective. Some other popular sales promotion techniques are:

- Special displays
- Offering premium
- Running contest
- Distribution of free samples
- Offering free introductory services
- Demonstrating products

In spite of all efforts spent in doing market research, sales forecasting and advertising and sales promotion, some one ultimately must do some personal selling of products or services.

Selling through Agent Middlemen

- *Broker:* A broker represents either the buyer or usually, the seller for negotiating packages or sales without physically handling the goods. A broker possesses only limited authority in setting prices and terms of sales.

After the sale is over, the seller transport the goods directly to buyer and the broker receives commission.

- *Selling Agent:* The selling agents perform on the basis of an extended contracts and negotiates all sales of a specialized line of merchandise or the manufacturer's entire output. Usually, the agent has full authority concerning prices and terms and is the sole seller for the line represented and is not given market area.
- *Manufacturer's Agent:* The manufacturer's agent or representative is an independent business person who sells a part of output of two or more client manufacturers whose products are related but non-competing, on a continuous or contractual basis in a limited or exclusive territory. Manufacturers use agents more often than any other type of agent middlemen. The agents do not take title to the goods, are paid a commission and have little or no control over prices, credit or other terms of sales.
- *Firm's Sales Representative:* Sales are effected through the firm's own sales representative.

The Marketing Mix

In considering the needs of their customers, companies must think in terms of the *product* itself, the *price* of the product and the *place* where the customers needs it, while making sure that the existence of the product is known through effective *promotion.* These various components are described in more detail below :

(i) Product

The product is the focus of marketing. Although many aspects of the product are not clearly known to the consumers, marketing is concerned with the product's attributes and what these mean to the customer. Such factors include quality, appearance and performance.

(ii) Price

Price creates sales revenue and is therefore important in determining the total value of the sales made. Price is really determined by what customers perceive as the value of a commodity or service. It is important to understand how customers value commodity or service as well as how much they are prepared to pay in relation to the benefit they expect to earn.

(iii) Place

The place factor deals with the various methods of transporting and storing commodities and then making them available to the customer. Getting the product to the right place at the right time depends on the distribution system. The choice of distribution method will depend on market circumstances and the nature of both the commodity and the customer.

(iv) Promotion

Promotion is the business of communicating with and influencing the customer. Although the cost associated with promotion can be a significant element in the overall cost of a product, successful product promotion increases sales so that costs are spread over a larger output. While increased promotional activity may be a response to competitor activity or a new product launch, it is important to maintain a constant flow of messages to the consumer as well as visibility in the market place.

Mix

Mix is an appropriate word to describe the marketing process, as it is a blending of ingredients to fulfill a common purpose. Each ingredient is vitally important and each depends upon the other for its contribution. Different markets will require a different balance of ingredients. The mix should comprise:

(i) A time scale

A company must have a plan, which indicates when it expects to achieve its objectives, in the short, medium and long term.

(ii) Strategic elements

These will involve the overall development strategy of the company and require considerable judgment and expertise; such decisions might involve the development of a new product range or a new distribution system.

(iii) Tactical or medium-term elements

The business environment requires constant monitoring; a company should have sufficient flexibility in order to react quickly to changing market circumstances, e.g. in response to competitor activity, which may require changes in pricing and promotional strategies or amendments to marketing plans.

(iv) Short-term operational elements

These involve predictable day-to-day decisions such as contacts with customers, organizing advertising and point of sale material, and planning distribution.

Key Terms and Concepts to Remember

Marketing functions, marketing segmentation, marketing policies, sales forecasting, product, price, place and promotion.

Chapter Summary

- Marketing management refers to the distribution of the firm's products or services to the consumers in order to satisfy their needs and to accomplish the firms objectives.

- Marketing functions include conceptualization of market and designing marketing policies and strategies.
- Marketing strategies mainly include i) market research and forecasting, ii) pricing the product and service, (iii) determining the channels of distribution and, iv) conducting advertising and sales promotion.
- In considering the needs of consumers, the companies must think in terms of marketing mix, i.e. product, place, price and promotion.

Chapter Highlights

This chapter deals with the definition of marketing management, various components of marketing functions like marketing concepts, polices and strategies. Marketing mix also has been discussed in this chapter.

Review Questions

Answer the following

1. Explain the concept 'Marketing Management'
2. Explain the 'marketing' concept
3. Discuss the marketing policies
4. What are the marketing strategies? Explain briefly.
5. Explain 'Marketing Mix'

References

Koontz.H., H. Weihrich and A.Ramachandra Aryasri. 2004. Principles of Management, New Delhi: Tata McGraw-Hill Publishing Company Ltd.

Koontz.H., and H. Weihrich . 1990. Essential's of Management, (Fifth Edition), New York : McGraw-Hill International Edition.

Further Reading Material

Heller.R. and T.Hindle.2000. Essential Manager's Manual, London: Color Library Direct Ltd.

Dinakar Pagare. 1995. Business Management (Fifth Edition), New Delhi: Sultan Chand & Sons.

Kotler.P. 2003. Marketing Management (Eleventh Edition), New Delhi: Prentice Hall of India Pvt. Ltd.

Wader.L.K. and C.Murthy.2003. Text Book of Agricultural Marketing and Co-operation, New Delhi: ICAR Publications.

Acharya.S.S. and N.L.Agarwal.2004. Agricultural Marketing in India (Fourth Edition), New Delhi: Oxford & IBH Publishing Company Pvt. Ltd.

Usha.K.R.2007. Export-Import and Logistics Management, New Delhi: Prentice-Hall of India Pvt. Ltd.

Chapter 11

PERSONNEL MANAGEMENT

Every small business manager is a personnel manager in the sense that work is done through people, with people and for the people. Consequently, the owner-manager should be personally capable of handling employee relations until the company becomes large enough to afford a personnel manager. Planning personnel requirement, developing sources from which new employees can be recruited, choosing (recruiting) the needed people, training and developing them into productive workers, evaluating their performance, compensating them and dealing with various personnel relationship, including industrial relation are included under personnel management.

Staffing

Staffing is a critical function of organizing and managing a successful business. All companies, whether large or small, are involved in the staffing process. All businesses run the same risk every time they hire a new employee. The staffing function is generally divided into four major categories (1) staffing needs, (2) acquisition, (3) motivation, and (4) retention.

Planning Personnel Requirements

As both quantity and quality of work force are important, personnel planning should be complete and detailed, but flexible and updated at least half-yearly. The following statement is frequently made that one should organize around 'what is to be done 'rather than 'who is to do it'.

Job specification are written statements covering duties, authority, responsibility and working conditions of the job and of qualifications required for a person to perform the job successfully. The use of job specification will help the manager to match the person to the job to be filled up.

Finding New Employees

There are two basic sources, one from the firm itself through promotion, upgrading or transfer; and the other from outside the company through recruitment and selection. More specifically, there are four sources usually used by managers of independent business. They are:

- Qualified people from within the organization
- Personnel from competing firms in the industry
- Organization outside the industry
- Educational institutions

There should be a balanced policy of promotion from within and recruitment from outside when the need arises.

Filling Jobs from within the Firm

There are three methods of securing employees internally; upgrading the employees' holding position, promoting an employee from a lower level of job and transferring an employee from a similar position elsewhere in the organization. The *advantage* is that the concerned person's capabilities are strengthened and their morale is built up. The *disadvantage* are non-availability of capable person and possibility of inbreeding development.

Recruitment

To recruit means to obtain fresh supplies or restore and replenish. Recruitment may be described as an activity that aims to bring job seekers (applicant) and job giver (employer) in contact with one another.

Selection

Selection of candidates begins after completion of recruitment process. In other words, the process of selection begins only after an adequate number of applications have been secured through different sources of recruitment - internal and or external. Selection involves a careful screening and testing of candidates who have put in their applications for any job in the enterprise. This is necessary for two reasons, first, many of the applicants may not really be suitable for employment in the enterprise and secondly, even where applicants are duly qualified and experienced, the enterprise, may not have adequate number of vacancies to accommodate all of them.

Recruitment and Selection

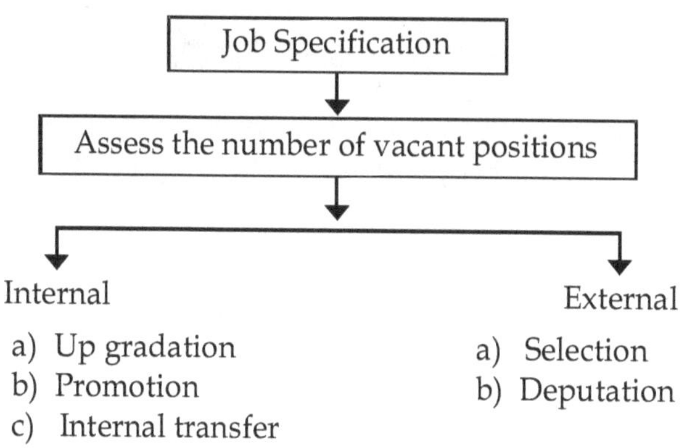

Reasons for Using External Sources

- At least lower level jobs be recruited from outside.
- New blood is to be infused into an organization to prevent inbreeding, conformity and stagnation.
- Mechanization and automation require new skilled workers.

External Sources

- Former employees
- Friends and relatives of employees
- Personal application received in person or through mail
- Competing firms
- Labour organization
- Employment agencies, either public or private
- Educational institutions
- Leased manpower- deputation
- Paper advertisement
- *Job posting:* Exihibition of available job opportunities on a notice board to give present employees a chance to bid for them.

Selection procedure involves two things, namely, recruiting or attracting a group of employees and then selecting the needed person.

Recruiting New Employees

- Campus selection
- Advertising using trade journals, newspaper, radio, television, bill boards, window displays, etc.
- Private and public employment agencies
- Employee referrals

Selecting Employees for a Given Job

Mistakes in selecting and placing personnel in the firm can be greatly reduced, if an orderly and systematic procedure for choosing the right person is used. One such procedure for effective filling up of position is given below.

- Reviewing the job specification for the position.
- Considering the present employees for one of them may be able to perform the job acceptably or become qualified if his abilities are upgraded.
- Looking outside the company and recruit applicants, if none of the present employees can fill up the job.
- Using an application bank or gathering information from applicants.
- Preparing for the interviews with applicants by using the points to be covered.
- Conducting interview.
- Using psychological tests to determine the applicant's knowledge, skills and attitudes.
- Check on qualified applicants with their employers.
- Arrange for the applicant to take physical examination.
- Decide whether the applicant should be hired on trial basis.
- Conduct an orientation programme for new employee.
- Decide whether the employee should be retained after a pre-arranged probationary period.

The personnel development may be defined as an attempt to increase employee's productive capacity up to highest level of the job to be performed.

Need for Training

Not only new employees be trained, but also the present employees must be trained in order to adjust to rapidly changing job requirements. This would result in increased productivity, less supervision and higher morale.

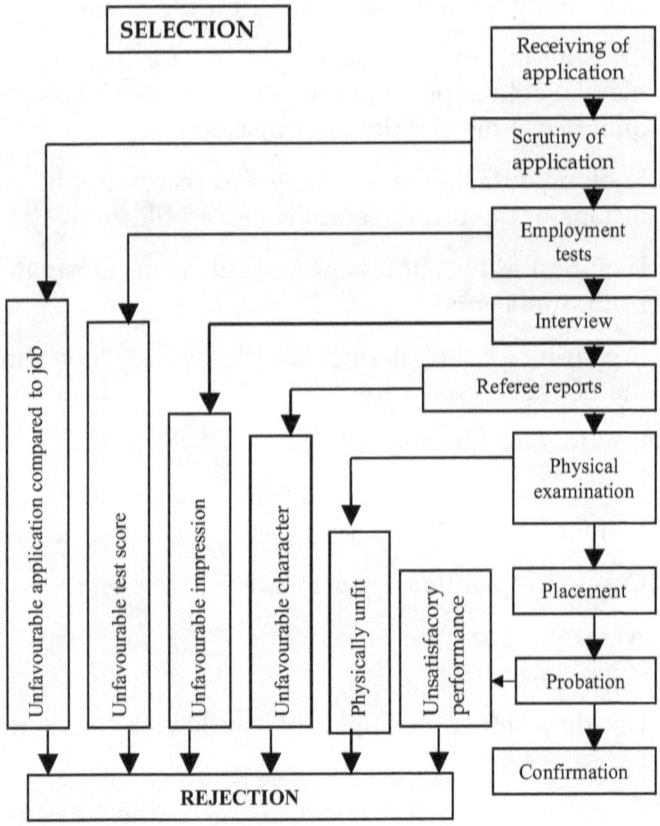

Fig. 11.1 : Recruitment and Selection Procedure

Methods of Training

Various methods of training to non-managerial employees are

- On the job training

- Apprenticeship
- Internship
- Outside Training

On the job training is a programme in which employees get training while they perform their jobs. Thus, they are both producers and learners.

The purpose of *apprenticeship* training is to develop well trained individuals who are capable of performing a variety of jobs. It involves learning a variety of skills that when combined, qualify one to practice a trade. The programme is usually a long - term process covering from two to seven years and a union is often involved in administering it.

Internship training is a combination of school and on the job training. It is usually used with employees who are aspiring for marketing or clerical positions or who are being prepared for management positions.

In the *outside training,* the employees receive training at schools outside the company. Usually the company reimburses the employees for all or part of their tuition expenses.

Performance Appraisal

Performance appraisal is a form of counseling and coaching employees. Performance appraisal is the process by which owners gather information about each employee's performance and effectiveness and communicate this information to them. Evaluating employee's performance is essential if managers wish to help their employees raise their level of performance. In the small business, managers do not spend much time on employee appraisal because they are usually occupied with the daily matters of trying to sell the product or service to the customer.

Performance appraisal includes (1) establishing standards, (2) recording performance, (3) reviewing performance in accordance with standards, and (4) taking corrective action wherever and whenever necessary.

Employee's performance in the small business is evaluated daily by owners on an informal basis while working directly with employees. However, there should be a regular schedule for performance reviews, such as once or twice a year. When the company is small, the owner-manager does the evaluation. However, as the company grows, the employees should be evaluated by their immediate supervisor and owner. These appraisals enable the owner to chart employees' progress and suggest areas that need improvement. The following guidelines are recommended for anyone conducting performance reviews.

- Decide in advance on the purpose of your performance reviews; evaluation, criticism, training, coaching, morale building, etc.
- Don't wait until the review occurs to let your staff know what you expect from them. Tell them early on exactly what the job requires; what specific goals, standards, and deadlines, you expect them to meet; and how you plan to evaluate and reward their performance.
- Keep a written record of your subordinates' performance throughout the year so that you can cite specific examples to back up any criticisms or comments you make during the review.
- The review should not be a one - way process. Let the employees participate, and listen to what they say.
- Go over the evaluation with each employee. They don't have to agree completely with your ratings, but if they strongly disagree, they are not likely to try to improve.

- When criticizing an employee's performance, make sure you also do some "stroking". Reinforce the good habits with praise.
- Be specific and constructive in your criticism. Don't just tell someone (s) he is not productive enough. Tell him or her how (s) he has fallen short and what you expect in the future.

Purpose of Performance Appraisal

The success of performance appraisal and follow-up counseling depends on whether employees comprehend and accept the purposes of the review. By observing the guidelines listed, a number of important functions can be served by the appraisal.

- Evaluation of performance over a specific time.
- Motivation of employees by providing them with relevant feedback of job performance.
- Evaluation of potential for growth and development of each employee, such as the potential for promotion to a position of more authority and responsibility.
- Accumulation of data for decisions concerning the distribution of rewards for outstanding performance, such as merit increases.
- Accumulation of information for decisions concerning transfers and terminations.
- Evaluation of effectiveness of training programmes and training needs.
- Effective method for communicating the goals of management.

The results of the appraisal should be communicated to each employee. Because most people are apprehensive about any type of evaluation, the owner should create an atmosphere that will put employees at ease throughout the counseling session. If the evaluation reveals that a worker's performance is below standard, steps are to be taken to improve performance, such as giving the employee additional training. If standards have been met, the employee should be recommended; if standards have been exceeded, employees should be rewarded, with a bonus or merit rise.

Key Terms and Concepts to Remember

Staffing, motivation, retention, job specification, on the job training, apprenticeship, internship, outside training and job performance.

Chapter Summary

- Personnel management deals with recruitment and selection, training them to develop efficient workers, evaluating their performance and compensating them.
- Staffing function involves i) assessing the staffing needs, ii) acquisition, iii) motivating and, iv) retention.
- Recruitment aims to bring job seekers and job giver in contact with one another.
- There are many internal and external sources to strengthen staff position.
- There are different methods of training such as on the job training, apprenticeship, internship and outside training.
- The main purpose of performance appraisal is to motivate the employees.

Chapter Highlights

In this chapter, staffing which include the process of selection and recruitment, training and performance appraisal of employees have been discussed.

Review Questions

Answer the following

1. What are the different components of personnel management ?
2. a) Define staffing, b) What are the staffing functions?
3. Explain the internal and external methods of selecting employees.
4. Why selection of employees becomes important?
5. Explain different steps involved in recruitment and selection procedure.
6. Explain the different methods of training.
7. Explain the purpose of performance appraisal.

References

Koontz.H., H. Weihrich and A.Ramachandra Aryasri. 2004. Principles of Management, New Delhi: Tata McGraw-Hill Publishing Company Ltd.

Koontz.H., and H. Weihrich . 1990. Essential's of Management, (Fifth Edition), New York : McGraw-Hill International Edition.

Further Reading Material

Heller.R. and T.Hindle.2000. Essential Manager's Manual, London: Color Library Direct Ltd.

Dinakar Pagare. 1995. Business Management (Fifth Edition), New Delhi: Sultan Chand & Sons.

Chapter **12**

FINANCIAL MANAGEMENT

Financing the Business

The capital of a business consists of those funds used to start and run the business. Capital may be of two types: fixed and working.

Fixed capital refers to items bought once and used for a long period of time. This includes such things as building, fixtures and equipment. Fixed Capital does not vary with the level of output.

Working capital is the type of funds, which is needed for carrying out day-to-day operations of the business smoothly. The management of working capital is no less important than the management of 'long term' financial investment. Working Capital varies with the level of output.

Working Capital Management

Significance of Working Capital

Every running business needs working capital. Even a business which is fully equipped with all types of fixed assets required, is sure to fail without i) adequate supply of raw materials for processing, ii) cash to pay wages, power and other costs, iii) creating a stock of finished goods to feed the market demand continuously and iv) the ability to extend credit to customers. All these require working capital. Thus, working capital is the lifeblood of a business without which a business will be unable to function. No business will be able to carry on day-to-day activities without adequate working capital.

Components of Working Capital

The working capital has following components, which are in several forms of current assets. The basis for assigning value to each component is shown against each.

Components of working capital	Basis of valuation
Stock of cash	Present value
Stock of raw materials	Prime cost
Stock of finished goods	Cost of production
Miscellaneous current assets like short term investment loans and advances, etc	Working expenses

Each component of the working capital is valued on the basis of valuation enumerated above of the holding period estimated. The total of all such valuation becomes the total estimated working capital requirement.

Factors Influencing Working Capital Requirement

The important factors that influence the working capital requirements of business are furnished below.

- Nature of business
- Seasonality of operations
- Production policy
- Market condition
- Conditions of supply

- Growth and expansion
- Price level changes
- Manufacturing cycle

Accurate Calculation of Working Capital

The working capital has very close relationship with day-to-day operations of a business. Neglecting proper assessment of working capital can therefore affect the day-to-day operations severely. It may lead to cash crisis and ultimately to liquidation. Inaccurate assessment of working capital may cause either under assessment or over assessment of working capital and both of them are dangerous.

Consequences of under Assessment of Working Capital

- Growth may be stunted. It may become difficult for the firm to undertake profitable projects due to non-availability of working capital.
- Cash crisis may emerge due to paucity of funds.
- Optimum capacity utilization of fixed assets may not be achieved due to non-availability of working capital.
- The business may fail to honour its commitment in time there by adversely affecting its credibility. This situation may lead to business closure.
- The business may be compelled to buy raw materials on credit and self finished goods on cash. In the process, it may end up increasing cost of purchases and reducing selling prices by offering discounts. Both these situations would affect profitability adversely.
- Non-availability of stocks due to non-availability of funds may result into production stoppage.

While inadequate working capital has disastrous implications on the business, excessive working capital also has its own dangers.

Consequences of over Assessment of Working Capital

- Excess of working capital may result into unnecessary accumulation of inventories.
- It may lead to excessively liberal credit items to buyers and very poor recovery system and cash management.
- It may take management complacent leading to its inefficiency
- The over investment in working capital makes the capital less productive and may reduce return on investment.

Planning Financial Needs

Planning the financial needs of a business is very important. The owner or manager needs to be able to ask the following questions :

Why Do I Need the Money?

The general area of need for money is: (a) starting a new business, (b) inventory, (c) expansion, (d) remodeling, and (e) improving working capital.

How Much Money Will I Need?

It is important to be able to specify how much money you will need. It is advisable, when doing any financing, to be able to stipulate the amount of money that you will be using and to specify if it is to purchase inventory, pay salaries or wages or even to be used to purchase a new equipment.

When I Will be Able to Repay the Money?

Friends, bankers, and business associates are always interested in knowing when and how you anticipate repaying the loans. The majority of loan repayments come from sales of merchandise, inventory and payments received for services rendered.

Factors that increase loan repayments

Amount of payments → Increases when
- → Amount borrowed increases
- → No. of years of loan increases
- → Interest rate increases

Where Will I Obtain Money?

Compare the advantages and disadvantages of obtaining money from different sources in terms of interest payment and control over business.

Sourcing of Capital for Business

There are two major forms of financing any business; equity financing and debt financing.

Equity capital (ownership) may come from personal savings, from partnership or by selling stock in a corporation. Equity financing involves giving up ownership to the investors of the business. It also involves dividing of the business ownership among the various investors. That is, instead of repaying an investor or one who is giving money to the business, the investor now becomes an owner and receives money from business primarily through dividend or profit sharing system.

- *Common stock* : This is the most widely used form of equity financing, and provides the greatest potential return on investment for the investor. It is important to remember that if the firm does fail, all of the creditors, and investors would be repaid before the common stockholders are repaid.
- *Preferred stock* : It provides a preference for stock holders during failure or bankruptcy. Preferred stockholders must be paid in full before other common stockholders are repaid. Because of this preferential treatment, the preferred stockholders receive smaller

dividends or returns on investment than do common stockholders; therefore, convertible preferred stock may be used, allowing the investors to convert their preferred stock at any time in the company's future.

- *Convertible debentures :* This is a long-term debt that would be paid off by an investor, with the option of the investor to convert the debentures to common stock before being repaid.
- *Debt warranties* are similar to convertible debentures but would allow the investor or creditor the option to purchase a specified stock at a specific set price. This option to purchase is available to the investor or creditor, even after the debt has been repaid but before the warranty has expired. This generally provides a longer time period for investment (ownership) for one who is providing debt financing to a corporation. That is, the debt warranty would allow someone loaning money to a business the opportunity to own part of the business even after the debt has been repaid until the time when the warranty expires.

Both debentures and debt warranties are debts and, therefore, must be paid before either common stockholders or preferred stockholders are paid, in case the business fails. All four of these opportunities are good opportunities to invest in business and provide potential ownership to investors who are interested in that specific business.

Venture capital has become an increasing source of equity funds for new business ventures. Individuals or firms supply funds for a percentage ownership of the new business. This source of capital has been popular in business start-ups involving new technology.

Source of debt capital are commercial banks, co-operative banks, mutual funds, vendors, equipment manufacturers and distributors, i.e., private investors, special type of finance lending institutions.

Commercial banks in India include State Bank of India and its Associate Banks, all nationalised banks and private commercial banks. Many of the commercial banks have industrial branches. They provide both fixed capital and working capital with over draft facility.

Special financial institutions like

- Industrial Development Bank of India (IDBI)
- Tamil Nadu Industrial Investment Corporation (TIDCO)
- Small Industries Development Bank of India (SIDCO)
- Mutual Funds (MFs)
- National Bank for Agricultural and Rural Development (NABARD)
- Co-operative banks
- Industrial Credit Investment and Investment Corporation of India (ICICI)
- National Agricultural Co-operative Marketing Federation (NAFED)
- Export-Import Bank (Exim Bank)

Vendors can be an important source of short - term credit for small business firms. Firms that sell inventories to a business usually will finance the purchase of these goods for short periods of time, usually 30 to 90 days.

Documents Required to Apply for Loan

Bankers generally look for three things for considering a loan application: (1) ability to repay the loan, (2) collateral, and (3) record.

Collateral refers to the personal or business possessions an owner is willing to assign to the lender as a contract for debt repayment. If the borrower does not repay the debt, all collateral remits to the lender to repay the loan.

The small business entrepreneur should take along three recent financial statements when applying for a loan or a line of credit : (1) a balance sheet, (2) an income statement, and (3) a cash flow statement.

Financial Analysis

Financial analysis is one of the roots of management used to carry out its controlling function. Proper interpretation of data presented by the financial statement helps in judging the profitability of operations during given time periods, in determining the soundness of financial condition at a specified date, in determining future potential to meet existing or anticipated credit obligations and in developing performance trends to be used as a basis for future decision making. The term financial statement refers to two basic statements that an accountant prepares at the end of a specified period of time for a business enterprise.

- *Balance sheet:* It is a statement of financial position of a firm at a particular point of time.
- *Income statement:* It is also called profit and loss statement. It shows firm's earnings for the period covered, usually half yearly or yearly.

Balance Sheet

From an analyst point of view, it is a written representation of resources and liabilities of the business firm. It shows the financial condition of the business firm at a given date. The balance sheet contains and reports on assets, liabilities and net worth of a firm. Assets must always equal the sum of liabilities and net worth. What is owned by or owed to firm (assets) must equal what the firm owes to its creditors plus what is owed to its owners (net worth). Balance sheet indicates the sources from which business obtained capital for its operations and the form in which that capital is invested on a specific date. *Net worth* represents owner's equity in the business.

Limitation

It is an interim statement between two operating periods. It summarizes solvency of business at a given time rather than financial transactions occurred in business during an accounting period.

Balance Sheet of Ramakanth as on 31.12.2008.

Assets			Liabilities		
No.	**Current Assets**	**Rs.**	**No.**	**Current Liabilities**	**Rs.**
1.	Bank Balance	30,000	16.	Operating loan payment	15,000
2.	Cash on hand	300	17.	Forthcoming principal due on long term loan	3,000
3.	Accounts receivables	800			
4.	Cocoon for sale	5000			
5.	Crops & supplies	3000			
	Total current Assets	39,100	18.	Total current liabilities	18,000
	Intermediate Assets			**Intermediate liabilities**	
6.	Bullock pair	6,000	19.	Balance of sheep loan	7,000
7.	Milch Animal	3,000			
8.	Oil engine	7,000			
9.	Bullock cart	4,000			
	Total intermediate Assets	20,000	20.	Total interm. liabilities	7,000
	Long term Assets			**Long term Liabilities**	
10.	Land Dry land 10 Ac	80,000	21.	Mortgage of land	25,000
11.	Garden land 3 Ac	60,000			
12.	Wet land ½ Ac	15,000			
13.	Mango garden	25,000	22.	Total long term liabilities	25,000
14.	Total long term Assets	1,80,000	23.	Net Worth	1,89,100
15.	Total Assets	2,39,100	24.	Total liabilities	2, 39, 100

How Beneficial to Owners?

- It determines the safety of their investments.
- The probability of making additional capital requirements.
- Possibility of withdrawals or dividends.
- Need for reorganization or liquidation.

How Useful to Creditors?

- Help in determining the extent of granting credit.
- How much money safely be granted as loan.

How Helpful to Management?

- Helps to judge the results of its operating activities and in planning for proper financing of future operations.

Income Statement

It is also called profit and loss statement. It states the source of firm's incomes, describes the nature of the expenses, and shows the net profit earned (or net loss incurred) during an accounting period. It is a supporting evidence to balance sheet, in the sense that it explains the change in retained earnings on the balance sheet.

Uses of Income Statement

- Can determine how much profit is earned by the business.
- Can find particular causes of low profit or operating losses.
- Management can take action to prevent the occurrences of future losses or to prevent further decline in profits.

Comparison of Balance Sheet and Income Statement

Balance sheet or Net worth statement	**Income statement or profit or loss statement**
Net worth statement is a summary of assets, liabilities and owner's equity at a given point of time.	Income statement is a summary of both cash and non cash financial transactions of farm business accrued during the selected accounting period.
The most commonly requested document by a lender in reviewing a loan request.	It is used to measure the financial profitability of business during a period of time.
It is used in preparation of income statement and tax returns.	It is used in making an analysis of the business profitability, efficiency and financial stability.
Net worth statement offers a little insight into financial transactions occured in business during an accounting period.	Information from this document is used in preparation of cash flow summary.

Cash Flow Statement

The cash flow statement is a measure of changes in cash the business has on hand from month to month. It records or projects all cash receipts less all cash disbursements. A business may use the cash flow statement as a record of what has occurred to cash or as a projection into the future to determine future needs for cash or as both.

The cash flow statement is accurate when it is a record of past receipts and disbursements and an estimate when it is projected for future months. The cash flow statement is usually calculated on a monthly basis for an entire year.

Profit and Loss Statement (Income Statement)
of Farm B for the Period Jan 1, 2001 to Dec 31,2008.

S.No.	Particulars	Amount in Rs.		
	Income			
	Cash Receipts			
1.	Paddy sales 30 qtl.	7,500		
2.	Sugarcane sales 16 tonnes	5,500		
3.	Groundnut sales 20 qtl.	12,000		
4.	Milk sale 100 ltr.	3,800		
5.	Broiler sales 200 birds	10,500		
6.	Miscellaneous income	1,500		
7.	**Total cash receipts**		**40,800**	
	Net Capital gains Income			
8.	Sale of purchased milch animal	2,000		
9.	Home bred animal sale	2,000		
10.	Machinery sale	150		
11.	**Total net capital gains**		**4,150**	
	Changes in Inventory Value			
12.	Crops in inventory	6,000		
13.	Livestock in inventory	-1,000		
14.	Total changes in inventory value		5,000	
15.	**Gross farm income**			**49,950**
	Expenses			
	Operating expenses			
16.	Hired labour	3,000		
17.	Hired bullock labour	4,000		
18.	Machinery, fuel, repairs	2,500		
19.	Fertilizers	500		
20.	Other crop expenses	1,400		
21.	Livestock, machinery, veterinary and marketing expenses	1,000		
22.	Interest on current debts	600		
23.	Miscellaneous expenses	700		
24.	**Total operating expenses**		**13,700**	

	<u>**Fixed Expenses**</u>			
25.	Land rent	3,000		
26.	Land revenue	500		
27.	Improvement repairs	4,200		
28.	Interest on intermediate and long term loans	1,000		
29.	Equipment depreciation	1,500		
30	Livestock depreciation	1,000		
31.	Attached farm servants wages	1,000		
32.	Depreciation on buildings,	600		
33.	**Total fixed expenses**		**12,800**	
34.	**Total expenses**			**26,500**
35.	**Net farm income**			**23,450**

Financial Tests

Ratio analysis: It has the following advantages :

- Has no units
- Compares numerator with respect to denominator
- Relative and comparable

Ratio analysis will explain what strength, weakness, pressures and forces are currently at work in the business operation. Farm business managers will need a full time job accountant for measuring the change accruing in his capital structure and net worth as revealed in his balance sheet.

Ratio analysis of properly calculated rates can be readily compared with i) firm's past ratio in order to show trends, ii) ratio of other firms of similar size, large size or of smaller size with which the manager is familiar, iii) industrial standards and iv) projected goals as reflected in plans for the future.

Fundamental difference between ratio analysis and trend is that the ratio analysis measures the movement in absolute terms whereas the trend indicates the relationship. The marginal analysis is used in determining the most profitable combination of resources and products. The concern here is with last added or marginal unit of input and product.

There are three types of financial tests and they are : a) tests of liquidity, b) tests of solvency and c) tests of profitability.

a) Tests of liquidity

Tests of liquidity are usually conducted to determine the firm's ability to meet its current financial obligations. The current ratio is the most commonly recognized indicator of a firm's liquidity.

$$\text{i) Current ratio} = \frac{\text{Current assets}}{\text{Current liabilities}} = \frac{\text{Rs. } 39{,}100}{\text{Rs. } 18{,}000} = 2.17$$

Nature of current assets determines the value whether the firm is able to meet promptly the current liabilities. The reasonableness of any current ratio can be tested by comparing current ratios of similar firm in the industry.

ii) Acid test ratio (ATR) or quick current ratio

$$\text{ATR} = \frac{\text{Current monetary assets}}{\text{Current liabilities}} = \frac{\text{Rs. } 31{,}100}{\text{Rs. } 18{,}000} = 1.73$$

The difference between current ratio and acid test ratio is the elimination of inventories in current assets used in acid test ratio. If a firm's cash marketable securities and accounts receivable are more than sufficient to meet its current liabilities, then inventories may be viewed as a buffer to absorb any subsequent deficiency in the receivables, such as unexpected bad debt.

iii) The inventory to receivable ratio

$$\frac{\text{Inventory}}{\text{Total receivables}} = \frac{\text{Rs. } 8{,}000}{\text{Rs. } 800} = 10.00$$

It is also associated with the acid test ratio. Inventory represents cost items while receivables presumably include profit. Hence, a favourable change in this ratio may be due to the execution of profitability which convert its inventory into liquid cash. It also has relevance in identifying a firm's current position in a business cycle since inventory generally is more subject to the value changes than the receivables are.

b) Tests of Solvency

Tests of solvency are designed to measure a firm's ability to meet both interest change and repayment of loans associated with its long-term financial commitments. Tests of solvency tell the manager how well his firm will survive a crisis but will provide little information as to the firm's normal operational viability.

i) Net worth to total debt ratio

$$\frac{\text{Net worth}}{\text{Total liability}} = \frac{\text{Rs. } 1{,}89{,}100}{\text{Rs. } 2{,}39{,}100} = 0.79$$

In general, the larger the net worth to total debt ratio, the less a firm's creditors concern themselves with thoughts of fore closure. It should be noted that some business may attempt to improve their current ratio, though not necessarily their financial health, through a simple funding operation. They decrease their current obligations by increasing long term debt and leave the total debt used by the manager as a valuable supplement to the current ratio. Where a very large proportion of a firm's total debt is funded, a manager may choose to use an auxiliary ratio of net worth to current liabilities, there by emphasizing the relative size of funded debt and its effect on solvency.

ii) Net worth to fixed asset ratio

$$\frac{\text{Net worth}}{\text{Fixed assets}} = \frac{\text{Rs. } 1{,}89{,}100}{\text{Rs. } 1{,}80{,}000} = 1.05$$

This ratio indicates the proportion to the owner's equity invested in fixed assets. The ratio of above one, if it exists, represents the proportion of owner's equity involved in the firm's working capital. A raising net worth to fixed asset ratio indicates that management may be less concerned with insolvency. A declining ratio serves to warn management that the firm possibly may be expanding its physical plant beyond its current ability to support it financially. This would be particularly important to management during a general period of declining business.

c) Tests of Profitability

Two subgroups of financial ratios are generally used by management to test the profitability of a business. The first sub-group involves those ratios that measure profitability of a business as related to investment. The second is more concerned with measuring profitability as related to sales. Both these sub-groups of ratios are helpful to managers in identifying performance trends over time and/ or comparing profit performance among similar business firms.

i) The earnings to investment ratio

$$\frac{\text{Net income}}{\text{Net worth}} = \frac{\text{Rs. 8,00,000}}{\text{Rs. 80,00,000}} = 0.1 \text{ (Hypothetical figure)}$$

This ratio is investor oriented and is of particular interest to the stock holders in so far as it has a direct impact on dividends.

ii) The earnings to sales ratio

$$\frac{\text{Net income}}{\text{Sales}} = \frac{\text{Rs. 8,00,000}}{\text{Rs. 90,00,00}} = 0.89 \text{ (Hypothetical figure)}$$

This ratio measures profit margin to sales. Higher the ratio, the more profitable the firm is. However, in comparing two or more enterprises, extreme care should be taken that net income excludes depreciation, taxes and outside earnings.

Agricultural Credit System in India

Farmers get external financial assistance from two sources namely, i) non-institutional or unorganized agencies, and ii) institutional or organized agencies. It is a fact that agriculture has been financed by non-institutional agencies for a long time and institutional agencies were started functioning only during the early part of this century.

Non-Institutional Sources of Finance in India

Non-institutional sources include money lenders, land lords, traders, commission agents, friends and relatives.

Money Lenders

There are two types of money lenders in rural areas. a) agricultural money lenders and b) professional money lender.

Agricultural money lender's main occupation is farming and money lending is secondary one. Professional money lender's main profession is money lending. Although the reliance on money lender by rural poor declined over the years, the credit disbursed by money lenders still forms a major portion of the total credit obtained by the farmers.

Advantages

- Unrestricted supply of credit for any purpose.
- Easy access by farmers as money lenders maintain close relationship with rural families.

- Method of business adopted are simple and flexible.
- Timely availability of credit without much formalities.
- Knowledge on local conditions and experience of money lender facilitate his business.
- Money lenders do not insist upon any particular type of security for the grant of loans.

Unfair Practices of Money Lenders

Money lenders deceive the farmers through many ways such as:

- They manipulate bonds and promissory notes obtained from debtors and enter large sum than what was actually lent.
- They give no receipt for repayments and often they deny such repayments.
- They charge very high rate of interest
- They give loans for both productive and unproductive purposes which results in indebtedness.

Land Lords

Small farmers and tenants rely on land lords for finance to meet out their productive and unproductive expenses. This source of finance has all the defects associated with money lenders. Interest rates are exorbitant. Often small farmers are forced to sell out their lands to these land lords and they become land less labourers. Landless labourers eventually become bonded labourers in the farms of land lords.

Traders and Commission Agents

They are functioning either to get regular supply of products for their trade or to have a control over the provision of credit by other creditors. Though the rate of interest charged by them is not as high as charged by the money lenders, they charge more in the form of concessions and service charges, They mostly finance for the cultivation of commercial crops like sugarcane, cotton, ground-nut, tobacco, onion, etc.

Relatives

Farmers borrow from their relatives for temporary exigencies. It is simply a mutual help. Since all farmers are living under similar conditions, they can not lend large sums as loans. Normally, no interest is paid on such loans.

Although, the private agencies satisfied some of the criteria of a good system of credit, their loan were not related to production purposes, they never cared for the end use of the loan extended and the loan is often used for wasteful purposes. However, institutions adopt a productive and purpose oriented credit policy while providing credit. So this policy made the institutions to discourage the provision of credit to consumption purpose. But it is evident that the need for consumption loan in rural households continues to persist. As the institutions deny consumption loans to farmers, the non-institutional agency continues to dominate the rural credit system. Moreover, the institutional agencies could not provide more than 61 per cent of the total credit needs of the farmers (vide Table given on next page). Therefore, the private credit agencies should be brought under a more realistic system of state regulation. Otherwise, the rural people would continue to suffer from indebtedness in spite of various efforts taken by the government to uplift their economic conditions.

Institutional Credit Agencies

As compared to the quantum of credit requirement and the capacity of institutions to meet these credit demands under multiagency system, it is impossible to completely wipe out the private agencies from the rural scene.The

Banking committee, (1931) and the Banking Commission (1972) offered suggestions to get over the evil aspects of private lending agencies and bring them under sound credit system.These suggestions may be adopted till the institutional agencies attain the capacity to meet the full demand for credit.

Share of Debt# of Cultivator Households from Different Sources: 1951-2002 (%)

Sources of Credit	1951	1961	1971	1981	1991	2002
I Institutional	**7.3**	**18.7**	**31.7**	**63.2**	**66.3**	**61.1**
i) Cooperative Societies / Banks, etc	3.3	2.6	22.0	29.8	30.0	30.2
ii) Commercial Banks	0.9	0.6	2.4	28.8	35.2	26.3
II Non-Institutional	**92.7**	**81.3**	**66.3**	**36.8**	**30.6**	**38.9**
i) Money lenders	69.7	49.2	36.1	16.1	17.5	26.8
ii) Unspecified	-	-	-	-	3.1	-
Total	**100.0**	**100.0**	**100.0**	**100.0**	**100.0**	**100.0**

Debt refers to outstanding cash dues.
Source: Reserve Bank of India (RBI), *All-India Rural Credit Survey, 1951-52*; RBI, *All India Rural Debt and Investment Survey, 1961-62* and NSSO, *All India Debt and Investment Surveys, 1971-72, 1981-82, 1991-92* and *2003*.

The major institutions supplying credit to agricultural sector are : i) Government, ii) Co-operatives, iii) Commercial Banks, iv) Regional Rural Banks, v) Reserve Bank of India (RBI) through National Bank for Agriculture and Rural Development (NABARD).

Government

The Government provides both direct and indirect finance to farming sector.

Direct Finance

The government provides taccavi loans in times of distress like famine, flood, drought etc. Land Improvement

Act of 1883 and the Agriculturists Loans Act of 1984 were enacted to extend long and short term financial assistance to farmers for agricultural development and also as relief measures during distress times.

Merits

- They are granted for long period of time.
- Low interest is charged.
- The repayment plan is convenient, i.e., repayment in equal annual installments.

Demerits

- Quantum of loan is determined an the basis of value of security offered, by which, large farmers receive more credit than small and marginal farmers.
- As these loans are not production oriented, they do not satisfy the standard needed for sound system of farm credit.
- The loan amount is inadequate.
- The land less labourers were left out in the lurch at the time of distress. The taccavi loans are not popular among farmers due to:
  - delay in sanctioning of loan.
  - imposition of irrelevant conditions.
  - incompetent supervision
  - in convenient recovery methods.

In view of these demerits, it was recommended to channalise these loans through co-operatives.

Indirect Finance to Agriculture by Government

- It allocates subsidized fertilizer to states according to their needs.

- It provides technical assistance to farmers through various agricultural development programmes implemented by the State Department of Agriculture.
- It implements price stabilization schemes for various crops.
- In consultation with the RBI, the government prescribes the rates of interest to be charged on loans granted to weaker sections of rural areas.
- It contributes to the share capital and debentures of co-operatives.

Co-operative Credit

Co-operative Credit Institutions

The co-operative credit structure in India is characterized by two types of institutions: one, involved in the dispensation of short and medium term credit and the other in the provision of long term credit.

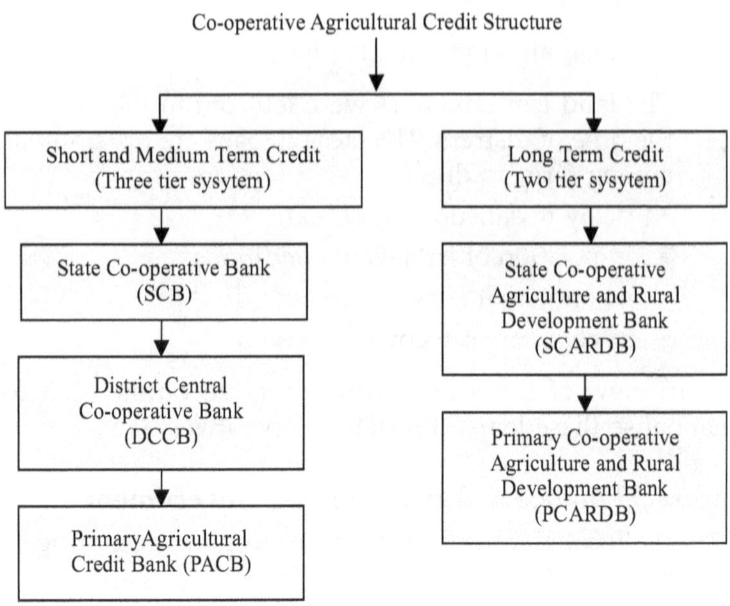

The Primary Agricultural Credit Banks (PACBs) is the foundation stone on which the whole co-operative credit structure is built up. These societies are federated to District Central Co-operative Bank (DCCB), generally at the district level. The DCCBs are federated to State Co-operative Bank (SCB) which is an apex instituion at the state level having close link with the RBI and NABARD. Long term credit is provided by Co-operative Agriculture and Rural Development Bank (CARDBs). The State / Central Co-operative Agriculture and Rural Development Bank (SCARDB) is the apex institution which operates through Primary Co-operative Agriculture and Rural Development Bank (PCARDB) at district / taluk / block level in some states or through its own branches where Primary Co-operative Agriculture and Rural Development Bank (PCARDB) do not exist.

Commercial Bank

Financing agriculture by commercial banks was not significant till 1950. However, the Rural Banking Enquiry Committee (1950) recommended that banking facilities should be extended to rural areas. The commercial banks were reluctant to enter the field of agricultural finance as they felt that it would be risky and costly.

The Imperial Bank of India was established in 1921 by the amalgamation of three Presidency Banks, (Bank of Bengal, Bank of Bombay and Bank of Madras). Until the establishment of the Reserve Bank of India in 1935, the Imperial Bank of India was the sole banker to the government. There was no branch for RBI and therefore, the Imperial Bank of India acted as an agent of the RBI for the purpose of transacting businesses of government.

In 1955, the State Bank of India Act was passed and Imperial Bank India was named as the State Bank of India. In 1959, State Bank of India (subsidiary Banks) Act was passed and seven Associate Banks or subsidiary banks of SBI were started functioning. They are:

- State Bank of Mysore
- State Bank of Travancore
- State Bank of Sourashtra
- State Bank of Hydrabad.
- State Bank of Bikaner and Jaipur.
- State Bank of Patiala.
- State Bank of Indore.

The role of commercial banks in rural credit was negligible till the sixties as is evident from the All India Debt and Investment survey Report, 1961-62 and 1971-72. They had shown little interest in direct financing of agriculture and had confined their financing activities to the movement of agricultural produces only.

To serve better the credit needs of rural society, fourteen commercial banks with deposits worth Rs.50 crores or more were nationalised on July 19, 1969. In her broadcast address of July 19, 1969 on bank nationalisation, Prime minister Mrs. Indira Gandhi stated that nationalisation was meant for an early realisation of the objectives of social control which were spelt out as:

- removal of control of money market by a few,
- provision of adequate credit for agriculture, small industry and export,
- encouragement of a new class of entrepreneurs, and
- strengthening the professional banking management system.

The banks nationalised were:

- Central Bank of India
- Bank of India.
- Punjab National Bank

- Bank of Baroda.
- United Commercial bank.
- Canara Bank.
- United Bank of India
- Dena Bank
- Syndicate Bank.
- Union Bank of India
- Allahabad Bank
- Indian Bank
- Bank of Maharashtra
- Indian Overseas Bank

This was followed by nationalization of six more commercial banks in April 1980. They were:

- New Bank of India.
- Vijaya Bank.
- Corporation Bank.
- Andhra Bank.
- Punjab and Sind Bank.
- Oriental Bank of Commerce.

This institutional change was effected to pursue the goals of growth and social justice.

Functions of Commercial Bank

The objectives of the changes in the banking structure and the banking policy since the nationalization of commercial banks were:

- Wider territorial and regional spread of branch net work;
- Faster mobilisation of savings through bank deposits; and
- Deployment of bank credit in favour of neglected sectors the economy.

In order to achieve these objectives, the commercial banks involved in the following activities:

- Commercial banks provide both direct and. indirect finance to farmers. Banks provide direct finance to farmers for the purchase of pump-sets, tractors and other agricultural machineries, for sinking and deepening wells, for land development, for raising crops, and for setting up of dairy, sheep/goat, poultry, fishery, piggery and sericulture units. Commercial banks also provide indirect finance which includes loan for distribution of fertilizers and other inputs, loan to electricity boards, loan to Primary Agricultural Co-operative Banks and subscribing to debentures of Land Development Banks.
- They extend financial assistance to small / marginal farmers identified by District Rural Development Agency (DRDA).
- They established specialized branches exclusively for rural lending.
- They finance Primary Agricultural Co-operative Banks ceded to them and organize them into Farmers' Service Societies since 1973-74.
- They have set-up Regional Rural Banks, Farmers' Service Society (FSS) and Large-Sized Adivasi Multi-Purpose Co-operative Societies (LAMPS) in selected areas to cater to the credit needs of the weaker sections.

Regional Rural Banks

The need for evolving a hybrid type of credit agency which combines the resource orientation of the commercial banks and the rural orientation of the co-operatives has been expressed in the reports of a few of the committees which have looked into rural credit problems.

To review the flow of institutional credit especially to the weaker sections of the rural community, the

Government of India appointed a working Group in 1975 under the chairmanship of Narasimhan. The Group identified certain deficiencies in the functioning of co-operatives and commercial banks and recommended the setting up of state-sponsored, regionally based and rural oriented banks called Regional Rural Banks (RRBs) which would encompass local feel and familiarity with several problems which the co-operatives possess and the degree of business organization, ability to mobilize the deposits, access to central money markets and a modernized outlook which the commercial banks have. The Government of India accepted this recommendation and RRBs were established in 1976.

The main objective of RRB is to provide finance to small and marginal farmers, agricultural labourers, artisans and small entrepreneurs whose annual income is less than Rs.10,000.

The idea behind the establishment of RRBs is to develop a comparatively backward area where the commercial bank and co-operative bank is relatively poor. The main difference from the commercial bank is that the area of operation of RRB is confined to a region comprising one or two contiguous districts. One of the tasks envisaged for the RRBs is to maintain their cost of operations at a lower level than that of the commercial banks. So the salary structures of the Staff were comparable to that of the State government employees.

RRBs are sponsored by schedule commercial banks. A few non-public sector commercial banks and state co-operative Banks are also allowed to sponsor RRBs. The sponsoring bank provides managerial assistance to RRBs for the first five years. The management of RRB is through a nine member Board of Directors headed by a chairman who is an officer of the sponsor bank. The Board consists of three nominees of Government of India, two nominees of the concerned State government, four including the chairman by the sponsor commercial bank.

The authorized share capital of a RRB has been fixed at Rs.5 crore and issued capital is Rs. one crore of this, 50 per cent is subscribed by the central government, 15 per cent by the concerned state government and 35 per cent by the sponsor bank.

RRBs have been advised to render other banking services like collection of cheques and bills, issue of drafts, collection of insurance premia, safe custody etc.

National Bank for Agriculture and Rural Development (NABARD)

On the basis of the views expressed by the All India Rural Credit Review Committee (1969), the Administrative Reforms Commission (1970), the Banking Commission (1972), and the National Commission on Agriculture (1976) and also the Committee to Review the Arrangements for Institutional Credit for Agriculture and Rural Development (CRAFICARD) which was appointed by the RBI under the chairmanship of B. Sivaraman in 1979 considered the desirability and the feasibility of establishing a national bank for rural development in the context of integrated rural development. While examining the activities of the ARDC and the RBI in the delivery of rural credit against massive credit needs for rural development over the coming years, the CRAFICARD felt that the present national level institutions had certain deficiencies affecting their capacity to meet the stupendous task of integrated rural development aimed at the uplift of the weaker sections in the rural areas within a given time horizon.

The CRAFICARD considered that the Agricultural Credit Department (ACD) of RBI was unable to ensure the necessary supporting short term credit and also the ARDC could not support non-land based activities which are also to be promoted in the context of implementation of

Integrated Rural Development Programme (IRDP). The committee considered whether the top management of the RBI in the midst of its multifarious functions could devote sufficient attention to the complex credit problems involved in the integrated rural development. The committee also felt that the Agricultural Credit Board (ACB) which was established in 1970 in the place of the then standing advisory Committee on Rural Co-operative credit could not solve the complex issues of rural credit by holding a few meetings in a year. For all these reasons, the committee recommended for the establishment of NABARD and hence it was started, functioning since 12th July 1982

As such it has replaced by merging in itself, the Agri Cultural Referance and Development Corporation (ARDC) and the two credit related constituents of the RBI, namely Agricultural Credit Department and the Rural Planning and Credit Cell (RPCC) which was initially dealt with by DBOD till 1979). Thus, NABARD is conceived as an exercise of decentralization of the RBI's functions relating rural credit and that it would take over the ARDC and the refinancing functions of RBI in relation to state co-operative banks and RRBs.

Resources

The share capital of NABARD is Rs. 100 crores and is held by the RBI and GOI in equal proportion. The NABARD draws funds from the RBI for its short-term operations, and for long-term operations, it draws from the Government of India, floats bonds in the open market and also draws from its National Agricultural Credit (Long Term operations) Fund and National Agricultural Credit (Stabilization) Fund. The NABARD is also authorised to accept deposits with maturity period of not less than twelve months from the central and state governments, local authorities, scheduled banks etc. and also to borrow forgein currency with the approval of central government.

Management

The management of NABARD is vested with 15 member Board of Management which consists of a chairman, a Managing Director and 13 Executive Directors. The chairman is the ex-officio Deputy Governor of RBI. The Managing Director is the Chief Executive of the Bank with operational responsibility for the performance of various tasks. The Executive Director will be in charge of each of the major functional divisions i.e., three Directors from central Government, three sitting Directors from co-operative and commercial Banks and two experts on rural economy and rural development.

The two Directors from State Governments will be appointed by rotation to give representntion to five Zones, viz., Northern, Southern, Eastern, Western and North-Eastern. NABARD will be, thus, broadly divided into five zones with its head quarters at Mumbai and 16 regional offices located in i) Jammu ii) Chandigarh iii) Lucknow, iv) Patna, v) Gwahati, vi) Calcutta, vii) Bhubaneshwar viii) Hyderabad, ix) Bangalore, x) Chennai, xi) Trivandram, xii) Mumbai xiii) Indore, xiv) Ahmedabad, xv) New Delhi and xvi) Jaipur. The Board of Directors can constitute an Advisory Council.

Functions of NABARD

i) Provision of Finance

NABARD provides different types of refinance to the following eligible institutions:

a) Short Term Credit

The eligible institutions to get short term credit are State Co-operative Banks, Regional Rural Banks and other financial institutions approved by RBI. The purposes for which short term credit extended are:

- Seasonal Agricultural Operations (SAO) and marketing of crops
- Marketing and distribution of inputs like fertilizers, pesticides, etc.,
- Production and marketing activities of artisans, small scale industries, village and cottage industries,
- Any other activity connected with agricultural / rural sector.

The repayment period is up to 18 months.

b) Medium Term Credit

The eligible institutions to get medium term credit are State Cooperative Banks, State Co-operative Agriculture and Rural Development Banks, Regional Rural Banks and other financial institutions approved by RBI. The purposes for which medium term credit extended are:

- Any investment connected with agriculture and rural sector requiring MT credit assistance

The repayment period is between 18 months and 7 years

c) Long Term Credit

The eligible institutions to get long term credit are State Cooperative Banks (SCB), State Co-operative Agriculture and Rural Development Banks, Regional Rural Banks, Commercial Banks, and other financial institutions approved by RBI. The purposes for which long term credit extended are:

- Refinance for investment in agriculture and allied activities such as minor irrigation, land development, soil conservation, dairy, sheep, poultry, piggery, farm mechanization, plantation/horticulture, forestry, fishery, storage and market yards etc.

ii) Refinances loans meant for artisans, small-scale industries, village and cottage industries and others (non-farm sector)

iii) Loans to state government for contributing share capital to co-operative institutions.

The repayment period is upto to a maximum of 25 years.

Major Functions

- Co-ordinates operations of rural credit institutions.
- Assists governments, RBI and other institutions in rural development efforts.
- Contributes to the share capital and securities of eligible institutions concerned with agriculture and rural development.
- Assists state government to enable them to contribute to the share capital of eligible institutions.
- Frames overall rural credit policies
- Provides facilities for training, research and dissemination of information in the fields of rural banking, agriculture and rural development.
- Undertakes the inspection of RRBs and co-operative credit institutions.

Small Farmers' Agri-Business Consortium (SFAC)

The Small Farmers' Agri-Business Consortium (SFAC), an autonomous body for the promotion and development of small farmers' agri-business activities, was set up in 1994. Such a body would be funded by institutions such as the RBI, NABARD, IDBI and the like. It was much clear that the Consortium's membership would include inter-alia, various Development Banks, Public Sector Corporations, Private Sector Companies, and Scientific Institutions, besides Farmers' Associations.

The SFAC was envisaged as a catalytic/facilitating agent to promote the type of activities enumerated on the principles of economic efficiency, environmental soundness and social equity, so that the country began a new chapter in its agricultural history, where farm enterprises would yield not only more quality products but also more productive jobs and higher income in rural areas.

SFAC has the following investment opportunities to promote agri-business in the country.

1. *Venture Capital*

In order to facilitate agribusiness development in the country, SFAC venture capital scheme will:

- Assist agripreneurs to make investments in setting up agribusiness projects through equity participation, and
- Provide financial support for preparation of bankable Detailed Project Reports (DPRs) through Project Development Facility (PDF).

Venture capital is made available to the agripreneurs to promote investments in agri-business projects with the participation of banks as detailed below.

- Equity participation in agri-projects upto 10% of the total project cost, or 26% of the total project equity or Rs.75 lakhs whichever is lower.
- In special cases, higher equity possible for Projects located in hilly and North Eastern States and in Projects recommended by State agencies/ State SFACs.

2. *Project Development Facility (PDF)*

This facility is offered to provide financial assistance to farmers, Producer Groups, Agripreneurs, Units in Agri-

Export Zones, Organizations and Agriculture graduates for the preparation of bankable Detailed Project Reports (DPR).

3. *Eligible Criteria for Funding by SFAC*

- Project should be in agriculture or allied sector namely horticulture, floriculture, medicinal and aromatic plants, minor forest produce, sericulture, organic farming, vermi compost, apiculture, plantation crops, and fisheries. However, poultry and dairy projects will not be covered under the scheme.
- Project should provide assured market to farmers / producer groups.
- Project should encourage farmers to diversify into high value crops, to increase farm incomes.
- Project should be accepted by banks for grant of term loan.

Agribusiness activity for a particular crop can start in the clusters of surplus producing zones/districts. Based on the information available from potential linked plans of NABARD, action plan of National Horticulture Mission and Horticulture Technology Mission for North Eastern States, Jammu & Kashmir, Himachal Pradesh and Uttaranchal, the Potential States and districts have been identified. Action plan for agribusiness development, in close association with commercial banks and State SFAC, have been drawn for the next two years in these districts.

Key Terms and Concepts to Remember

Working and fixed capital	Equity capital
Common stock	Preferred stock
Convertible debentures	Debt warranties
Venture capital	Balance sheet
Income statement	Cash flow statement
Tests of liquidity	Tests of profitability

Chapter Summary

- Financial management refers to acquisition and use of funds to start and run the business.
- Capital may be of two types : fixed and working.
- Working capital is required to ensure adequate supply of raw materials, payment of wages, purchase of other inputs and to extend credit to customer for the purchasing the product of the firm.
- Working capital requirement has to be accurately assessed, as under or over estimation of working capital hamper the functioning the firm.
- Equity capital and debt capital are available to the entrepreneurs to run the business.
- Financial analysis is done to carry out the firm's controlling function. Balance sheet, income statement and cash flow statement are required for the financial analysis.
- Financial ratio analysis will explain the strength and weakness of the business.
- Institutional and non - institutional financial agencies cases to the credit needs of rural people.
- Small farmers' Agri - Business Consortium (SFAC) provide venture capital for the development of Agri - Business in the country.

Chapter Highlights

This chapter highlights definitions of capital, significance, components and assessment of working capital influencing working, source of acquiring capital, documents required to apply the loan. Preparation of documents for carrying out financial analysis like balance sheet, income statement and cash flow statement, and estimation of financial ratios.

Review Questions

1. Distinguish between fixed and working capital
2. How working capital is important to run the business?
3. What are the factors influencing working capital requirement?
4. What are the components of working capital?
5. Explain how under estimation of working capital will affect the business?
6. Explain the different forms of debt and equity capital?
7. Explain the different financial statements required to carry out financial analysis?
8. Discuss the different tests of financial analysis?

References

Koontz.H., H. Weihrich and A.Ramachandra Aryasri.2004. Principles of Management, New Delhi: Tata McGraw-Hill' Publishing Company Ltd..

Koontz.H., and H. Weihrich . 1990. Essential's of Management, (Fifth Edition), New York : McGraw-Hill International Edition.

http://rbi.org

Further Reading Material

Heller.R. and T.Hindle.2000. Essential Manager's Manual, London: Color Library Direct Ltd.

Dinakar Pagare. 1995. Business Management (Fifth Edition), New Delhi: Sultan Chand & Sons.

Chapter **13**

MANAGEMENT INFORMATION SYSTEM

A management information system (MIS) is an organized collection of people, procedures, software, databases, and devices used to provide routine information to managers and decision makers. The focus of an MIS is primarily on operational efficiency. Marketing, production, finance, and other functional areas are supported by MIS and linked through a common database. MIS typically provides standard reports generated with data and information from the transaction processing system (Fig. 13.1)

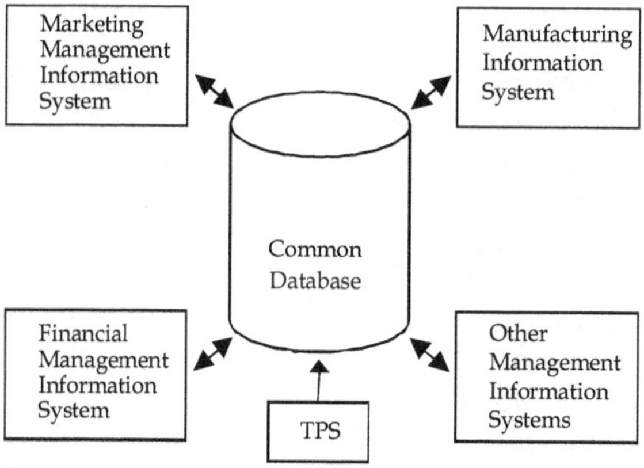

Fig. 13.1 : Functional Management Information Systems Linkage with Organization's Transaction Processing System (TPS).

MIS began to be developed in the 1960s and is characterized by the use of information systems to produce managerial reports. In most cases, these reports were produced periodically - daily, weekly, monthly, or yearly. Because they were printed on a regular basis, they were called *scheduled reports*. These scheduled reports helped managers perform their duties. Other scheduled reports could be used to help managers in controlling and monitoring customer credit, payments to suppliers, the performance of sales representatives, inventory levels, and more.

Other types of reports were also developed during the early stages of MIS. *Demand reports* were developed to give decision makers certain information upon request. For example, prior to closing a sale, a sales representative might seek a demand report on how much inventory exists for a particular item. This report would tell the representative if enough inventory of the item is on hand to fill the customer order. *Exception reports* describe unusual or critical situations, like low inventory levels. The exception report is produced only if a certain condition exists - in this case, inventory falling below a specified level.

Information Systems in the Functional Areas of Business

Information systems are used in all the functional areas and operating divisions of business. In finance and accounting, information system is used to forecast revenues from different business activities, determine the best sources and uses of funds, manage cash and other financial resources, analyze investments, and perform audits to make sure the organization is financially sound and that all financial reports and documents are accurate. In sales and marketing, information systems are used to develop new goods and services (product analysis), determine the best advertising and sales approaches (promotion analysis), and set product prices to get higher total revenue (price analysis).

In manufacturing, information systems are used to process customer orders, develop production schedules, control inventory levels, and monitor product quality. Information system is also used in the human resource management to screen applicants, administer performance tests to employees, monitor employee productivity and more. Legal information systems are used to analyze product liability and warranties and to develop important legal documents and reports.

Information System Principles

Assembling an effective and efficient computer system requires an understanding of its relationship to the information system and the organization.

The components of all information systems - such as input devices, people, procedures, and goals - are all independent. Because the performance of one system affects the others, all these systems should be measured according to the same standards of effectiveness and efficiency, given issues of cost, control, and complexity.

When selecting computer system, you also must consider the current and future needs of these systems. Your choice of a particular computer system should always allow for later improvements in the overall information system. Reasoned forethought - a trait required for dealing with computers, information, and organizational systems of all sizes- is the hall mark of true systems professional. Determine your hard ware needs based on how the hardware will be used to support the objectives of the information systems and goals of the organization. Consider the trade- offs between overall systems performance and cost, control and complexity.

Characteristics of a Management Information System

In general, management information system performs the following functions:

- Provide reports with fixed and standard formats.
- Produce hard - copy and soft- copy reports.
- Use internal data stored in the system.
- End users are able to develop their own custom reports.
- Require formal requests from users.

Information Technology and Management Information System

During last decade, the tremendous progress in information technology (IT) is affecting all spheres of our life. For India, this progress in IT provides new opportunities to improve the utilization and performance of livelihood technologies such as agriculture, education, library, health and medical services, and artesian technologies. The research challenge here is to build cost-effective IT based systems to improve the living standards of Indian rural population. Center for Data Engineering at International Institute of Information Technology, Hyderabad is carrying out research to build cost-effective IT based systems to accelerate Indian agricultural and rural development.

Agricultural Projects

Information technology specifically applied for agricultural development as discussed below.

- *e-Sagu* : Web-based Agricultural Expert Advice Dissemination System

  In this project, by exploiting advances in Information Technology (IT), we are making an effort to build a cost-effective agricultural information dissemination system to disseminate expert agriculture knowledge to the farming community so as to improve the crop productivity.

- *Pest Prediction Systems* : In this project, we make an effort to understand pest population dynamics and build pest prediction systems by applying data mining techniques on pest surveillance data set of *Helicoverpa*

Armegira, Bacterial Leaf Blight, Groundnut leaf miner regarding Chickpea, Pegionpea, Cotton, Groundnut, and Rice crops. This project is carried out in collaboration with International Crop Research Institute for Semi-Arid (ICRISAT), Patancheru, Hyderabad (India) and CRIDA, Hyderabad (India).

Indian Technology Corporation (ITC) has over the last 98 years established a very close business relationship with the farming community in India and is currently in the process of enhancing the Indian farmers' ability to link to global markets, through the e-Choupal initiative, and produce the quality products as demanded by its customers. This long-standing relationship is being leveraged in sourcing best quality agricultural produce for ITC's Foods business.

The Foods business is today represented in 4 categories in the market. They are:

- Ready to eat foods
- Staples
- Confectionery
- Snack foods

In order to assure consumers of the highest standards of food safety and hygiene, ITC is engaged in assisting outsourced manufacturers in implementing world-class hygiene standards through Hazard Analysis Critical Control Point (HACCP) certification. The unwavering commitment to internationally benchmarked quality standards enabled ITC to rapidly gain market standing in all its 6 brands:

- Kitchens of India
- Aashirvaad
- Sunfeast
- Mint-o
- Candyman
- Bingo

Agribusiness Division

ITC's Agri Business Division, one of India's largest exporters of agricultural commodities, has conceived e-Choupal as a more efficient supply chain aimed at delivering value to its customers around the world on a sustainable basis.

The e-Choupal model has been specifically designed to tackle the challenges posed by the unique features of Indian agriculture, characterised by fragmented farms, weak infrastructure and the involvement of numerous intermediaries, among others. The Value Chain - Farm to Factory Gate:

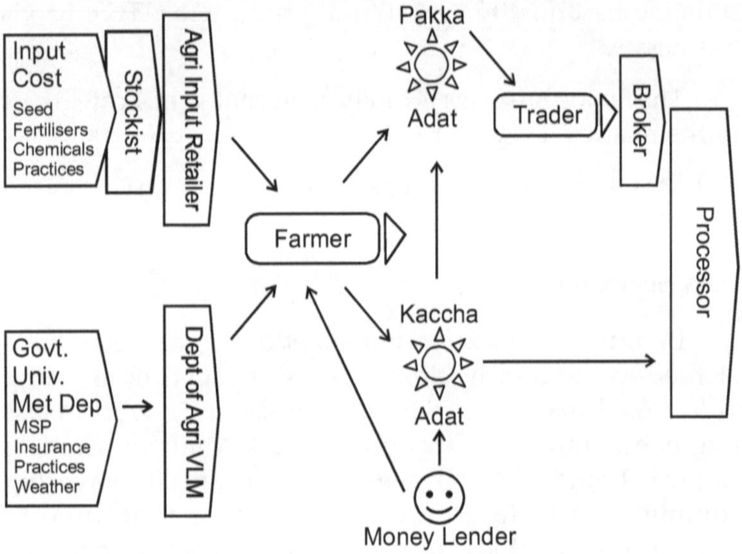

Source: WWW.e-choupal.com

'e-Choupal' also unshackles the potential of Indian farmer who has been trapped in a vicious cycle of low risk taking ability, low investment, low productivity, weak market orientation, low value addition, low margin low risk taking ability. This made him and Indian agribusiness sector globally uncompetitive, despite the availability of rich and abundant natural resources.

Such a market-led business model can enhance the competitiveness of Indian agriculture and trigger a virtuous cycle of higher productivity, higher incomes, enlarged capacity for farmer risk management, larger investments and higher quality and productivity.

Further, a growth in rural incomes will also unleash the latent demand for industrial goods so necessary for the continued growth of the Indian economy. This will create another virtuous cycle propelling the economy into a higher growth trajectory.

Appreciating the imperative of intermediaries in the Indian context, 'e-Choupal' leverages Information Technology to virtually cluster all the value chain participants, delivering the same benefits as vertical integration does in mature agricultural economies like the USA.

'e-Choupal' makes use of the physical transmission capabilities of current intermediaries - aggregation, logistics, counter-party risk and bridge financing -while disintermediating them from the chain of information flow and market signals.

With a judicious blend of click and monitor capabilities, village internet kiosks managed by farmers - called sanchalaks - themselves, enable the agricultural community access ready information in their local language on the weather and market prices, disseminate knowledge on scientific farm practices and risk management, facilitate the sale of farm inputs (now with embedded knowledge) and purchase farm produce from the farmers' door steps (decision making is now information-based).

Real-time information and customised knowledge provided by 'e-Choupal' enhance the ability of farmers to take decisions and align their farm output with market demand and secure quality and productivity. The aggregation of the demand for farm inputs from individual farmers gives them access to high quality inputs from established and reputed manufacturers at fair prices. As a direct marketing channel, virtually linked to the 'mandi' system for price discovery, 'e-Choupal' eliminates wasteful intermediation and multiple handling. Thereby, it significantly reduces transaction costs.

'e-Choupal' ensures world-class quality in delivering all these goods and services through several product / service specific partnerships with the leaders in the respective fields, in addition to ITC's own expertise.

While the farmers benefit through enhanced farm productivity and higher farm gate prices, ITC benefits from the lower net cost of procurement (despite offering better prices to the farmer) having eliminated costs in the supply chain that do not add value.

Progress

Launched in June 2000, 'e-Choupal', has already become the largest initiative among all Internet-based interventions in rural India. 'e-Choupal' services today reach out to over 4 million farmers growing a range of crops - soybean, coffee, wheat, rice, pulses, shrimp - in over 40,000 villages through nearly 6,500 kiosks across ten states (Madhya Pradesh, Haryana, Uttarakhand, Karnataka, Andhra Pradesh, Uttar Pradesh, Maharashtra, Rajasthan, Kerala and Tamil Nadu).

The problems encountered while setting up and managing these 'e-Choupals' are primarily of infrastructure inadequacies, including power supply, telecom connectivity and bandwidth, apart from the challenge of imparting skills to the first time internet users in remote and inaccessible areas of rural India.

Several alternative and innovative solutions - some of them expensive - are being deployed to overcome these challenges e.g. Power back-up through batteries charged by Solar panels, upgrading BSNL exchanges with RNS kits, installation of VSAT equipment, Mobile Choupals, local caching of static content on website to stream in the dynamic content more efficiently, 24x7 helpdesk etc.

Going forward, the roadmap includes plans to integrate bulk storage, handling and transportation facilities to improve logistics efficiencies.

As India's 'kissan' Company, ITC (Indian Tabucco Company) has taken care to involve farmers in the designing and management of the entire 'e-Choupal' initiative. The active participation of farmers in this rural initiative has created a sense of ownership in the project among the farmers. They see the 'e-Choupal' as the new age cooperative for all practical purposes.

The enthusiastic response from farmers has encouraged ITC to plan for the extension of the 'e-Choupal' initiative to altogether 15 states across India over the next few years. On the anvil are plans to channelise other services related to micro-credit, health and education through the same 'e-Choupal' infrastructure.

Another path-breaking initiative - the 'Choupal Pradarshan Khet', brings the benefits of agricultural best practices to small and marginal farmers. Backed by intensive research and knowledge, this initiative provides Agri-extension services which are qualitatively superior and involves pro-active handholding of farmers to ensure productivity gains. The services are customised to meet local conditions, ensure timely availability of farm inputs including insurance and credit, and provides a cluster of farmer schools for capturing indigenous knowledge. This initiative, which currently covers 43,500 hectares, has a multiplier impact and reaches out to over 1 million farmers.

Traditional Farmers to New-Age Marketers

ITC has continued to build new infrastructure by supplementing the farm gate presence of e-Choupal with new physical infrastructure - rural marketing hubs called Choupal Saagars, positioned within tractorable distance of 30 e-Choupal centres and their user communities.

The e-Choupal - Choupal Saagar hub and spoke combination is unprecedented grassroots click and monitor infrastructure transporting rural local economies to a new level of productivity and consumption.

Choupal Saagar offers a combination of services to rural India. Made-to-design agri-business hubs, they function as:

- ITC agri-sourcing centres providing farmers a transparent best price sales window,
- Shopping centres bringing a range of products comparable to urban levels of choice, and
- Facilitation centres delivering a host of farm-related services - training, soil testing, product quality certification, medical and clinical services, and cafeteria and fuel station. 24 Choupal Saagar hubs are already in operation in 3 states, to grow to 100 by 2010.

Springboard for Competitive Farming

The digital and physical infrastructure has a third dimension. It galvanizes ITC's constant agency for propagating adoption of best practices in farming and soil and water management.

In 2006-07, ITC's unique paid Choupal Khet Pradarshan farm extension service conducted over 15,000 Field demonstrations in 9 states. This continuous interaction sustains the rising tide of productivity channeled by the click and mortar infrastructure.

The 1 million tonne of wheat sourced by ITC over e-**Choupal** - strategically supporting its packaged foods business - makes e-Choupal robust and open, a successful application of business logic to serve a larger cause.

Agmarknet

Market information is needed by farmers in planning production and marketing, and equally needed by other market participants in arriving at optimal trading decisions. The existence and dissemination of complete and accurate marketing information is the key to achieve both operational and pricing efficiency in the marketing system.

Advancement in Information and Communication Technology (ICT) has made the world a smaller place and a larger market at one go. To fully utilize the new emerging trade opportunities for the benefit of farming community, there is a felt need to establish an ICT based "Agricultural Marketing Information Network' in the country.

Ministry of Agriculture has launched the ICT based Central Sector Scheme of Agricultural Marketing Information Network (AGMARKNET) in March, 2000, to link important agricultural produce markets spread all over the country and the State Agriculture Marketing Boards and Directorates. The project is being executed with the technical support of National Informatics Centre (NIC). The scheme has made rapid strides and by the end of X Five Year Plan, a total number of 2965 nodes have been covered under the scheme comprising of 2784 agricultural produce markets, field offices of Directorate of Marketing and Inspection (DMI) and State Agricultural Marketing Boards/ Directorates and their attached offices, etc. Necessary Computer hardware and system software tools have been supplied to all the nodes and as many as 1976 market nodes have become functional with internet connectivity by March, 2007. A user friendly software package 'AGMARK', developed to facilitate organization and transmission of market data, has been implemented in the markets. In order to strengthen interface with farmers and other beneficiaries, AGMARKNET portal *(http://agmarknet.nic.in)* has been evolved, 1700 plus markets are regularly reporting price related data which is being disseminated through the portal. The AGMARKNET portal also serves as a single window for accessing websites of various organizations concerned with agricultural marketing. It provides weekly trend analysis for important markets in respect of major commodities. It is also linked with Online Commodity Exchange of India Limited, providing futures prices in respect of oilseeds, fiber crops, etc. International price trends of various agricultural commodities available on Food and Agriculture Organisation (FAO) website are also accessible through the portal. The portal is constantly being enriched.

In order to facilitate wider market access to farm produce and better price discovery through value addition, the scheme is additionally disseminating information on market requirements in terms of quality, packing, standards, sanitary and phyto-sanitary conditions, etc.

Following activities are also proposed to be undertaken while implementing the Scheme during the XI Plan to fully achieve various objectives of the Scheme:

- Information regarding export documentation, export infrastructure, transportation facilities, exporters, marketing experts, agri-business corporates, quality standards, grading/pack house infrastructure, plant quarantine facilities, package of best marketing practices, seasonality of commodities will be provided on the portal.
- Information on contract farming, direct marketing opportunities, value addition facilities etc. to be enriched and tie-ups between farmers/ growers and sponsors/ buyers will be facilitated through the portal by evolving a specific software system through

outsourcing of work to an expert agency. It would be developed as an interactive query based system to educate the farmers on issues raised by them and would serve as a national clearing house for buyback and contract farming arrangements.

- Information on warehouses along with addresses, accreditation facilities and their distance, pledge financing facilities, etc. will also be provided on the portal.
- Area specific Success Stories will be loaded at the portal so that farmers can get knowledge and plan for trading their produce.
- Geo Information System (GIS) based Atlas will be expedited for the content enrichment and system will be put in place for regular data updating.
- A data validation software will be developed to identify the wrong reporting and for removal of undesirable data from the central data base.
- Electronic display boards will be provided at every networked market for displaying minimum and maximum price of important commodities, arrivals, temperature, etc. These efforts would be dovetailed, as far as possible, with the action being taken by the Forward Market Commission under the Scheme of the Department of Consumer Affairs.
- An aggressive publicity campaign of Agmarknet will be launched for efficient and timely utilization of information by the farmers, traders, etc.
- The programme of capacity building of different stakeholders of the Scheme will be taken up with the help of National Institute of Agriculture/Marketing (NIAM), National Institute of Agricultural Extension Management (MANAGE), State Agricultural Management and Extension Training Institutes (SAMETIs) Agricultural Technology Management

Agencies (ATMAs), KVKs. The programmes for sensitization of farmers and training of stakeholders and extension functionaries of the States will also be taken up under the Scheme.

- The translation of contents of portal into regional languages is necessary and this work are undertaken through the concerned State Marketing Boards/ Directorates.
- Strategic alliances will be developed with corporate, telecom players and private users for strengthening market intelligence services.
- The programme initiated under Common Service Centers (CSC) Scheme of DIT would help in achieving wider dissemination of information on establishment of linkage of Agmarknet portal with the proposed Information Technology (IT) kiosks at CSCs.
- To ensure timely collection and regular transmission of market information from each node, the personnel engaged by State Marketing Directorates/ Boards would be given monetary incentive and best market functionaries/ Boards/ Directorates would be given recognition (awards).
- DMI will collaborate with the agencies of Ministry of IT and Communications and others for facilitating dissemination of market information at grass root level through mobile telecom service providers.
- The price forecasting software developed by NIAM will be strengthened by outsourcing the work to a competent agency and will be integrated with Agmarknet.
- After ensuring consistent and timely reporting of data with the help of the State Governments/Marketing Boards and achieving the optimum coverage,

> infrastructure and strength for the portal, the revenue model recommended in the evaluation study will be evolved and implemented towards the end of the XI Five Year Plan. In this regard, a strategy would be evolved in consultation with respective State Marketing Boards, for adopting public-private partnership (PPP) models, to maintain the portal beyond XI Plan period. As recommended in the Evaluation Study, the Ministry would consider to adopt Buy - Build - Own - Operate (BBOO) model.

The revenue generation model for Agmarknet portal will be a mix of two established models i.e., advertising model and subscription model which would be coined as Advertising - cum - Subscription (AS) model.

Promotion of nationally and internationally acceptable standards of grading and standardization, packaging and labeling, storage and warehousing and sanitary and phyto-sanitary requirements and quality certification in farm sector will enable trade and processing sector to undertake large scale agricultural marketing operations in domestic as well as international markets.

The information relating to the schemes in respect of agricultural marketing implemented by Government Departments and Central Agencies, viz., Commerce, Food and Public Distribution, Consumer Affairs, Health and Cotton Corporation of India (CCI), Jute Corporation of India (JCI), National Cooperative Development Corporation (NCDC), National Agricultural Co-operative Marketing Federation Ltd. (NAFED), National Tobacco Growers Federation (NTGF), Tribal Cooperative Marketing Development Federation of India Ltd. (TRIFED), National Co-operative Consumers' Federation of India Ltd (NCCF), National Dairy Development Board (NDDB), National Horticultural Board (NHB), Agricultural Processed food

Export Development Authority (APEDA), Marine Products Export Development Authority (MPEDA) will also be disseminated in user friendly manner.

An e-directory of AGMARKNET nodes will be published over the portal to facilitate effective and timely exchange of information among markets and other users. Once the farm produce is standardized and labeled, backed by quality certification, it can be directly offered for sale on web site in national and international markets.

Aim of the Scheme

- To establish a nation-wide information network for speedy collection and dissemination of market information and data for its efficient and timely utilization.
- To facilitate collection and dissemination of information related to better price realization by the farmers. This would cover:
    - Market related information such as market fee, market charges, costs, method of sale, payment, weighment, handling, market functionaries, development programmes, market laws, dispute settlement mechanism, composition of market committees, income and expenditure, etc.;
    - Price-related information such as minimum, maximum and modal prices of varieties and qualities transacted, total arrivals and dispatches with destination, marketing costs and margins, etc.;
    - Infrastructure related information comprising facilities and services available to the farmers with regard to storage and warehousing, cold storage, direct marketing, contract farming, buy-back arrangements, grading, re-handling and repacking etc.; and

- Promotion related information covering accepted standards and grades, labeling, sanitary and phyto-sanitary requirements, pledge finance, marketing credit and new opportunities available in respect of better marketing;

- ❑ To sensitize and orient farmers to respond to new challenges in agricultural marketing by using ICT as a vehicle of extension.
- ❑ To improve efficiency in agricultural marketing through regular training and extension for reaching region-specific farmers in their own language.
- ❑ To provide assistance for marketing research to generate marketing information for its dissemination to farmers and other marketing functionaries at grass-root level so as to create an ambience of good marketing practices in the country.

Implementation Plan

The agencies involved in execution of the scheme will be Directorate of Marketing and Inspection (DMI), National Informatics Centre (NIC), State Governments through State Agriculture Marketing Boards (SAMB)/ Departments, National and State level institutions, individual market committees/ authorities, local bodies, private market operators, wherever applicable in the country. NIC will make available computer hardware, develop software, train market personnel in handling computer hardware and software, update the software package from time to time, provide internet connectivity and develop and commission State level portals. It will also arrange to harmonize/ integrate software package developed by the State with AGMARKNET to bring uniformity in database. It will continue to manage AGMARKNET portal. Management of State level portals could be outsourced wherever considered necessary by respective competent authorities.

Market Committees/ Controlling authorities of AGMARKNET node at market level would continue to collect relevant data and information, feed it and transmit it to the State level and AGMARKNET portal. NIC will train suitable persons from each node in operating computer and handling software package.

Key Terms MIS, TPS

Scheduled reports, e- sagu, e - choupal, Choupal-Saagars, AGMARKNET, NIC.

Chapter Summary

- Marketing, production, finance and other functional areas are supported by MIS and linked through a common data.
- MIS in specifically used in finance and accounting, and functional areas and operating decisions of business like sales and marketing.
- Assembling on effective and efficient computer system requires a understanding of its relationship to the information system and the organization.
- MIS provides reports with fixed and standard formats required for decision making.
- E - sagu is a web based Agricultural Expert Advice Dissemination System.

Chapter Highlights

Management information system (MIS) linkages with organizations transaction processing system. Characteristics of MIS, applications of MIS for agricultural development, a brief discussion on ITC's e – choapul, AGMARKNET and Information and Communication Technologies (ICT) activities proposed to be undertaken in this chapter, XI plan have been highlighted in this chapter.

Review Questions

1. Define Management Information System.
2. How MIS could be linked with the organizations transaction processing system?
3. What are the characteristics of MIS ?
4. Explain e - saagu and e - choupal ?
5. Discuss the role of AGMARKNET in disseminating agricultural information to farmers.

References

Gordon S.R. and J.R. Gordon.2004. Information Systems: A Management (3rd Edition), USA: Wiley & Sons Inc.

Murdick.R.G., J.E.Ross and J.R. Claggeff.2006. Information Systems for Modern Management (Third Edition), New Delhi: Prentice Hall of India Pvt. Ltd.

http://agmarknet.nic.in

http://agris.nic.in

www.echoupal.com

http://itcportal.com/ruraldevelopment

Further Reading Material

Stair.R.M.G.W.Reynolds.1999. Principles of Information Systems: A Management Approach (Fourth Edition), Cambridge: Course Technology ITP.

Laudon K.C. and J.P. Laudon.1991. Business Information Systems: A Problem Solving Approach (Second Edition), Fort Worth: Harcourt Brace Jovanovich College Publications.

Chapter 14

GOVERNMENT PROGRAMMES AND REGULATIONS FOR AGRIBUSINESS

Government Programmes for Agribusiness

Both the central and state governments have devised programmes to luve the entrepreneurs for setting up agribusiness in India. They may be classified as programmes falling under small-scale industries, Khadi and village industries, small and medium industries, large industries based on the finance required for investment. Apart from these many efforts were taken especially after signing, the WTO agreement to harness the export market. They include conversion of Export Processing Zones (EPZ) into Special Economic Zones (SEZ), establishment of Agri-export zones for which government is attracting private investors to make investment in infrastructure development of cold storage chains, improvement in road, rail, sea and air transport systems.

The Ministry of Small Scale Industries & Agro and Rural Industries designs and implements the policies through its field organizations for promotion and growth of small and tiny enterprises, including the coir industries.

The Ministry also coordinates with other Ministries/ Departments on behalf the Small Scale Industries (SSI) sector.

The implementation of policies and various programmes/schemes for providing infrastructure and support services to small enterprises is undertaken through its attached office, namely the Small Industry Development Organization (SIDO), statutory bodies/other organizations likely Khadi and Village Industries Commission (KVIC) & Coir Board a Public Sector Undertaking - National Small Industries Corporation (NSIC) and three training institutes - National Institute of Small Industry Extension Training (NISIET), Hyderabad, National Institute for Entrepreneurship and Small Business Development (NIESBUD), New Delhi and Indian Institute of Entrepreneurship (IIE), Guwahati.

Entrepreneurial Training Institutes

There are three institutes engaged in training of small-scale entrepreneurs. They are Indian Institute of Entrepreneurship (IIE), Guwahati, National Institute of Small Industry Extension Training (NISIET), Hyderabad, National Institute for Entrepreneurship and Small Business Development (NIESBUD), New Delhi.

Fragrance & Flavour Development Centre (FFDC), Kannauj

Fragrance & Flavour Development Centre (FFDC) set up as an autonomous body in the year 1991 by Govt. of India with the assistance of UNDP/UNIDO and Govt. of U.P/UNDP/UNIDO has provided technical expertise and imported equipments. Main objectives of the Centre is to serve, sustain and upgrade the status of farmers and industry engaged in the aromatic plants cultivation and their processing, so as to make them competitive both in the local and global markets.

Export Processing Zones

The export zones (EPZ) set up as enclaves, separated from the Domestic Tariffs Areas by fiscal barriers, are intended to provide a competitive duty free environment for export production. There are four EPZs set up by the Government at Noida(Uttar Pradesh), Chennai (Tamil Nadu), Palta (West Bengal) and Vishakapatnam (Andhra Pradesh).

Export Oriented Units (EOU)

The export Oriented units(EOU) scheme introduced in 1981, is complementary to the EPZ scheme. It adopts the same production regime but offers a wide option in locations with reference to factors like source of materials, ports of export, hinter land facilities, and availability of technological skills, existence of industrial base and the need for a large area of land for the project. And 1,536 units are in operation under the EPU scheme as on March, 2001.

Product range: EOUs are mainly concentrated in textiles and yarn, food processing, electronics, chemicals, plastics, granites and minerals/ores. Majority of units are located in Tamil Nadu, Andhra Pradesh, Karnataka, Maharashtra and Gujarat.

Export Promotion Industrial Park (EPIP) Scheme: A centrally sponsored "Export Promotion Industrial Park (EPIP) Scheme has been introduced in 1993-94 with a view to involving the State Governments in the creation of infrastructure facilities for export oriented production. The scheme provides that 75 % of the capital expenditure incurred towards creation of such facilities, ordinarily limited to Rs. 10 crores in each case, will be met from a central grant to the State Governments.

New Anna Marumalarchi Thittam: The State Government of Tamil Nadu has introduced the New Anna Marumalarchi Thittam in April 2002 to set up agribusiness units with a minimum investment of Rs 35 lakhs at the rate of one unit in each block. This scheme provides scope for setting 385 agribusiness units in Tamil Nadu.

AgriClinic and Agribusiness Centres: Small Farmers Agribusiness Consortium in co-operation with MANAGE has drawn plans to provide training on management capacity building for those willing to set up Agriclinics and Agribusiness Centres either as individual or a group of five entrepreneurs (four agricultural and allied graduates and one management graduate) with a maximum loan assistance of Rs. 10 lakhs for individuals and Rs 50 lakhs for a group of five entrepreneurs.

Regulations

Legal Regulations

Decisions are strongly affected by laws pertaining to competition, price setting, distribution arrangements, advertising, etc. It is necessary for a manager to understand the legal environment of the country and the jurisdiction of its courts. The following laws affecting business in India are important.

- Indian Contract Act, 1872
- Factories Act, 1948
- Minimum Wages Act, 1948
- Securities Contracts Regulation Act, 1956 (Now replaced by SEBI Act)
- The Companies Act, 1956
- Trade and Merchandise Marks Act, 1958
- Monopolies and Restrictive Trade Practices Act, 1969
- The Water (Prevention and Control of Pollution) Act, 1974
- The Air (Prevention and Control of Pollution) Act, 1981

- Sick Industrial Companies (Special Provision) act, 1985
- Environment Protection Act, 1986
- Consumer Protection Act, 1986
- Securities and Exchange Board of India Act, 1992
- Taxation laws covering Corporate tax, indirect taxes like Excise, Customs, Sales tax and Wealth tax).

Food Control Orders

Fruit Products Order (FPO), 1995

Fruit Products Order -1955, promulgated under Section 3 of the Essential Commodities Act - 1955, aims at regulating sanitary and hygienic conditions in manufacture of fruit, vegetable products. It is mandatory for all manufacturers of fruit, vegetable products to obtain a license under this Order. To ensure good quality products, manufactured under hygienic conditions, the Fruit Product Order lays down the minimum requirements for:

- Sanitary and hygienic conditions of premises, surrounding and personnel.
- Water to be used for processing.
- Machinery and equipment.
- Product standards.

Besides this, maximum limits of preservatives, additives and contaminants have also been specified for various products.

This order is implemented by Ministry of Food Processing Industries through the Directorate of Fruit & Vegetable Preservation at New Delhi. The Directorate has four regional offices located at Delhi, Mumbai, Calcutta and Chennai, as well as sub-offices at Lucknow and Guwahati. The officials of the Directorate undertake frequent inspections of the manufacturing units and draw random samples of products from the manufacturers and markets which are analyzed in the laboratories to test their conformity with the specifications laid under FPO.

The Central Fruit Advisory Committee comprising of the officials of concerned Government Departments, Technical experts, representatives of Central food Technology Research Institute, Bureau of Indian standards, Fruits and Vegetable Products and Processing Industry, is responsible for recommending amendments in the Fruit Product Order. In view of the demands of the industry, and the liberalized economic scenario, major amendments were made in FPO during 1997.

Meat Food Products Order (MFPO)

Meat Food Products Order, 1973 (MFPO) promulgated under the provisions of Essential Commodities Act, 1955 provides for sanitary and other requirements, limits of heavy metals, preservatives, insecticides, residue, etc., for meat food products. This order was being implemented by Ministry of Rural Development in the Ministry of Rural Area & Employment. As on 31st March 1998, there were 128 licenses issued under MFPO 1973.As per the recent amendment to the Allocation of Business, Ministry of Agriculture (Deptt. of Agriculture & Cooperation) would now be the Administrative Ministry for this Order.

Milk & Milk Products Order (MMPO)

Milk and Milk Products Order, 1992 administered by the Department of Animal Husbandry & Dairying under Ministry of Agriculture was promulgated on 9th June, 1992 under the provision of Section 3 of the Essential Commodities Act, 1955 with a view to maintain an increased supply of liquid milk of desired quality to the general public. This order regulated production, supply and distribution of milk and milk products throughout the country. The order also seeks to ensure the observance of sanitary requirements for dairies, machinery and premises, and quality control standards for milk and milk products. So far, 254 registration certificates under MMOP, 1992 has been issued by the Department of Animal Husbandry and Dairying.

CODEX Alimentarius

The term Codex Alimentarius is taken from Latin and it means food code. Codex Alimentarius brings together all the interested parties-scientists, technical experts, governments, consumers and industry representatives to help develop standards for food manufacturing and trade. These standards, guidelines and recommendations are recognized worldwide for their vital role in protecting the consumers and facilitating international trade. As Codex Alimentarius represents a consensus of food and trade experts from around the world, these standards are more and more being used in international trade negotiations and also for settling of disputes by WTO

The Codex Contract Point in India is the Directorate General of Health Services (DGHS) in the Ministry of Health; however, the Ministry of Food Processing Industries is closely associated with the activities of Codex Alimentarious. Under the Plan schemes, a scheme for setting up of Codex Monitoring Cell in the Ministry with the allocations of Rs. 58.00 lakhs in 1998-99 has been formulated for creating data base, technical examination of various standards in association with experts.

The Pulses, Edible Oilseeds and Edible Oils (Storage) Order, 1977 empowers the government to put maximum stock limits on wholesalers and retailers of pulses, oilseed and oils and is designed to maintain supplies and ensure equitable distribution and availability at fair prices of these items.

Food Safety and Quality

The Food Processing Ministry cleared a proposal for release of Rs. 59.2 lakhs to Food Research and Analysis Center, New Delhi for up gradation of its Food Analysis and Quality Control Laboratory for analysis of food products. The main objective of the proposal is to upgrade the existing analytical laboratory and bring it on par with any other modern analytical laboratory in the country. During the year under review, the Ministry cleared a proposal in principle for release of 12.32 lakhs to Choudhry Charan Singh (CCS) Haryana Agriculture University, Hissar for up gradation of quality control and food analysis laboratory of the Department of Food Science and Technology of the university. The main objective of the proposal are to provide quality assurance and analytical services to the food processing industries, to undertake micro biological examination of various pathogen and mycotoxins and to estimate nutritional parameters including minerals, vitamins, food value in calories, protein, carbohydrates, fats etc.

Hazard Analysis and Critical Control Point (HACCP)

Hazard Analysis and Critical Control Point (HACCP) is an important quality assurance system. This system ensures that the products are safe and of good quality. The system is extremely desirable in view of the changing scenario in the international trade. The Ministry provides a grant of 50% subject to a limit of Rs.10 lakhs towards the cost of implementing Total Quality Management (TQM) including HACCP and ISO-9000 certifications.

This Ministry sponsored a one-day seminar and five day training programme organized by APEDA from 30th November to 5th December 1998 in collaboration with NSF-International strategic Registration Limited, USA, which is the main authority for certifying HACCP-9000. HACCP is an important requirement for ensuring the quality of products from health and safety aspects and is crucial for exports.

Laws Relating to Food Processing Industries

There are a number of food laws being implemented by various Ministries/Departments. These are primarily meant for two purposes namely (1) Regulation of Specifications of food and (2) Regulation of Hygienic condition of Processing/Manufacturing. Some of these food laws are mandatory and some are voluntary. The details of various food laws in operation in India are as under:

Food Laws

1. Prevention of Food Adulteration Act (PFA) Ministry of Health

The Act lays down specifications for various food products and is mandatory. The Ministry of Health in 1995 had constituted a Task Force under the chairmanship of Shri E.S. Venkataramaiah, Chief Justice of India (retired). The Task Force recommended that there should be emphasis on good manufacturing practices instead of detection of adulteration and prosecution. It also expresses concern about lack of laboratory equipments and quantified persons. In addition, it also suggested that the name of PFA Act be changed to Food Safety Act.

2. Agriculture Produce (Grading & Marking) Act (Ministry of Rural Development)

This Act is commonly known as AGMARK and is voluntary. The Act lays down the specifications for various agricultural commodities including some processed foods to be graded as AGMARK Products.

3. Laws being operated by Bureau of Indian Standards (BIS)

BIS is the largest body for formulating standards for various food items. These standards are also voluntary.

4. *Essential Commodities Act*

A number of quality control orders have been issued under Essential Commodities Act such as FPO, MMPO, Meat Food Product Order and Vegetable Oils Control Order. These orders are mandatory and primarily meant for regulating the hygienic conditions. They were clubbed under one order which is called Food Products Order.

Whom to approach for what

Steps Involved	**Persons/ Officers to be Contacted**
Product selection and assistance in preparation of project report/ feasibility/report/market survey	Small Industries Service Centre, Chennai
Obtaining provisional /permanent registration certificate	District Industries Centre of the concerned district where the unit is to be set up
Registration under sales tax	The Commissioner of Commercial Taxes, Chennai
Registration under central excise	The Collector of Central Excise & Customs, Chennai
Obtaining Finance	Nationalized banks, Private Commercial banks Tamil Nadu Industrial Investment Corporation Small Industries Development Bank of India
Obtaining water supply	Tamil Nadu Water Supply & Drainage board
Obtaining Power connection	Tamil Nadu Electricity Board
Registration under ESI Act (applicable for units employing 20 or more workers)	Employee's, State Insurance Corporation, Chennai
Obtaining ISI Certificate	Bureau of Indian Standards, Nanak Bhavan, New Delhi
Obtaining the Trade Mark registration	Registrar of Trade Marks, 9 Judge Jumbulingam Mudaliar Road, Chennai

contd....

Obtaining Patent Right	The Controller of Patents and Design, 776 Triplicane High Road, Chennai
Obtaining license under Food Products Order for manufacture of food products	Deputy Director, Directorate of Marketing & Inspection, Ministry of Food & Agriculture, Sastry Bhavan, 35, Haddows Road, Chennai-600006.
Obtaining Information on manufacturing of essential oils	Central Institute of Medicinal & Aromatic Plants, Regional Centre, UAS, GKVK Campus, Hebbal, Bangalore
License for Drug & Cosmetic manufacture	Drug Controller Office of the Drug Controller, Chennai
Pollution control License	Tamil Nadu Pollution control Board, Chennai
Setting up of Rice Solvent Extraction Units	Tamil Nadu Civil Supplies Department, Chennai

Evolution: From Export Processing Zones (EPZs) to Special Economic Zones (SEZs)

Special Economic Zones (SEZs) are geographical regions that have economic laws different from a country's typical economic laws. The goal is to increase in foreign direct investment (FDI) in the country. Traditionally, SEZs are created as open markets within an economy that is dominated by distortionary trade, macro and exchange regulation and other regulatory governmental controls. SEZs are believed to create a conducive environment to promote investment and exports. And hence, many developing countries are promoting the SEZs with the expectation that they will provide the engines of growth for their economies to achieve industrialization.

To achieve its three-fold objectives of attracting FDI, increasing exports and accelerating the country's economic growth, the Government of India announced the introduction of SEZs in its Export-Import Policy of March, 2000.

The EXIM Policy (1997-2002) introduced a new scheme from April 1, 2000 for establishment of the Special Economic Zones (SEZs) in different parts of the country.

Salient Features of the Indian SEZ Initiative Include

- Unlike most of the international instances where zones are primarily developed by Governments, the Indian SEZ policy provides for development of these zones in the government, private or joint sector. This offers equal opportunity to both Indian and international private developers.
- For green field SEZs, the Government has specified a minimum preferable area of 1,000 hectares. However, for sector specific SEZs, there is no restriction of minimum area.
- 100 per cent FDI is permitted for all investments in SEZs, except for activities under the negative list.
- SEZ units are required to be positive net foreign exchange earners and are not subject to any minimum value addition norms or export obligations.
- Goods flow into the SEZ area from Domestic Tariff Area (DTA) will be treated as exports and goods coming from the SEZ area into DTA are treated as imports.

Currently, a number of SEZ projects are coming up in the country. The government has given a go-ahead for around 17 SEZs to be set up in the private sector or the joint sector. Of these, the projects at Positra (Gujarat), Vishakhapatnam (Andhra Pradesh), Indore (Madhya Pradesh) and Navi Mumbai (Maharashtra) are in advanced stages of planning and development, while the others are preparing to get off the ground.

Incentives and Benefits

Besides providing state-of-the-art infrastructure and access to a large well-trained and skilled work force, the SEZ policy also provides enterprises and developers with the following favourable and attractive framework of incentives:

- 100% Income Tax Exemption for a block of five years and an additional 50% tax exemption for two years thereafter
- 100% FDI in the manufacturing sector permitted through automatic route, barring a few sectors.
- External commercial borrowings by SEZ units up to US$500 million in a year without any maturity restrictions through recognized banking channels.
- Facility to retain 100% foreign exchange receipts in Exchange Earners' Foreign Currency Account.
- 100% FDI permitted to SEZ franchisee in providing basic telephone services in SEZs.
- No cap on foreign investment for small scale sector reserved items.
- Exemption from industrial licensing requirements for items reserved for the SSI sector.
- No import license requirements
- Exemption from customs duties on import of capital goods, raw materials, consumables, spares etc
- Exemption from Central Excise duties on procurement of capital goods, raw materials, consumable spares etc., from the domestic market.
- No routine examinations by Customs for export and import cargo.
- Facility to realize and repatriate export proceeds within 12 months.

- Profits allowed to be repatriated without any dividend-balancing requirement.
- Job work on behalf of domestic exporters for direct export allowed.
- Subcontracting both domestic and international is permitted; this facility is available to jewellery units as well.
- Exemption from Central Sales Tax and Service Tax
- Facilities to set up off-shore banking units in SEZs.

Incentives to Developers

- Exemption from duties on import /procurement of goods for the development, operation & maintenance of SEZ.
- Income tax exemption for a block of 10 years in 15 years.
- Exemption from Service Tax
- FDI to develop townships within SEZs with residential, educational, health care and recreational facilities permitted on a case-to-case basis. As per the policy-
    - From November 1, 2000 the Export Processing Zones at Kandla, Santa Cruz (Mumbai), Cochin and Surat have been converted into SEZs.
    - In 2003, other existing EPZs namely, Noida, Falta, Chennai, Vishakapatnam were also converted into SEZs.
    - As on June 2005, 53 SEZs have been approved by the Government of India out of which 11 SEZs are functional and the rest 42 SEZs are under establishment.
    - However, the area norms for multi-product SEZs in the northeastern states like Assam, Meghalaya,

Nagaland and the states of Jammu and Kashmir, Himachal Pradesh and Uttaranchal have been limited to 200 hectares, and 50 hectares in the case of sector-specific SEZs.

SEZ Act, 2005

According to the SEZ Act, 2005, the GOI has proposed that multi-product SEZs must have an area of at least 1,000 hectares, while sector-specific zones including ports and airports, must have a minimum area of 100 hectares.

Export Performance of SEZs

Exports from SEZs grew by 16.4% from 2000-01 to 2004-05. In the same period, total exports in India grew only by 12.1%. This clearly signifies the importance of SEZs in India. However, the share of exports from SEZs in the total exports of the country has only increased from 4.2% in 2000-01 to 5.1% in 2004-05.

Key Focus Areas

The zones' performance in attracting investment and promoting export competitiveness seems to be directly related with the location, infrastructure facilities, quality of governance and the incentive packages.

The Road Ahead

- There should be a vision on the design, establishment and operations of the SEZ.
- It is necessary to develop zones as industrial clusters of specific products so that backward linkages would benefit the growth of accessories units as well.
- The zones should specialize in terms of economic activities depending on the availability of human capital, resources and infrastructure in the region. They thus tend to transform into horizontally-

integrated industrial clusters, which include industries that might share a common market for the end products, use a common technology or labor force skills, or require similar natural resources. It seems, therefore, that it would be desirable to develop zones as industrial clusters of specific products. This may encourage downstream industries also.

Zones in the long run need to give way to industrial clusters of horizontally and vertically integrated industries in general, high tech industries in particular. This would not only help to jump-start the manufacturing processes but would also improve export competitiveness with greater returns.

At present, there is no autonomous authority responsible for the development of zones and for providing single window clearances in India. The zone administration functions as a government department office. Ideally, the SEZs should be managed by autonomous authorities, which should be constituted under specific Acts and should be assigned the responsibilities to promote the zones.

In India, SEZs are managed by a single government department. At the zonal level, there is no fine tuning and division of responsibilities. Ideally, there should be specific departments managing specific issues within SEZs. There should be a general administration department and other departments dedicated to specific issues. For example, there can be an Investor Services department for all the investment processing issues, an Industrial Relations Deparment handling labour issues, etc.

The government needs to enact legislation, create a focused administrative infrastructure to govern SEZs, offer highly attractive incentives and locate zones in the best possible locations. Overall investment climate (infrastructure, governance) in a country matters in the success of its SEZs in terms of competitiveness. Generally, it is argued that the SEZ concept is attractive because it is much easier to resolve the problems of infrastructure and governance on a limited geographical area than it is to resolve them countrywide. The zones cannot be insulated from the broader institutional and economic context of the country and be treated as an economy within the economy. Zones are a part of the economy and require overall improvement in the investment climate to ensure success in the long run. They should not, therefore, be viewed as an alternative to the overall development model. This is perhaps the reason why SEZs failed to fulfill the role of engines of industrialization in most countries on a sustainable basis.

Agri Export Zones - Genesis

With the removal of almost all the quantitative restrictions on imports and with the decks cleared for integration of Indian economy with the global one, a need was felt to harness our competitive advantage in international trade. Agriculture was perceived as one sector where such a potential existed. The provisions of agreement on agriculture, implemented in letter and spirit, could create such an opportunity. However, despite the potential, there was a lot to be done to get the supply chain going. The objective, therefore, was to take a look at an agriculture produce in a comprehensive manner- right from farm to the palate so as to be able to deliver an appropriately priced and attractively package quality product in the international market. Thus emerged the concept of Agri Export Zone, which found a place in the exim policy announced for the year 2001- 2002 as a separate chapter.

Concept

The concept of Agri Export Zone attempts to take a comprehensive look at a particular produce/product located in a contiguous area for the purpose of developing and sourcing the raw material, its processing/ packaging, leading to final exports. However, the entire effort begins with market analyses to assess the market potential for that produce. Subsequently, steps are taken to ascertain the quality parameters that are required for making this produce/product acceptable in the international market. The attempt then is to see what sorts of interventions are required at each stage of the value chain to come up with such a produce/product.

These interventions commence right from availability of inputs like seeds, fertilizers, pesticides, credit etc. This would then entail research into the pre-harvest protocols, if they do not already exist and application and extension of these protocols and practices in the fields of identified farmers. Development of harvesting protocol, its implementation and the post-harvest management are all critical links in the value chain. These would include activities like storage (both intermediate and final), grading, sorting, processing, packaging and transportation. Each of these activities would involve a specialized intervention, which could be technological (hence would involve research) or financial.

Finally, it is the marketing, which is the key to the success. The capability to position the product in an appropriate market and getting an appropriate price would ultimately determine whether the AEZ could get going.

Objective

In a fast changing international trade environment and with a view to providing remunerative returns to the farming community in a sustained manner, efforts will be made to provide improved access to the produce/ products of the Agriculture and Allied sectors in the international market.

State Governments may identify product specific Agri Export Zone for end to end development for export of specific products from a geographically contiguous area. State Government may evolve a comprehensive package of services provided by all State Government Agencies, State Agricultural Universities and all institutions and agencies of the Union Government for intensive delivery in these zones.

Such services be managed and co-ordinated by State Government would include provision of pre/post harvest treatment and operations, plant protection, processing, packaging, storage and related research and development, etc. APEDA will supplement, within its schemes and provisions, efforts of State Governments for facilitating such exports.

Export Promotion Credit Guarantee (EPCG) Scheme

Agriculture exporters shall be eligible for the facility of EPCG scheme and the export obligation shall be determined in accordance with export of the Policy but the licence holder shall not be required to maintain the average level of exports.

Exporter shall have the facility to move or to shift the capital goods within the zone provided he maintains accurate record of such movements. However, such equipments shall not be sold or leased out by the license holder. This facility shall also be available to service providers, setting up common infrastructural facilities such as sorting, grading, polishing, packaging, cold storage, transport equipment/ refrigerated vans, vapour treatment and heat treatment plant, X-ray screening facility, etc.

The units setup in the notified Agri Export Zone shall be entitled to the benefits available under the scheme. A service provider in the Agri Export Zone may import equipment under the EPCG scheme for supplying services to agri exports. The export obligation may be offset by the service provider by earning foreign exchange in lieu of services rendered.

Duty Exemption and Remission Scheme

The agriculture exporter shall be entitled to the facility for import of inputs like fertilizers, pesticides, insecticides, packing material etc. under Advance Licence/Duty Free Replenishment Certificate (DFRC), Duty Entitlement Pass Book (DEPB) scheme as given in three of the Policy subject to the eligibility criteria and conditions enumerated under the scheme.

Status

The agri exporter shall be eligible for recognition as Export House/Trading House/Star Trading House/ Super Star Trading House on achieving the performance level.

Benefits of Agri Export Zones

The concept of Agri Export Zone attempts to take a comprehensive look at a particular produce/products located in a contiguous area for the purpose of developing and sourcing the raw materials, their processing/ packaging, leading to final exports. Thus, the entire effort is centered around a cluster approach of identifying the potential products, the geographical region in which these are grown and adopting an approach of integrating the entire process, right from the state of production till it reaches the market.

The anticipated benefits to accrue as a consequence of setting up of such zones are as follows:

- Strengthening of backward linkages with a market oriented approach.
- Product acceptability and its competitiveness abroad as well as in the domestic market.
- Value addition to basic agriculture produce.

- Reduction in cost of production through economies of scale.
- Better price for agricultural produce.
- Improvement in product quality and packaging.
- Promotion of trade related research and development.
- Increase in employment opportunities.

Novelty of Agri Export Zones

Convergence of all ongoing schemes of Central and State Governments is the special feature of Agri Export Zone. The extension and inputs related assistance from Ministry of Agriculture schemes, funds for vans, marketing assistance from APEDA, purchase refrigerated funds for establishing cold storage by NHB and processing plant by Ministry of Food Processing are made available in Agri Export Zones.

List of Agri - Export Zones

States	AEZs for Products	Total
Andhra Pradesh	Chilli, Gherkins and Mangoes, Mango pulp and Fresh Vegetables.	5
Assam	Fresh and Processed Ginger	1
Bihar	Lychee and Vegetables	1
Gujarat	Dehydrated onion, Sesame seeds, Mangoes and Vegetables	3
Himachal Pradesh	Apples	1
Jammu & Kashmir	Apples and Walnut	2
Jharkand	Vegetables	1
Karnataka	Gherkins, Flowers, Rose Onion and Vannila	4
Kerala	Horticulture Producet; Medicinal Plant	2

contd....

Madhya Pradesh	Lenthil and Grams, Wheat (including sharbati wheat for Bhopal zone) Potatoes, Onion and Garlic, Seed Spices and Oranges.	5
Maharashtra	Mangoes, Grape and Kesar mango, Flowers, Onion, Pomegranate, Banana and Oranges.	8
Orissa	Ginger and Turmeric	1
Punjab	Potatoes, Basmati rice, Vegetables (Cabbage Broccoli, Okra, Peas, Carrot, Baby Corn, Green Chillies, Green Beans and Tomato)	3
Rajasthan	Coriander and Cumin	2
Sikkim	Flowers (Orchids) and Cherry Pepper and Ginger	2
Tamil Nadu	Mangoes, Flowers, Cashew nut, Cut flowers	4
Tripura	Pineapple	1
Uttaranchal	Lychees, Flowers, Basmati Rice, Medicinal and Aromatic plants.	4
Uttar Pradesh	Basmati Rice, Mangoes, Vegetables and Potatoes.	4
West Bengal	Pineapple, Lychee, Potatoes, Mango, Vegetables, and Darjeeling tea	6
	Total	**60**

Agri Export Zones, A Partial Success

The Agri Export Zones (AEZs) set up in 2001-02 and numbering 60 spread over in 20 States have so far garnered an investment of Rs 866.40 crore and achieved exports of Rs 5,412.81 crore over the last five years, against an envisaged investment of Rs 1,717.95 crore and exports of Rs 11,821.47 crore.

The AEZ scheme thus, achieved "a partial success." One of the reasons for shortfall in the performance pertains to the lack of any extra special benefit to exporters from AEZs.

A peer evaluation shows that there is no single entrepreneurial agency running an AEZ. The success of any AEZ depends on coordinated efforts of various Central and State Government agencies along with private entrepreneurs. Following this, it has been resolved to accord priority of funding of projects in the AEZs under Assistance for State Infrastructure Development for Export (ASIDE) of the Department of Commerce. It has also been decided that in the absence of separate funds for AEZs under the ASIDE scheme, the States might spend 15-20 per cent of the ASIDE funds allocated to them on AEZ projects. Some 29 projects entailing financial support amounting to Rs 97.95 crore are under consideration for funding from the ASIDE scheme.The private financial institutions such as Yes Bank and ILFS have also evinced interest in making public-private partnership projects for some of the AEZs. According to the sources, the Department is extending fillip to build infrastructure and enable export of agri produce under the Plan schemes of the Agricultural and Processed Food Products Export Development Authority (APEDA). Various schemes being operated by APEDA for development of infrastructure, market development, quality development, R and D and transport assistance would get an enhanced outlay of Rs 750 crore in the 11th Plan (2007-12), against the actual expenditure of Rs 272.20 crore for such schemes during the 10th Plan. In the context of the technical barriers to trade and stringent sanitary and phyto-sanitary standards of major importing countries impacting the competitiveness of Indian produce, persistent efforts of the authorities had paid off, with both the US and Japan recently lifting the ban on import of Indian mangoes. However, Japan insists on vapour heat treatment for mangoes before exports, while the US wants irradiation.

Food Safety and Quality Year 2008-09

The year, 2008-09 has been pronounced as the "Food Safety and Quality year", in order to give more emphasis on safety and quality standards for food products.

Plan of Action

The ministry of Food Processing Industries is celebrating the year as "Food Safety and Quality year"

Food safety is a growing concern across the world. There is an increasing need to provide greater assurance about the safety and quality of food to consumers. Food standards are expected to acquire greater importance, given increasing concerns on food safety on the one hand, and growing consumer demand for products which are healthy on the other. The concept of food safety and quality is important for all stakeholders starting from the farmers to the processors, to the retailers and to the consumers. The present initiative of the Ministry aims to meet certain requirements of the sector.

This initiative was primarily to bring together the proposed initiatives of this Ministry as well as related Schemes proposed by other Ministries such as Ministry of Agriculture, Department of Commerce, Ministry of Health, and Department of Consumer Affairs which are all directly involved in the implementation of the Food Safety and Standards Act, 2006. The close cooperation of various State Governments would also be required for the implementation. All the concerned Ministries/ Organizations will identify such initiatives relating to food quality and safety either in the form of existing schemes or which are proposed to be taken up by them during the course of the year.

This will give us an opportunity to focus on the thrust areas of Food Safety & Food Quality to be achieved through a clearly defined set of steps, with timelines for each.

The following are the components of a Food Safety and Quality Year 2008-09.

Implementation of Food Safety and Quality Year under 11th Plan

Schemes

- Under the new scheme of upgradation of hygiene and quality of street food of the Ministry, 10,000 street vendors across the nation would be identified, profiled and steps would be taken up to upgrade the safety and quality of food.
- National and regional industry associations would be involved in identifying units and launching a programme for capacity building through HACCP or ISO 22000 for the food processing units who are members of their Organizations. 10,000 units could be targetedin order to compile their profiles and detailed programmes drawn up for upgradation and follow up steps launched. Certification would be achieved within a period of 18 months.
- Preparation of a protocol based on best international trade standards and conducting checks against the prepared protocol in HACCP certified units. The field protocol will be evaluated and companies graded into Platinum, Gold and Silver categories.
- 50 food safety laboratories will be identified who would be benchmarked against industry best practices and a plan of action drawn up for their upgradation. Steps will be initiated to bring them up to best practice levels within the next 2 years.
- Good Agricultural Practices (GAP) have already been identified as a thrust area for improving traceability, hygiene and safety of food items. For the country as a whole, 10,000 farmers would be identified (approximately 500 in each State) who would be taken in a step by step process to achieve certification of

GAP or for organic food. Viable projects would be created so that the agri-horticultural produces from these farms are marketed and the returns accrue to the farmers.

- 10 abattoirs would be taken up either by modernization of existing abattoirs or setting up new abattoirs in a public private partnership mode. The programmes for their upgradation would be approved and worked out. These would also be linked through cold chain, to a retail network so that there is discernible impact on the quality and safety of processed meat.
- Fruit Products Order and Meat and Meat Food Products Order would be reviewed in consultation with stakeholders and modern forward linking and internationally benchmark marked regulatory systems prepared for consideration of the Central Food Authority.

Gender Sensitivity of Food Processing Units

- The Ministry will undertake a Gender Sensitivity Programme by developing a standard for gender sensitivity for food processing units. The minimum facilities to be provided and the certification process in this regard would be developed and compliance rewarded.

Updating Food Laws and Regulations

- The current Food Safety Standards under the Prevention of Food Adulteration Act would be reviewed in consultation with stakeholders and the revised proposals drawn up for consideration of the Central Food Authority.

Awards for Innovation in Food Safety and Quality

- The Ministry will draw up a programme to identify innovative food products and practices by a process of rigorous selection.

Commissioning Studies

- A micro level study and survey to be commissioned to estimate the level of wastages under various crops and the steps which are required to eliminate them.
- State level studies to be initiated to estimate the level of pesticide and other residues in food products as well as estimate the nutritional contents of diet in various parts of the country.
- APEDA has already initiated preparation of a directory of exporters of agricultural processed food which will be distributed.
- A study to be commissioned to prepare an action plan for a rapid response system for identification and responding to safety issues in the food processing sector.
- FICCI has already prepared the details of an international portal to assist investors in the food processing sector. This will be expanded to cover the sub sects of investor interest and made more informative and operational.
- Bureau of Indian Standards have been working on developing standards for the street food sector. This will be finalised and used as an input of the street food sector programmes of the Ministry.
- A study will be commissioned to identify the standards prescribed under Codex Alimentarius which are relevant to Indian markets, the gap with existing local standards and action points.

Awareness Programmes on Food Safety and Quality

- A brochure will be brought out on the food safety issues faced by a housewife and safe practices required in the kitchen. This will be widely disseminated.
- Food safety issues need to be introduced into the school curriculum. Proper teaching material will be drawn up through an expert group.
- A book on Indian cuisine and its relation to cultural aspects will be brought out in collaboration with private corporates. Alternatively, the best few books in the area of cuisine and food will be identified and rewarded.
- Food clusters will be identified which will be taken up for HACCP and quality upgradation through CII and FICCI. At least 3 organic food clusters will be identified and the farmers linked to sustainable market outlets.
- A year long programme for holding short duration workshops and seminars at various places in the country on topical issues relating to food safety and quality will be organized.
- A postage stamp to commemorate the Food Safety and Quality Year 2008-09 will be launched.

Radiation Processing of Food

Irradiation technology is widely used in scientific as well as commercial applications in the field of agriculture and animal science, pharmaceuticals and medical science, etc. One of the important applications of the radiation technology in the services of mankind is post harvest handling and management of foods. Food Irradiation involves treating certain types of foods with ionizing energy or radiation. Radiation processing of food strengthens food conservation, improves food hygiene and helps food exports overcome quarantine barriers. It facilitates packing, storage, transport and distribution of foods.

Uses of Radiation Processing of Foods

- Extension of shelf-life of food products by killing micro-organisms causing spoilage.
- Enhancement of safety by killing food borne pathogens and parasites.
- Inhibiting sprouting in tubers, bulbs and rhizomes.
- Delaying ripening of fruits.
- Destroying insect pests in stored products and fruits.

Food irradiation has been thoroughly and extensively studied in order to ensure its toxicological, nutritional and microbiological safety. The data available from the world wide research including that from India over the last four decades were jointly reviewed by the experts of WHO and FAO Expert Committee on the Wholesomeness of Irradiated Food, convened in Geneva concluded that any food irradiated up to a maximum of 10 kg is safe for human consumption. Independent technical and scientific committees constituted by several countries including Canada, Denmark, France, India, Sweden, the U.K. European Economic Community (EEC) and, the USFDA have declared that irradiated food is safe for human consumption.

Three international agencies viz., the World Health Organization, the Food and Agricultural Organisation of the United Nations, and the International Atomic Energy Agency accept the safety and usefulness of food irradiation. The process is also endorsed by the American Medical Association, the Scientific Committee of the European Union, and the American Spice Trade Association, Spice Board of India, APEDA (GOI), Ministry of Food Processing Industries (GOI), Ministry of Health, among others.

Current Status

Over 42 countries in the world including developed countries like USA, Canada, UK, France as well as developing countries like Bangladesh and Thailand have given clearance for radiation processing of Food. The Government of India has also permitted use of irradiation technology in preservation of food items such as potato, onion, rice, semolina (sooji or raws), Wheat atta or maida, mango, rasins, dried dates, ginger, garlic, shallots (small onion) and meat products including chicken.

In India, Bhabha Atomic Research Centre (BARC) has done extensive RandD work on preservation of foods by radiation. Board of Radiation and Isotope Technology (BRIT) of the Ministry Atomic Energy has set up a facility for radiation processing of spices at Navi Mumbai. BARC is also setting up the first demonstration plant for radiation processing of onions and potatoes at Lasal Gaon in Nasik Distt. of Maharashtra. It is proposed to use the same plant for low dose radiation processing of other foods with alterations in throughput and source utilization efficiency.

The Ministry of food processing industries (MFPI) has interest in radiation processing technology as a means of preservation of perishable fruits and vegetables, pest control and enhancement of quality. The MFPI is now encouraging entrepreneurs for setting up of facilities for radiation processing of foods in private sector.

Cost of Irradiated Food

The cost of food depends upon many variables, and one of them is cost of processing. But processing results into a number of benefits to consumers in terms of availability, storage life, distribution and improved hygiene of food. Irradiation can have a stabilizing effect on market price of foods by reducing storage losses resulting in increased availability of produce. Irradiation cost may range from Rs. 0.25 to 0.50 per kg. for a low dose application such as sprout inhibition of potato and onion and insect disinfestations in cereals and pulses to Rs. 1-3 per kg. for high dose application such as treatment of spices for microbial decontamination. The cost could be brought down in a multipurpose facility treating a variety of products round the year.

Technology/assistance available Irradiation clearance by Various countries.

North America and South America	**Asia and Africa**	**Europe**
America, Argentina, Brazil, Cuba Mexico, Uruguay United States, Canada	Africa, Bangladesh, China, India, Indonesia, Iran, Israel, Japan, Pakistan, Philippines, South Africa, Syria, Thailand, South korea, Vietnam,	Belgium, Croatia, Czech Rep.Denmark, Finland, France, Italy, Netherlands, Norway, Poland, Russian Federation, Spain, United Kingdom, Yugoslavia

Source: Ministry of Food Processing, Industry, GOI

Public sector undertaking/private sector/cooperative/individual entrepreneurs/industrialist desirous of setting up of irradiation facility/demonstration plant in India may approach the following:

- *Bhabha Atomic Research Centre (BARC)* : BARC is the Nodal agency for assistance and guidance on processed technology. BARC/BRIT may be approached for information on availability, cost and possible alternative of essential/critical machinery, pollution and other environmental aspects, utilization/disposal of radioisotopes. Guidance on legal and regulatory aspects, techno-economic advantages, project configuration, financing and other relevant aspects, can also be obtained from them. BARC will also provide help in standardization of dosimeter procedure and carrying out of dosimeter. BARC/BRIT can provide training to the staff on one of the existing plant on various aspects of operation and safety.

- *Board of Radiation and Isotope Technology (BRIT):* BRIT also provides technological inputs and guidance for formulation of irradiation projects. It has set up a plant at Indore (Centre for Advanced Technology) based on electron radiation, and has the capacity to set up the irradiation processing plant totally indigenously.
- *Ministry of Food Processing Industries (MFPI):* MFPI is willing to support food processing by radiation in the public and private terms to promote the commercial use of technology in India. Under the Plan Scheme for Development of Infrastructure facilities, financial assistance in the form of a loan will be provided to a private sector organisation to the extent of 50% of the cost of capital equipment and technical civil works upto Rs.50 lakhs in general areas and upto Rs.75 lakhs in difficult areas.

  Under above said scheme financial assistance in the form of grant will be provided to the entrepreneurs upto Rs.4 crores for creation of common facility in a food park, such as cold chain, quality control laboratory, effluent disposal unit and the like, of which, common irradiation facility may be one.

List of Nodal Officers of State/U.T. Governments for Food Processing Industries

S.No	State/Union Territory	Nodal Agency	Tel. No.	Fax. No
1	Andaman and Nicobar Islands	Director, Agriculture, Port Blair	03192-33257	-
2	Andhra Pradesh	Secretary, Agriculture and Cooperation Ministry Secretariat Building, Hyderabad - 500 022	0842-231798	-
3	Arunachal Pradesh	Chief Secretary Government of Arunachal Pradesh, Itanagar.	03781-22595	-

4	Assam	Secretary Ministry of Industries Government of Assam, Guwahati.	0361-561307	561176
5	Bihar	Industrial Development Commissioner, Ministry of Industries Government of Bihar, Vikas Bhawan, Patna - 800 001.	0612-221462	224992
6	Chandigarh	Director, District Industries Centre, Dadra and Nagar Haveli, Silvasa - 396 210.	0172-707343	-
7	Dadra and Nagar Haveli		02638-42367	
8	Daman and Diu	Deputy Director of Agriculture, Secretariat Moti Daman - 396 220	02638-54875	
9	Delhi	Commissioner (Industries), C/O Commissioner of Industries, Delhi Administration Kashmiri Gate, Delhi		
10	Goa	Development Commissioner, Government of Goa, Panaji.	0832-223196	
11	Gujarat	Managing Director, Gujarat Agro Industries Corporation Ltd., Khet Udyog Bhavan,Opp. Old High Court,Navrangpura, Ahmedabad	02712-25841	
12	Haryana	Managing Director, Haryana Agro Industries ,Corporation Chandigarh.	0172-707343	
13	Himachal Pradesh	Director of Industries, Government of Himachal Pradesh, Shimla.	0177-213414	
14	Jammu and Kashmir	Jammu and Kashmir State Industrial Development Corporation, Government of J and K, Drabu Houses, Ram Bagh Srinagar.	0194-30036	
15	Karnataka	Technical Consultancy Services Organisation Of Karnataka (TECSOK), Directorate of Industries and Commerce, Rashtrothana Parishat Bhawan, Nrupathunga Road, Bangalore - 560 002.	080-2266134	
16	Kerala	Managing Director, Kerala Industrial Infrastructure Development Corp., KINFRA House, 31/2312 Sastha-mangalam, Trivandrum - 695010	0471-2726585	2724773
17	Lakshadeep	Managing Director, Lakshadweep Development Corporation, 40/5598 II Floor, Near Padma Junction M.G. Road, Ernakulam Cochin - 682 035	0484-361630	373635

18	Madhya Pradesh	Managing Director, Madhya Pradesh State Agro Industries Development Corporation, 'Panchanan' 3rd Floor, Malviya Nagar, Bhopal	0755-551807	557305
19	Maharashtra	Managing Director, Maharashtra Agro Industries Development Corporation Ltd., Rajan House, Prabha Devi Mumbai	022-4305122	4308618
20	Manipur	Director of Industries, Industries Ministry, Secretariat Government of Manipur, Imphal.	0385-310220	310550
21	Meghalaya	Managing Director Meghalaya Industrial Development Corporation, Kismat, Upland Road,Shillong	0364-224965	224763
22	Mizoram	Managing Director, Mizoram Food and Allied Industries Corporation Ltd., (MIFCO), Aizwal.	0389-323680	323680
23	Nagaland	Secretary Ministry of Industries Government of Nagaland Kohima	0370-22919	22534
24	Orissa	Managing Director, Agricultural Promotion and Investment Corporation of Orissa Ltd., 326, Brahmunda, Bhubneshwar.	0674-420526	420506
25	Punjab	Managing Director, Punjab Agro Industries Coporation, 2-A Sector-28A, Madhya Marg, Chandigarh - 160 002	0172-651386	651576
26	Pondicherry	Director of Industries, Industries Ministry, Thattachavady, Pondicherry - 605 009	0413-34145	35512
27	Rajasthan	Director of Industries, Ministry of Industries Government of Rajasthan, Jaipur	0141-380727	380796
28	Sikkim	Director of Industries, Ministry of Industries, Government of Sikkim, Gangtok - 737 101	03592-22853	
29	Tamil Nadu	Managing Director, Tamil Nadu Agro Industries Corporation Ltd., Agro House, Industrial Estate Guindy, Chennai - 600 032.	044-2341664	2342375

Agricultural and Processed Foods Export Development Authority (APEDA)

Under the Plan Scheme of APEDA, financial assistance to the extent of 50% of the cost subject to a ceiling of Rs.50 lakhs per beneficiary is given for setting up of irradiation facilities.

Food Parks

The Government has sanctioned 45 food parks across the country. Food parks are set up with financial assistance from the Ministry of Food Processing Industries. The quantum of subsidy is 25 per cent for general areas and 33.33 per cent for difficult areas. The maximum amount of assistance is Rs.4 crore. The assessment report on the progress of ten food parks prepared by the Entrepreneurship Development Institute of India, Ahmedabad, has been received by the Ministry. The following break up of the food parks approved by his Ministry.

Number of food parks approved

S.No.	Name of the State	No. of Food Parks Approved
1	Andhra Pradesh	1
2	Assam	1
3	Bihar	1
4	Chhattisgarh	1
5	Haryana	2
6	Jammu and Kashmir	3
7	Karnataka	3
8	Kerala	3
9	Madhya Pradesh	6
10	Maharashtra	5
11	Manipur	2
12	Mizoram	1
13	Orissa	1
14	Punjab	1
15	Rajasthan	3
16	Tamil Nadu	1
17	Tripura	1
18	Uttar Pradesh	4
19	West Bengal	5
	Total	**45**

Source: Lok Sabha, Replies to queries by Minister for Food Processing Industries, GOI

Food Labelling

Consumers in Indian markets are switching over to buy only the products with labels containing information about the product, safety and its quality of specified standard. The labels must provide information on the name of the food item, date of manufacture and storage instructions.

Key Terms

Export processing zones (EPF), Special Economic Zones (SEZ), Agri Export Zones (AEZ), Food Safety and Quality, Fruit Products Order, Meat Food Products Order, Codex Alimentations, Hayard Analysis Critical Control Point (HACCP).

Chapter Summary

- The Government of India has established Special Economics Zones (SEZ) and Agri - Export Zones (AEZ) for the promotion of agri business in the country.
- Export Promotion Industrial Part (EPIP), New Anna Marumalarchi Thittam in Tamil Nadu, Agri clinic and Agri Business centres, etc., are some of the schemes being implemented for the promotion of agri business.
- Fruit Product Order 1995; Meat Food Products Order 1973; and Milk and Milk Products Order, 1992 are being administered by different Government Agencies to ensure safety and quality of food products.
- HACCP is an important requirement for ensuring the quality of products from health and safety aspects and is crucial for exports.
- The Government has permitted to set up 17 SEZs and 60 AEZs in the country.
- The Ministry of Food Processing Industries is celebrating the year 2008-2009 as " Food Safety and Quality Year".

Chapter Highlights

The special features of Government programmes for promoting agri business, entrepreneurial training institutes in India, Export Processing Zones, Special Economic Zones and Agri - Export Zones, Legal Provisions for Promotion of Agri Business, Food Safety and Quality Schemes of the Government, Fruit Product Order, Meet Food Products Order, AACCP and Food Laws have been discussed in this chapter.

Review Questions

1. What are the entrepreneurial training centres establishes by the Government? Explain their roles.
2. What are objectives and functions of a) Export Processing Zones b) Special Economic Zones, c) Export Oriented.
3. List out the Acts which are regulating the agri business in India.
4. Explain: a) Fruit Products Order, 1995, b) Meat Food Products Order, 1973 c) Milk and Milk Products Order, 1992.
5. What is CODEX Alimentarius
6. Explain HACCP.
7. Explain the following Food Laws
   a) Prevention of Food Adulteration Act,
   b) Agricultural Produce (Grading and Marking) Act.
   c) Laws being operated by BIS.
   d) Essential Commodities Act
8. Explain the salient features, benefits and incentives and focus area of SEZs.
9. Explain the objectives, special features, benefits and reasons for partial success of AEZs.
10. Write short notes on Food Quality and Safety.

References

Mangaraj.S. and R.Singh.2008. Status of Food Processing Industry in India and its Future Outlook, Indian Food Industry,27(3): 35-42.

www.mospi.nic.in

http://dacnet.nic.in

http://mofpi.nic.in

Further Reading Material

http://www.sezindia.nic.in

http://exim.indiamart.com

Chapter **15**

AGRICULTURAL INPUTS AND AGRO-PROCESSING

Agro-inputs are either biological or chemical or inorganic compounds used in the production of agricultural and allied products. Some of the agro-inputs used in India are :

- In-organic fertilizers
- Pesticides which include insecticide, fungicide, nematicide and herbicide
- Seeds which include varieties, hybrids and genetically modified plant materials
- Vegetatively propagated planting materials
- Bio-fertilizers
- Organic inputs which include compost, vermi-compost, enriched farm yard manure, oil meals and farm yard manure
- Bio-pesticides
- Bio-control agents
- Plant Growth regulators

- Micro-nutrients
- Farm machinery and agricultural tools and implements
- Animal feed
- Poultry feed.

The production and distribution of above mentioned agricultural inputs create agri-business opportunities. The agricultural input production inputs and distribution firms may be big companies like Madras Fertilizers, SPIC, FACT, EID Parry, Monsanto, Syngenta or MAHYCO and the like. They may also be small business firms like vermi-composting, coir pith decomposing.

Seed

Seed is a critical and basic input for attaining sustained growth in agricultural production. Distribution of assured quality seed is necessary for attaining higher crop yields. Policy initiatives taken by Government of India during 1960s and 1970s for generating quality seed production and distribution of improved plant varieties developed by the scientists is one of the reasons for our self sufficiency in food grains. The Indian seed industry has shown impressive growth and should continue to provide further potential for growth in agricultural production. The role of the seed industry is not only to produce adequate quantity of quality seeds but also to achieve varietal diversity.

Indian Seeds programme largely adheres to the limited generation system for seed multiplication. The system recognises three generations, namely, breeder, foundation and certified seeds.

New Seeds Bill

Based on the changes that have taken place in the seed sector since 1966, the existing Seeds Act, 1966 is proposed to be replaced by a suitable legislation. Over the years, the following deficiencies have been noted in the existing Seeds Act :

- Registration of seed variety is not compulsory.
- Non-notified varieties are not covered.
- Commercial crops and plantation crops are not covered.
- Certification is only through State Seed Certification Agencies.
- No provision for regulation of transgenic materials.
- Penalties for infringement are very mild.

The revision of existing Seeds Act is proposed to (i) overcome its present deficiencies, (ii) create facilitative climate for growth of seed industry, (iii) enhance seed replacement rates for various crops and (iv) boost the export of seeds and encourage import of useful germplasm, (v) create conducive atmosphere for application of frontier sciences in varietal development and for enhanced investment in research and development. The draft Seeds Bill, 2004 is under consideration.

The highlights of the proposed Seeds Act are as under:-

- Compulsory registration of varieties based on agronomic performance data.
- Accreditation of ICAR centers, State Agricultural Universities and Private Organisations to conduct agronomic trials.
- Accreditation of Organisations for certification.
- Maintenance of National Register of varieties.
- To regulate the export and import of seeds.

- Exemption for farmers to save, use, exchange, share or sell their seed without registration.
- Accreditation of private seed testing laboratories.
- Enhancement of penalty for major and minor infringement.
- Inclusion of provisions to regulate GM crops and ban on terminator seed.

Implementation of Legislation on Plant Varieties and Farmers' Rights Protection

The scheme for implementation of Legislation on Plant Varieties and Farmers' Rights Protection was launched during the Ninth Five Year Plan. The Bill was passed by both the House of Parliament and was assented to by the President of India in October, 2001.

The Objectives of the Legislation are:

To stimulate investments for research and development both in the public and the private sectors for the development of new plant varieties by ensuring appropriate returns on such investments; and

To facilitate the growth of seed industry in the country through domestic and foreign investment which will ensure the availability of high quality seeds and planting material to Indian farmers.

The Salient Features of the Legislation are:

- The legislation extends to all categories of plants except micro-organisms.
- In order to be eligible for protection, a variety must be new, distinct, uniform and stable.
- The legislation contains provisions for compulsory licensing in the public interest.

- Farmers will continue to enjoy their traditional rights to save, use, exchange, share and sell their produce of the protected variety with the only restriction that the farmers will not be able to sell branded seed of the protected variety for commercial purposes.

Plant Varieties and Farmers' Rights Protection Authority to be set up will be vested with necessary executive powers to perform all functions relating to the protection of plant varieties.

The Rules under the "Protection of Plant Varieties & Farmers' Rights Act, 2001" have been notified in the Gazette. The Protection of Plant Varieties and Farmers' Rights Authority will administer the Act.

Strengthening of Seed Quality Control

The Scheme aims at strengthening of quality control arrangements for seeds to ensure that farmers get good quality seeds. The Seeds Act, 1966 regulates the quality of seeds sold/distributed to the farmers through voluntary certification and compulsory labelling of seeds of notified kind/varieties. The scheme i.e., Quality Control arrangements on Seeds has the following components:

- Setting up of National Seeds Research & Training Centre (NSRTC) at Varanasi.
- Secretariat support to Central Seed Committee/ Central Seed Certification Board.
- Strengthening of Seed Development Organisations, State Seed Certification Agencies and State Seed Testing Laboratories.
- Financial assistance to Central Seed Testing Laboratory (CSTL).
- Financial assistance to National Seeds Corporation (NSC)/ State Seeds Corporations (SSC)/SCAs/DOA for training of officials.

Table 15.1 : Type of Seeds

Share of Public Sector in Making Available/Supply of Certified/Quality Seeds in India (2005-2006 to 2007-2008) *(In Lakh Quintal)*

	Govt. Agencies		Private *	
Year	**Quantity**	**%**	**Quantity**	**%**
2005-06	73.67	52.43	66.84	47.57
2006-07	79.62	53.73	68.56	46.27
2007-08	111.59	57.43	82.72	42.57

Note : * : Including Multinational Companies.
Source : Rajya Sabha Unstarred Question No. 553, dated on 23.11.2007

Export/Import of Seeds and Planting Materials

In order to encourage export of seeds in the interest of farmers, the procedure for export permission for seed has been simplified. Seeds of privately developed varieties/ hybrids are being allowed to be exported freely, except where there is any emergency caused by the natural calamities and seed is required for meeting the demand within the country. Export against orders for which production of seed is organised, is allowed without restriction. In other cases, export is permitted freely subject to the provision of the EXIM Policy (2002-2007). Import of seeds and planting materials is also allowed subject to New Policy on Seed Development, 1988 read with Plant Quarantine (Regulation of Import into India) Order, 2003 and as per the Ex- Im Policy, 2002-07. During 2003-04, 61 applications for import and 41 applications for export of seeds of restricted nature were received of which 45 applications for import and 39 applications for export were cleared.

Production of Seeds

The production of breeders seed, foundation seed and certified seeds are respectively 54.70 thousand quintals, 7.40 quintals and 118.52 lakh quintals during 2005-06. All types of seeds production are steadily increasing from 2000-01 to 2005-06 (Table 15.2).

Table 15.2 : Production of Seeds

Programme	Unit	2000-01	2001-02	2002-03	2003-04	2004-05	2005-06
(i) Production of Breeder Seeds	Thousand Qtls.	42.69	45.54	48.42	61.82	66.46	-
(ii) Production of Foundation Seeds	Lakh Qtls.	5.91	5.44	6.14	6.50	6.90	7.40
(iii) Distribution of Certified/ Quality Seeds	Lakh Qtls.	86.27	91.80	98.03	108.59	113.10	118.52

Source: www.indiastat.com

Seed Replacement

The seed is the carrier of improved technology and replacement of seed is an indicator of adoption of latest technology for enhancing productivity. The seed replacement ratio is 55 to 69 percent for sunflower, rapeseed/mustard and pearl millet. In the case of rice, maize, jute and soybean it ranged from 25 to 40 per cent (Table 15.3).

Table 15.3 : Seed Replacement Ratio (%)

Crop	2001	2002	2003	2004	2005	2006
Wheat	13.04	13.00	13.000	16.48	17.64	18.03
Paddy	19.22	19.31	19.16	23.28	24.38	25.10
Maize Hybrid	20.98	21.35	24.41	31.50	35.39	36.23
Sorghum (v)	18.36	18.78	26.71	19.28	19.03	19.12
Pearl millet(v)	45.92	48.47	51.02	44.90	55.36	56.12
Bengal gram	4.17	4.23	7.09	9.87	9.41	9.54
Black gram	16.55	17.06	20.48	17.24	15.70	16.21
Green gram	13.47	13.80	19.48	12.34	12.50	12.82
Red gram	8.71	8.84	13.60	9.80	10.48	10.88
Groundnut	5.20	5.50	11.00	7.11	6.89	7.03
Rape seed/mustard	38.39	44.64	66.96	58.48	55.36	56.25
Soybean	12.44	12.45	15.58	27.00	28.88	32.34
Sunflower	13.73	15.69	19.61	60.15	67.67	69.17
Cotton	21.21	21.86	19.84	20.73	21.78	22.27
Jute	28.77	30.14	27.40	26.03	26.03	26.03

v - Variety

Fertilizers

Consumption and production of major fertilizers Nitrogen, Phosphorous and Potassium are increasing from 2000-01 to 2005-06, but there is always a gap between consumption and production in the case of N and P which necessitates there imports and entire K is imported (Table 15.4).

Table 15.4 : Consumption, Production and Import of Fertilizers from 1981-82 to 2005-06 *(Lakh Tonnes)*

Crop	2001	2002	2003	2004	2005	2006
Wheat	13.04	13.00	13.000	16.48	17.64	18.03
Paddy	19.22	19.31	19.16	23.28	24.38	25.10
Maize Hybrid	20.98	21.35	24.41	31.50	35.39	36.23
Sorghum (v)	18.36	18.78	26.71	19.28	19.03	19.12
Pearl millet(v)	45.92	48.47	51.02	44.90	55.36	56.12
Bengal gram	4.17	4.23	7.09	9.87	9.41	9.54
Black gram	16.55	17.06	20.48	17.24	15.70	16.21
Green gram	13.47	13.80	19.48	12.34	12.50	12.82
Red gram	8.71	8.84	13.60	9.80	10.48	10.88
Groundnut	5.20	5.50	11.00	7.11	6.89	7.03
Rape seed/mustard	38.39	44.64	66.96	58.48	55.36	56.25
Soybean	12.44	12.45	15.58	27.00	28.88	32.34
Sunflower	13.73	15.69	19.61	60.15	67.67	69.17
Cotton	21.21	21.86	19.84	20.73	21.78	22.27
Jute	28.77	30.14	27.40	26.03	26.03	26.03

The imports made after decanalization of phosphatic fertilizers (w.e.f.17.09.1992) and potassic fertilizers (w.e.f. 17.06.1993) include the quantities imported by private parties also.

Source: Annual Report 2005 - 06 Department of Fertilizers.

Pesticides Consumption

The pesticides constitute insecticide, fungicide, weedicide and rodenticide. Except the rodenticide other pesticides consumption are decreasing due to adoption of Integrated Pest Management practices and due to concern for environment, health and sustainability of farming (Table 15.5)

Table 15.5 : Consumption of Pesticides (Technical-Grade Insecticides) for Agriculture in India (2003-2004 to 2007-2008)

Pesticide Group	2003-04	2004-2005	2005-06	2006-07	2007-08
Insecticide	23304	24424	20882	18307	15719
Fungicide	8532	6639	13376	8305	7498
Weedicide	5054	6670	6222	4264	3615
Rodenticide Total	365	443	978	293	392
Indigenous	37290	38210	42297	31444.85	27440

Source: www.indiastat.com

Agro Processing

The agro and food processing industry in India is of utmost significance in terms of employment and income generation, poverty alleviation, export promotion and foreign exchange earning. The growth of the processed food sector is expected to make a quantum jump of Rs.1,75,000 crores by 2005. Although India is one of the largest producers of raw materials for the food processing industries in the world, the industry itself is underdeveloped in India. Less than 2 per cent of fruits and vegetable production is processed, when compared to 30 per cent in Thailand, 70 per cent in Brazil, 78 per cent in Philippines and 80 per cent in Malaysia. The value addition in food sector is as low as 7 per cent. There is a need for increasing food processing from 2 to 10 per cent by 2010. This will require an investment of Rs. 1,40,000 crores in the food processing sector. The investment will generate direct employment for 77 lakh persons and indirect employment for three crore people. This will also reduce wastage by

Rs.80,000 crores. Apart from these advantages, the value addition of food product will go up from 7 to 35 per cent which will be reflected in the corresponding increase in Gross National Product (GNP).

Types of Food Processing Industries

Primary Processing Industries

Rice milling

Roller flour milling

Pulse milling

Oil milling

Cereal based products (bread biscuits)

Cocoa products

Soft drinks

Alcoholic drinks

Horticultural products

Fruits and vegetables

Milk and milk products

Meat processing

Poultry processing

Fish processing

Food packaging

A strategic Assessment of Food, Beverage and Agribusiness Opportunities in India are furnished in (Table 15.6).

Table. 15.6 : Processed Food markets

Product	Volume (metric tonnes)	Value (US $ million)	Major players
Basic foods			
Packaged wheat flour(including branded flour)	1 million	8	Hindustan Lever Limited(HLL), Pillsbury, Best foods India Ltd.,
Spices	2.45 million	3780	Regional
Edible oil	8 million	8820	ITC agrotech, Marico Industries, HLL, NDDB, Ahmed Oil Mills Ltd
Salt	500,000	60	Gujarat Salt Federation, Hindustan Salt Works, Tata Chemicals, Bestfoods India Ltd.,
Sugar	15 million	7,150	Government, co-operatives and Private Sugar Mills
Eggs	33 billion eggs	780	Government Poultry Corporations, National Egg Co-ordination Committee
Poultry meat	550,000	n.a.	Govt. Poultry Corporations
Milk (total)	73.5 million		NDDB
Bakery products (including unorganized sector)			
Biscuits and cakes	1 million (biscuits) 500,000(cakes)	775	Britannia Industries Ltd.,, Parle Products, Bakeman's
Bread	1.5 million	350	Britannia India Ltd.,Modern Industries (now with HLL), Spencer's
Indian Dairy products			
Ghee (Butter oil) (organized sector only)	85,000	n.a.	Milk Co-operatives and Small Players.
Indian Milk sweets(including unorganized sector)	300,000	350	Small players

Western dairy foods (organized sector)			
Ice cream	50 million liters	120	HLL, Gujarat Co-operative Milk Marketing Federation, Hutsun Agro
Butter	80,000	200	Gujarat Co-operative Milk Marketing Federation, Britannia Industries Ltd.,
Cheese	12,000	30	Gujarat Co-operative Milk Marketing Federation, Britannia Industries Ltd.,
Dairy whitener	48,000	85	Nestle India Ltd., Gujarat Co-operative Milk Marketing Federation
Western dairy foods (organized sector) contd..	100,000	100	Gujarat Co-operative Milk Marketing Federation, Nestle India Ltd.,
Malted food drinks	65,000	140	Cadbury India Ltd., Smithkline Beecham Consumer products, Nestle India Ltd.,
Processed fruit and vegetable products			
Pickles	120,000	28	Nestle India Ltd., American Dry Fruits, Ruchi, Bedeker's, Priya
Fruit Beverages	130,000	80	HLL, Parle Products, Enkaye,Texofoods
Fruit spreads, sauces & ketchup	50,000	43	HLL,Marico Industries
Convenience foods (organized sector)			
Chocolate	20,000	95	Cadbury India ltd., Nestle India Ltd.,
Sugar-boiled confectionery	80,000	280	Parry's Confectionery, Nestle India Ltd.
Chewing /Bubble gum	25,000	55	Warner Lambert, Wrigley's Perfetti
Snack foods			
Traditional Indian snacks (incl. small players)	310,000	295	Haldiram's. Pepsi Foods
Western snacks (including branded potato chips = 5,000 metric tones)	40,000	30	Frito-Lay India, Uncle Chipps, Procter & Gamble

n.a - Not Available

Source: Promar International, 2001.Indian Food Industry,20(4), 29.

Changes in Food Processing

Government is at the forefront of forces for changes in the food processing industry and is also the least predictable of the forces. Other forces for changes include the productivity of agriculture, the emergence of an organized food retail sector, improving infrastructure and the changing Indian food consumer (Fig.15.1)

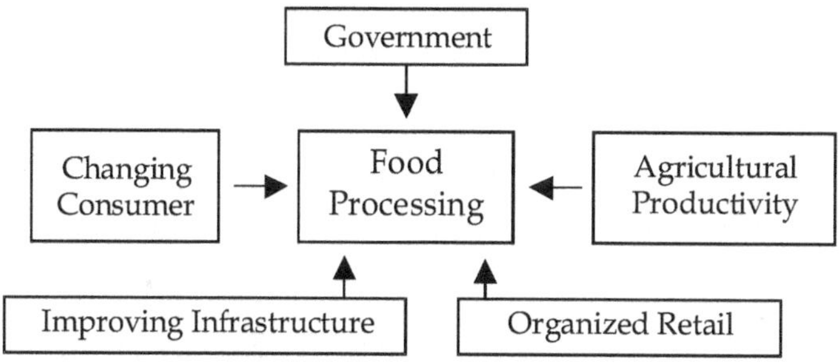

Fig. 15.1 : Forces for changes in Indian Food Processing Industry

The changing food consumer in India will be one of the most powerful forces for change in the food industry. Increasing incomes, literacy rates, small family sizes, women entering the work force, urbanization and increasing concern about health and hygiene will be motivating consumer changes in attitudes. The (Fig.15.2) depicts the markets for basic foods and processed food today and in the future, taking into account changing consumer attitudes. The triangles are not meant to be drawn to scale but illustrate an order of magnitude. These graphics also represent the markets for those Indians in the middle and upper income groups. Despite these changes, some consumer traits have not changed. For instance, the Indian consumer is still very price sensitive. Most Indians simply do not have enough money to lose this trait. Most Indians tend to save rather than spend money.

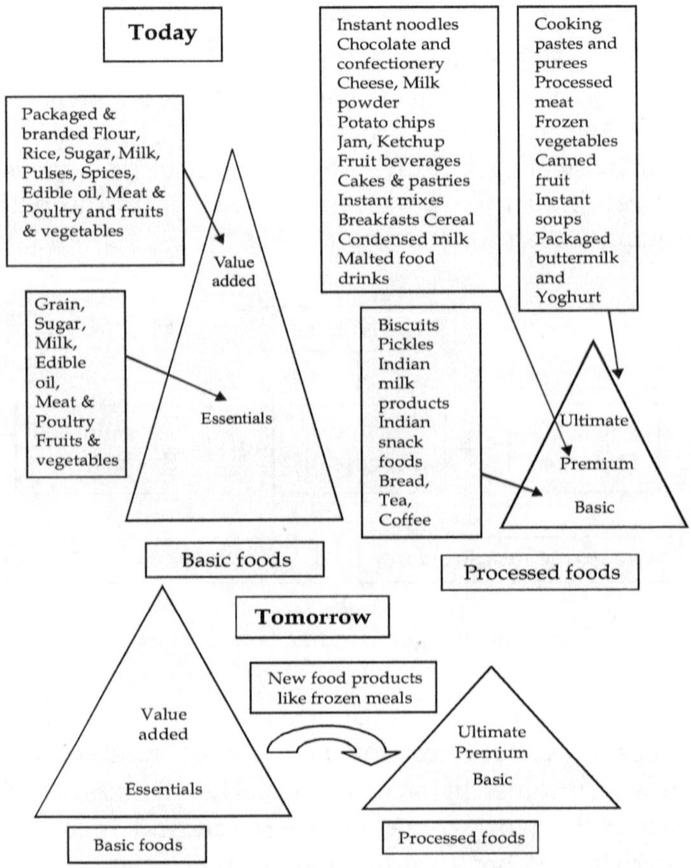

Fig.15.2 : Food processing today and tomorrow

Priorities

The opportunities in food markets depend on market growth, market size, government influences and infrastructure bottlenecks (Table 15.7).

Food Distribution in India

The flow chart (Fig. 15.3) depicts the distribution system in India. As the chart shows, there are several middlemen/ intermediaries / agents who come between the farmer and the consumer or food manufacturing company. Distribution of food products is also fragmented given the fact that food retailing in India is highly unorganized by small neighbourhood retailers and vendors. They are estimated to be over five million such small retail outlets in rural and urban India. These small retail outlets account for nearly 95 % of the total retail turn over in the country, and their number continue to grow despite a worldwide trend toward retail consolidation.

Large food markets or supermarkets are an emerging retail format, but only in metropolitan cities. According to USDA estimates there are between 50 and 100 privately owned supermarkets and about 350 convenience stores in all over India, and these stores only account for 1-2 % of food retail sales in urban areas of India.

Table 15.7 : Opportunities Basic Food & Branded Processed Food

Product	Market growth	Market size	Infrastructure bottlenecks	Government influences
Basic food				
Wheat flour	High	Medium	Some	Some
Poultry	High	Large	Many	Some
Milk	High	Large	Some/ Many	Many
Fresh fruits & Vegetables	High	Large	Many	Some/ Many
Edible oils	Medium	Medium/ Large	Some	Some/ Many
Branded processed food				
Bakery products	High	Large	Some/Few	Some
Indian dairy products	High	Large	Many / some	Many
Indian snacks	High	Large	Some	Some
Processed fruits & vegetables	Medium	Small/ Medium	Many	Some
Convenience foods	Medium/ High	Small/ Medium	Some/Few	Some
Western dairy products	High	Medium	Many/some	Many

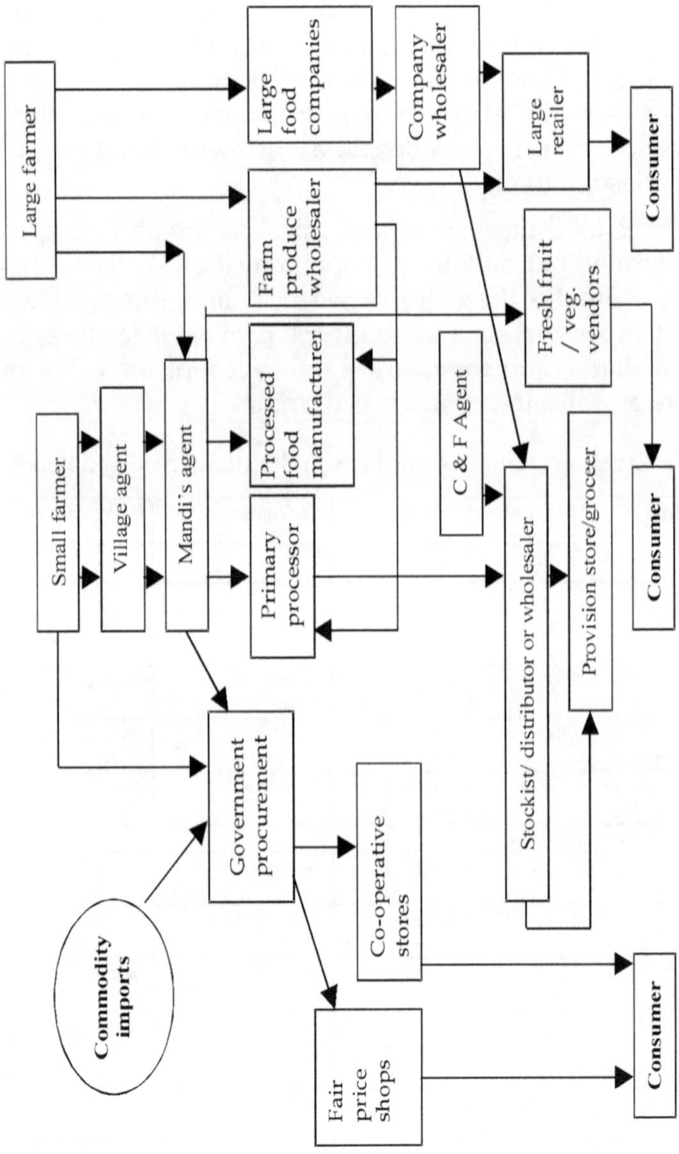

Fig.15.3 Indian Food Chain

Future Outlook of Food Processing Industries in India

The industry requires huge investments over the next five years to create necessary infrastructure, expand production facilities and state - of - the - art – technology to match the international quality standards. The present infrastructure for marketing of agricultural commodities and trade affairs are furnished below.

- The infrastructure for marketing of perishables
- Primary grading/ collection centers non-existent.
- Ware housing and cold storage inadequate.
- Cold chain non-existent.
- Quality certification system non-existent.
- Transportation for perishables non-existent.
- Rural markets lack infrastructure.
- Wholesale markets in government control, lack modern amenities.

Investment in Food Processing Sector

The potential for processed foods will be Rs 1,35, 000 crores by 2014-2015, of which Rs 57,000 crores for primary processing and Rs. 78,000 crores for value addition (Table 15.8).

Table 15.8 : Potential for Processed Foods in crores of Rupees at 2003-04 prices

Particulars	2009-10	2014-2015	Growth (%)
Processed food	82,000	1,35,000	10
Primary processed	42,000	57,000	7
Value added food	40,000	78,000	15
Share of value added products in processed food consumption	49 %	58 %	

Source: MOFPI Report.2005. Vision, Strategy and Action Plan for Food Processing Industries in India, Vol I

Market Potential

The market potential for types of food processing industries are furnished in (Table 15.9) Rice milling, milk processing, pulses, spirits, spices and fruits and vegetables have good potential.

Table 15.9 : Market potential for processed foods (Rs.crores)

Particulars	2009-10	2014-2015
Fruits & Vegetables	2,900	5,500
Dairy	25,000	44,000
Meat & Poultry		
Buffalo Meat	500	860
Poultry	370	1040
Non- Alcoholic Beverages		
Tea	1,360	2,110
Coffee	330	420
Grain based products		
Rice milling	9.800	11,500
Flour milling	6,500	7,600
Breads	950	1,980
Biscuits	1,820	3,930
Snack and ready to eat foods	1,500	4,860
Pasta based foods	360	1,020
Marine products	1,730	
Sugar and sugar based products	860	1,290
Sugar	3,200	1,390
Confectionery	300	700
Chocolates	250	590
Alcoholic Beverages		
Beer	1,100	1,930
Spirits	3,90	8,700
Wine	500	900

Contd...

Pulses	6,050	8,100
Aerated averages	1,370	2,010
Malted Beverages	350	750
Spices	4,500	8,860
Salt	530	900
Total	**82,000**	**1,35,000**

Source: MOFPI Report.2005. Vision, Strategy and Action Plan for Food Processing Industries in India, Vol I

Future Investments

The investment requirements during 2010-15 for various types of processing are furnished in (Table 15.10) Milk processing, chocolates, cold storage and fruits and vegetables require large investments. Alteraction of Foreign Direct Investments in food processing industries is furnished in (Table 15.11).

Table 15.10 : Future investment requirement for food processing

Particulars	**Investment in Rs. Crores during 2010-15**
Fruits & Vegetables organized	4,015.9
Packed Fruits & Vegetables	2,857.1
Other processed	1,158.7
Processing of milk	10,109.1
Edible oils	292.6
Buffalo meat processing	914.6
Poultry meat	162.1
Total processed meat	1,076.7
Freezing & ice facility	299.5
IQF	133.5
Pre-processing	622.2
Cold storage	5,367.8

Contd...

Sugar	
Confectionery	204.8
Chocolates	7,540.2
Grain and grain products	
Rice milling	1,899.9
Flour milling	1,807.7
Bread	481.3
Biscuits	1,253.1
Snack foods	642.1
Pasta based foods	179.4

Source: MOFPI Report.2005. Vision, Strategy and Action Plan for Food Processing Industries in India, Vol I

Foreign Direct investment in Food Processing Industries

Table.15.11 : Investment in Food Processing Sector

Processing sector	Total industrial Approval Nos.	Investment Rs. Crores	Foreign investment Rs. crores	Foreign investment share (%)
Grain Milling and products	472	6879	1207	17.55
Fruits & Vegetable products	2144	8491	1089	12.83
Meat and Poultry products	148	1778	267	15.02
Fish Processing and aquaculture	305	2688	548	20.39
Fermentation industry	883	11374	1094	9.62
Confectionery industry	931	13252	4423	33.38
Milk and Milk products	1130	14883	1004	6.77
Other including food beverages	71	934	535	57.28
Edible oil & oil seeds	1675	13416	-	-
Total	**7759**	**73645**	**10167**	**13.81**

Source : MOFPI 2001-02

Requirements of Post Harvest Requirements

The projections for 2010 are furnished in (Table 15.12). Cleaners and graders and flour units post harvest equipments will be the major requirements. This shows that consumers are concerned about clean and graded products in future.

Table 15.12 : Status of Post Harvest Equipments in India. (lakh units)

Name of the post harvest equipment	In 1991	In 2004	Projected in 2010
Flour units	2.66	4.00	4.25
Cleaners and graders	1.10	3.80	4.50
Dryers	0.07	0.25	0.50
Rice Mills	1.30	1.50	1.60
Maize shellers	0.65	1.18	1.23
Dal Mills	0.10	0.20	0.30
Oil expellers	2.22	4.50	5.50

Source :

1. Data Book on Modernizion and Agr-processing since Independence, 1997, CIAE, Bhopal.
2. Website of Ministry of Food Processing Industry, Annual Report, 2002-03.
3. *Souvenir of International Conference on Engineering Technology in Agricultural and Food Processing, held at Kharagpur during 14-17, 2004.*

Key Terms

Different agro - inputs used in India -breeder, foundation and certified seeds, Plant Varieties and Farmers' Rights Protection Act, Seed replacement ratio. Scope of Agro and Food Processing, basic foods, processed foods, convenience foods, food chain.

Public Private Partnership mode for food processing is furnished in Fig. 15.4.

Chapter Summary

- The Indian Seed Programme recognizes the generation of breeder, foundation and certified seeds.

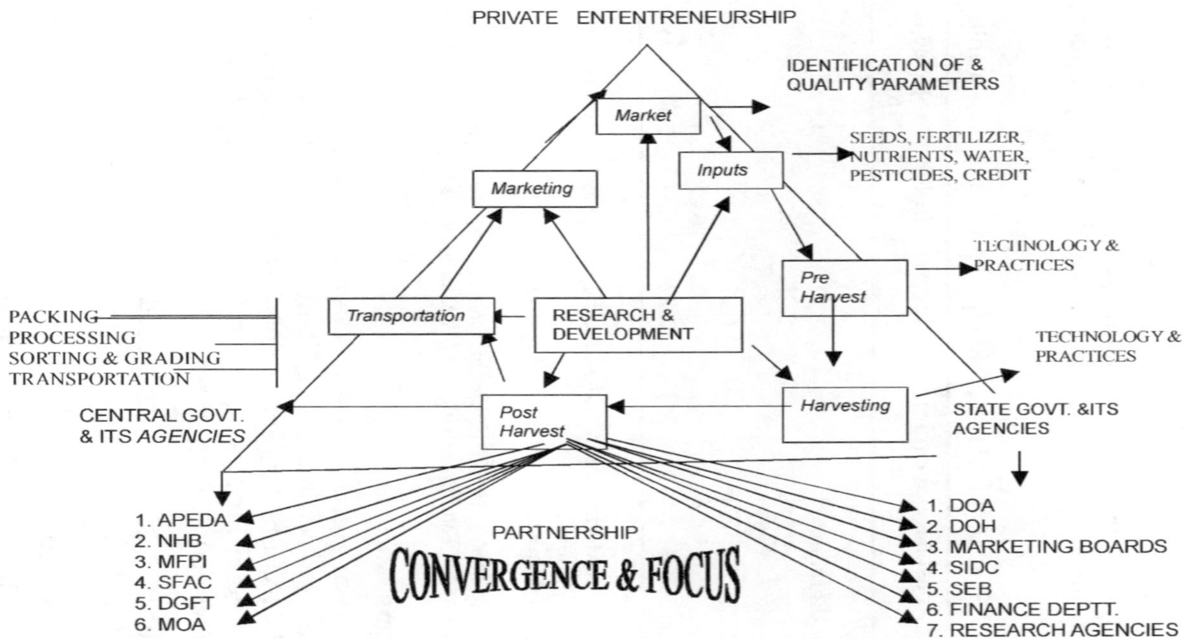

Fig. 15.4. Food Processing Entrepreneurship System with Govt. and Private Sector
Source: Mangarag. S. and R. Singh.2008. Status of Food Processing Industry and its Future Outlook, Indian Food Industry, 27 (3), May-June, p 41

- The existing Seeds Act, 1966 is proposed to be replaced by a suitable legislation considering the deficiencies noted in the existing Seeds Act.
- Plant Varieties and Farmers' Rights Protection Act, 2001 aims at stimulating investments for research and development both in the public and private sector for the development of new plant varieties by ensuring appropriate returns on such investments.
- Seed Replacement Ratio ranges from 7 to 69 per cent for different crops grown in India during 2006.
- Ferlizer imports increased from 21 lakh tonnes in 2000-01 to 53 lakh tonnes in 2005-06
- Pesticides consumption declined due to the adoption of Integrated Pest Management practices.
- There is a great market potential for rice milling, milk processing and Dal and Flour mills
- Agro and food processing industry in India is of utmost significance in terms of employment and income generation, poverty alleviation, export promotion and foreign exchange earning.
- Government at the forefront of forces for changes in food processing industry. Other forces for changes include the agricultural productivity, the emergence of an organized food retail sector, improving infrastructure and the changing Indian Food Consumer.
- Increasing income, literacy, small family, woman entering the work force, mechanization and increasing concern about health and hygiene are the motivating forces that change consumer attitudes.
- The opportunities in food markets depend on market growth, market size, Government influences and infrastructure bottle necks.

Abbreviation	Expansion
Central Govt.	
APEDA	Agricultural and Processed Products Development Authority
NHB	National Horticulture Board
SFAC	Small Farmers Agribusiness Consortium
DGFT	Director General of Foreign Trade
MOA	Ministry of Agriculture
State Govt.	
DOA	Department of Agriculture
DOH	Department of Horticulture
SIDC	State Industrial Development Corporation
SEB	State Electricity Board

Chapter Highlights

The provisions of new seeds bill, salient features of the legislation on Plant Varieties and Farmers' Right Protection, Schemes to strengthen the seed quality control, export / import of seeds, seeds replacement ratio, consumption of fertilizers and pesticides have been discussed in this chapter. Strategic assessment of food and agribusiness opportunities in India, forces influencing the changes in food processing, and Indian food chain model have been discussed in this chapter Also, future outlook of food processing industries in India, investments and market potential in food processing sector have been highlighted in this chapter.

Review Questions

1. What are the agro-inputs used in India ?
2. What are the deficiencies noted in the existing Seeds Act, 1966?
3. What are the highlights of the proposed Seeds Act?
4. What are the objectives of Plant Varieties and Farmers' Rights Protection Act, 2001?
5. What are the facilities created in India to strengthen the quality of seeds?

6. Write short note on (i) seed production in India and (ii) fertilizer and pesticides consumption in India.
7. Explain the market potential and investment requirement for the food processing sector in India.
8. Discuss the significance of agro and food processing industries in the context of Indian Economic Development.
9. What are the difference types of food processing industries ?
10. Briefly outline the strategic assessment of food, beverage and agri business opportunities in India ?
11. Explain the forces that influence the change in the food processing industry?

References

Vision 2015: Strategy and Action Plan for Food Processing Industries in India, Vol.1.Ministry of Food Processing Industries, Govt. of India, 2005.

Vision 2015: Strategy and Action Plan for Food Processing Industries in India, Vol.2.Ministry of Food Processing Industries, Govt. of India, 2005.

Further Reading Material

www.fai.delhi.org

Fertilizer Statistics 2207-08, FAI Publications.

http://mofpi.nic.in

http://agricoop.nic.in

Chapter **16**

INDIA'S AGRICULTURAL EXPORTS AND IMPORTS

There is sufficient support to view that foreign trade plays has a vital role in the economic development of a country. Its contribution to the growth of National Income can be quite substantial. If a country is pulled into world trade, then the country can and should maximize its real income by specializing along lines of comparative advantage. The volume and composition of foreign trade have a profound influence on the character and the extent of development of a country. From the point of view of economic development, both import and export are important. It is through import that a country could obtain plant, machinery and equipment, components, raw materials, technical know-how, etc., which are indispensable for accelerating economic development.

India's share in world exports was 0.54 per cent in 1970s, which has risen to 0.81 per cent in 2000s and exports has grown 700 times and imports more than thousand times during the course of economic development. It is clearly observed from Table 16.1 that import is greater than export. The rate of growth of export between 2001-02 and 2007-08 was 90 per cent, whereas import growth rate was 150 per cent in the corresponding period.

Agricultural Imports

The imports of food grains was necessitated by the growing demand for pulses and edible oil seeds due to stagnant production of these commodities. The import of agricultural commodities has increased from Rs. 12.09 thousand crores in 2000-01to Rs.21.03 thousand crores in 2005-06 (Table 16.1). The important items of agricultural commodities imported in 2007-08 is furnished in Table 16.2. The major imports are vegetable oils, pulses, wheat, fruits and nuts. The raw cashew nuts are the cashew nuts imported as raw nuts and they are processed in India and then exported as value added products.

Agricultural Exports

The agricultural exports has risen from Rs. 20.14 thousand crores in 2000-01 to Rs. 45. 48 thousand crores in 2005-06. Percentage of agricultural exports to total exports was in the range between 14.3 to 10.95 during the above mentioned period. A steady decline in share of agricultural exports to total exports can be observed (Table 16.1). The principal agricultural exports from India in 2005-06 are furnished in Tbale.16.3. The fish and fish preparations, cereals, oil cakes , cashew kernels and spices are major items of agricultural exports from India. The share of agricultural commodities in world exports in 2005 is furnished in Table 16.4. Among these items rice and tea exports from India occupy a major share of world agricultural exports.

Table 16.1 : India's Agricultural Exports and Imports
(in '000 Rs. Crore)

Year	Total Imports	Agril Imports	Agrl. Imports as percentage of total imports	Total Exports	Agrl. Exports	Agrl. Exports as percentage of total Exports
2000-01	22.84	12.09	5.29	20.14	28.66	14.23
2001-02	24.52	16.26	6.63	20.90	29.73	14.22
2002-03	29.72	17.61	5.92	25.51	34.64	13.58
2003-04	35.91	21.97	6.12	29.34	37.27	12.70
2004-05	48.16	22.06	4.59	35.61	39.86	11.20
2005-06	63.05	21.03	3.33	45.48	49.80	10.95

Note: Rounded off to two decimal places
Source: DGCI &S, Ministry of Commerce, Govt. of India

Table 16.2 : Principal Agricultural Imports in 2007-08

Commodity	Qty (in '000 tonnes)	Value (in Rs. Crores)
Vegetable oils Fix (Edible)	4,902.81	10,298
Pulses	2,792.10	5,278
Wheat	1,793.21	2,657
Fruits and Nuts Excl. Cashew nuts	-	1,857
Cashew nuts	5916	1,714
Spices	140.45	938
Cereal preparations	43.839	161
Oil seeds	0.00	147
Tea	19.84	131
Milk and cream	2.06	30
Other cereal	10.35	19
Sugar	0.51	2
Rice	0.15	0.42
Total	**10,295.92**	**23,237**

Source : DGCIS Annual Report

Table 16.3 : Principal Agricultural Exports from India in 2005-06

Commodities	Qty (in '000 tonnes)	Value (in Rs. Crores)
Coffee	177.7	1,539
Tea and Mate	162.9	1,731
Oil cakes	5976	4,875
Tobacco	142.7	1,330
Cashew kernels	131	2,594
Spices	400.2	2,116
Sugar and molasses	394.1	598
Raw cotton	614.8	2,904
Rice	4,088.2	6,221
Fish and Fish preparations	-	7,036
Meat and meat preparations	-	2,750
Fruits, Vegetables and pulses (excl. Cashew kernels, processed fruits and spices)	-	3,649
Miscellaneous processed foods (and processed fruits and vegetables)	-	1,589
Agricultural and Allied Products	-	46,703

Source : Economic Survey, 2007-08, Ministry of Finance, Govt. of India.

Table 16.4 : India's Share in World Exports of Agricultural Commodities in 2005
(US $ Million)

Commodity	World	India	India's share (%)
Meat and Meat Preparations	73,102	620	0.8
Fish, Crustaceans, and Mollusc and preparations	70,532	1,590	2.3

Contd...

Cereals and cereals preparations	70,686	1,753	2.5
Rice	8,930	1,411	15.8
Vegetables and Fruits	1,12,872	1,586	1.4
Sugar, Sugar preparations and Honey	23,961	196	0.8
Coffee, Tea, Cocoa and Spices	44,600	1,042	2.3
Coffee and Coffee substitutes	15,608	393	2.5
Tea and Mate	4,100	393	9.6
Spices	281	478	-
Feeding stuff for animals	30,335	1,127	3.7
Tobacco and Tobacco manufacture	24,425	232	0.9
Oilseeds and oleaginous fruits	22,857	319	1.4
Textile yarn, fabrics, made-up articles	2,12,992	8,462	4.0
Woven Cotton Fabrics	28,751	861	3.0
Woven Fabrics of man made fibres	32,269	981	3.0

Source: Economic Survey, 2007-08, Ministry of Finance, Govt. of India.

Markets for Indian Commodities

Japan, UAE, EU, USA, China, South / South East Asia, Middle East and Russia, were the major importing countries of agricultural commodities from India (Table 16.5).

Table 16.5 : Key Markets for Indian Commodities

Commodities	**Key Markets**
Marine Products	Japan, UAE,EU, China
Non Basmati Rice	South/ South East Asia, EU
Cashew	UAE, EU
Wheat	South/ South East Asia, Middle East
Tea	Russia, UK, Pakistan, USA, Japan, Egypt, Iraq
Spices	USA, EU
Buffalo meat	Middle East, South East Asia
Sugar	South Asia
Coffee	Italy, Germany, Russia

Contd...

Processed Fruit and Vegetables	Middle East, EU
Guar gum	EU, USA
Ground Nut	South East Asia
Dairy Products	South Asia, Africa
Poultry Products	South East Asia

Source: Vision, Strategy and Action Plan for Food Processing Industries in India, Vol I, Ministry of Food Processing Industries, Govt. of India.

Export of Cereals

As far as export of cereals was concerned, non - Basmati rice followed by Basmati rice were the major export commodities in terms of value during 2006-07 (Table 16.6)

Table 16.6 : Export of Cereals

Particulars	2005-06		2006-07	
	Qtry in '000 MTS	Value inin ;000 Rs. Lakhs	Qtry in '000 MTS	Value in in '000 Rs. Lakhs
Basmati Rice	1,166.56	304.31	1,045.71	279.28
Non Basmati Rice	2,921.60	317.82	3,702.19	424.31
Milled Products	50.90	6.47	69.94	9.59
Wheat	746.17	55.75	46.63	3.54
Other Cereals	567.21	45.38	730.28	59.93
Total of Cereals	5,452.45	729.73	5,594.76	776.64

Source : DGCIS Annual Report

Import of Spices by World

As far as spices imports were concerned, USA was the largest country importing around one - fifth of the total spices export from India (Table 16.7).

Table 16.7 : World Imports of Spices by Major Countries in 2003

Country	US $ million	Percent
USA	679.6	22.0
Germany	192.8	6.3
Japan	184.3	6.0
France	171.2	5.6
UAE	141.5	4.6
Netherlands	124.0	4.0
Saudi Arabia	111.2	3.6
UK	101.2	3.3
India	93.5	3.0
Spain	88.0	2.9
Total	**3,084.1**	**100.0**

Source: Compiled from data of UN, Year Book of International Trade Statistics, 2004, Geneva.

Chillies formed the major spice commodity exported to other countries from India and it was followed by mint products, spice oils and oleoresins during 2005-06 (Table 16.8).

Table 16.8 : Segment-wise India's Exports of Spices (in Rs.crores)

Segment	2004-05	2005-06
Chilli	499.01	1,131.74
Spice oils & Oleoresins	463.75	505.57
Mint products	407.77	813.21
Turmeric	156.50	152.86
Pepper	121.40	150.95
Cumin	101.90	98.19
Coriander	82.66	67.71
Curry powder / paste / condiments	66.10	73.83
Other spices	59.60	44.15

Contd...

Ginger fresh/ dry	59.50	42.95
Vanilla	27.59	12.27
Fenugreek	26.61	34.03
Other seeds	26.14	33.22
Fennel	25.30	27.82
Cardamom (small)	23.81	26.82
Nutmeg & mace	22.36	31.17
Celery	13.01	15.01
Cardamom (Large)	11.34	11.55
Garlic	5.61	47.98
Total	**2,200**	**2,627.62**

Source: Spice Board, Kochi

Destination of Indian Spices

During 2005-06, USA ranked first in import of spices from India in terms of quantity and it was followed by Malaysia and Bangladesh. In value terms, USA ranked first followed by China, Germany and so on (Table 16.9).

Table 16.9 : Major Destinations of Indian Spices in 2005-06

Country	Qty in '000 MT	Value in Rs. Crores
USA	43.24	582.32
Malaysia	43.17	148.36
China	4.95	225.00
Singapore	5.98	107.31
Germany	6.10	162.78
UK	17.74	153.77
Bangladesh	34.09	45.08
UAE	27.23	100.41
Sri Lanka	33.32	84.64
Japan	8.38	129.47

Source: Vision, Strategy and Action Plan for Food Processing Industries in India, Vol I, Ministry of Food Processing Industries, Govt. of India

World Floriculture Trade

As could be seen from the (Table 16.10), Netherlands ranked first in terms of floriculture trade accounting for almost half of the global trade in floriculture and India's share was only 0.4 percent.

Table 16.10 World Floriculture Trade

Country	Value (million US $)	Percent
Netherlands	3,399.20	49.9
Colombia	528.40	7.8
Italy	266.66	3.9
USA	251.90	3.7
Israel	201.55	3.0
Germany	145.20	2.1
France	130.39	1.9
Kenya	109.75	1.6
China	41.98	0.6
India	27.02	0.4
Australia	26.36	0.4
Total (World)	**6,815.94**	**100.0**

Source: United Nations Commercial Trade database. ITC, UNTAD / WTO

As far as export of floriculture products were concerned, foliage branches, grasses, cut flowers and flowers buds suitable for bouquets and ornamental purposes were the major exported products, (Table 16.11). These floriculture products were exported mainly to USA, UK, Netherlands and so on (Table 16.12).

Table 16.11 : Category-wise India's Exports of Floriculture Products in 2003-04

Item	Rs. Crores	Percent
Cut flowers and flower buds suitable for bouquets/ ornamental purposes (fresh, dried, dyed, bleached, impregnated, or otherwise prepared	111.07	44.3
Foliage branches and other plant parts, grasses, moses and lichens for bouquets / ornamental purposes (fresh, dried, dyed, bleached, impregnated or otherwise prepared)	114.14	45.6
Other live plants (Incl. roots) cuttings and slips, mushroom spawn	21.94	8.8
Bulbs, tubers, tuberous roots, corms, crowns and rhizomes, dormant, in growth / in flower, chicory plants and roots excluding roots of HS code 1212	3.30	1.3
Total (All India)	**250.45**	**100.0**

Destination of floricultural products

Table 16.12 : India's Exports of Floricultural Products to the Major Markets (2003-04)

Country	Rs. Crores	Percent
USA	73.10	29.2
UK	28.09	11.2
Netherlands	26.98	10.8
Japan	25.28	10.1
Germany	21.37	8.5
Italy	12.35	4.9
France	8.14	3.3
Australia	5.16	2.1
UAE	3.54	1.4
Total (All India)	**250.45**	**100.0**

Source: DGCI & S, Monthly Statistics of India's Foreign Trade; Exports and Re-exports, Vol 1, part1, March 2004 Issue .

Export of Vegetables and Processed Food Products

Export of agricultural commodities in terms of both quantity and value are given in (Table 16.13). Cereals followed by fruits and vegetables and animal products were the major commodities exported in terms of quantity to other countries during 2006-07. In terms of value, cereals, animal products and processed fruits and vegetables were the major exported agricultural commodities.

Table: 16.13 Export of Flowers, Vegetables and Processed Food Products

Particulars	2005-06 Qty in '000 tonnes	Value in '000 Rs. Lakhs	2006-07 Qty in '000 tonnes	Value in '000 Rs. Lakhs
Total of Floriculture and Seeds	-	39.22	-	77.13
Total of Fruits and Vegetables	1,465.04	165.87	1,983.87	241.17
Total of Processed Fruits & Vegetables	943.57	245.46	797.48	250.23
Total of Animal Products	1,730.15	371.40	1,257.26	406.30
Total of Other Processed Foods	673.58	262.99	1,065.88	363.58
Total of Cereals	**5,452.45**	**729.73**	**5,594.76**	**776.64**

Source: DGCIS Annual Report.

Export of Fruits and Vegetables

Among the fruits and vegetables fresh onions, fresh vegetables and fresh grapes were the major exported commodities during 2006-07 (Table 16.14).

Table 16.14 : Export of Fresh and Dried Fruits and Vegetables

Particulars	2005-06 Qty in '000 tonnes	Value in '000 Rs. Lakhs	2006-07 Qty in '000 tonnes	Value in '000 Rs. Lakhs
Fresh onions	960.51	70.82	1378.37	116.33
Other Fresh Vegetables	217.28	26.77	275.91	43.00
Walnuts	5.26	11.45	5.06	11.80
Fresh Mangoes	69.61	12.81	79.06	14.19
Fresh Grapes	54.05	21.46	85.90	30.19
Other Fresh Fruits	158.34	22.57	159.57	25.64
Total of Fruits and Vegetables	**1,465.04**	**165.87**	**1,983.87**	**241.17**

Source : DGCIS Annual Report

Processed Fruits and Vegetables

The details of export of processed fruits and vegetables are given in (Table 16.15). In 2006-07, processed pulses was exported to a larger extent, and they were followed by mango pulp, pickles and chutneys in terms of quantity. In terms of value of exports, pulses ranked first followed by mango pulp, dried and presented vegetables and so on. (Table 16.15).

Export of Animal Products

Buffalo meat topped the list of exported animal products and it was followed by dairy and poultry products in terms of value of export of animal products (Table 16.16).

Table 16.15 : Export of Processed Fruits and Vegetables

Particulars	2005-06 Qty in '000 tonnes	Value inin '000 Rs. Lakhs	2006-07 Qty in '000 tonnes	Value in in '000 Rs. Lakhs
Dried & Preserved Vegetables	124.45	36.41	118.79	42.41
Mango pulp	134.61	36.42	156.84	50.58
Pickles & Chutneys	135.38	27.00	145.22	29.36
Other Processed Fruits & Vegetables	107.34	37.02	129.11	50.81
Pulses	441.74	109.51	247.53	77.04
Total of Processed Fruits & Vegetables	**943.57**	**245.46**	**797.48**	**250.23**

Source : DGCIS Annual Report

Table 16.16 : Export of Animal Products

Particulars	2005-06 Qtry in '000 MTS	Value inin ;000 Rs. Lakhs	2006-07 Qtry in '000 MTS	Value in in '000 Rs. Lakhs
Buffalo Meat	459.94	262.96	494.11	321.17
Sheep / Goat Meat	7.18	8.04	5.48	6.30
Poultry Products	118.51	31.57	710.88	31.59
Dairy Products	59.75	55.23	37.39	39.59
Animal Products	1.12	1.75	0.44	0.95
Processed Meat	0.26	0.24	0.83	0.68
Natural Honey	16.77	11.62	8.14	6.09
Total of Animal Products	**1,730.15**	**371.40**	**1,257.26**	**406.30**

Source : DGCIS Annual Report

Processed Food

In case of export of other processed foods, guar gums, jaggery and confectionary were major export items in terms of value during 2006-07. In terms of quantity, jaggery and confectionery topped the list followed by groundnut, guar gum and so on (Table 16.17).

Table 16.17 : Export of Other Processed Foods

Particulars	2005-06 Qty in '000 tonnes	Value inin '000 Rs. Lakhs	2006-07 Qty in '000 tonnes	Value in '000 Rs. Lakhs
Groundnuts	190.05	51.37	251.43	79.85
Guar Gum	186.72	104.92	189.30	112.58
Jaggery & Confectionery	112.64	26.50	455.94	87.35
Cocoa Products	2.15	2.18	2.89	3.51
Cereal Preparations	76.88	39.40	79.85	46.27
Alcoholic Beverages	55.53	16.05	28.78	11.66
Miscellaneous Preparations	49.61	22.58	57.70	22.36
Total of Other Processed Foods	**673.58**	**262.99**	**1,065.88**	**363.58**

Source : DGCIS Annual Report.

Projection for Agricultural and Food Products

India's share of exports to global exports will likely to be increased by 2% in 2010 and d3% in 2015. The growth rate of India's exports will likely to be 14% in 2010 and 15% in 2015. (Table. 16.18)

Table 16.8 : Projected Exports of Agricultural and Food Products

Year	World Exports	India's Exports	India's Share	Growth rate
2010	770	15	2 %	14 %
2015	1020	30	3 %	15 %

Source : Vision, Strategy and Action Plan for Food Processing Industries in India, Vol I, Ministry of Food Processing Industries, Govt. of India.

Market Focus for Agricultural Exports

The destinations of agricultural commodities to different countries is given in (Table 16.19). USA, EU and Middle East countries were the major importing countries of agricultural commodities from India.

Table 16.19 : Product Market Focus

Commodities	USA	EU	Middle East	South East Asia	South Asia	Africa	CIS
Marine Products	....	....	....	....	....	....	....
Non Basmati Rice	....	....	....	....	....	....	....
Basmati Rice	....	....	....	....	....	....	....
Cashew	....	....	....	....	....	....	....
Wheat	....	....	....	....	....	....	....
Tea	....	....	....	....	....	....	....
Spices	....	....	....	....	....	....	....
Buffalo meat	....	....	....	....	....	....	....
Coffee	....	....	....	....	....	....	....
Vegetables	....	....	....	....	....	....	....
Guar gum	....	....	....	....	....	....	....
Mango Pulp	....	....	....	....	....	....	....
Dairy Products	....	....	....	....	....	....	....
Confectionery	....	....	....	....	....	....	....
Cereal	....	....	....	....	....	....	....
Preparations	....	....	....	....	....	....	....

Source : Vision, Strategy and Action Plan for Food Processing Industries in India, Vol I, Ministry of Food Processing Industries, Govt. of India

Key Terms

Agricultural Imports and Agricultural Exports.

Chapter Summary

- Import of agricultural commodities has increased to Rs. 21.03 thousand crores in 2005-06 from Rs. 12.09 thousand crores in 2000-01.
- Raw Cashewnut, vegetable oils, pulses and wheat were the major commodities imported during 2007-08.
- Agricultural exports has risen from Rs. 20.14 thousand crores in 2000-01 to Rs. 45.48 thousand crores in 2005-06.
- Fish and fish preparations, rice, oil cakes, fruits, vegetables, cashew and spices were the major commodities exported from India in 2005-06.

Chapter Highlights

Import of Agricultural Commodities and Export of Agricultural Commodities like, cereals, pulses, fruits and vegetables, flowers to different destinations have been highlighted in this chapter.

Review Questions

1. Explain the share of agricultural imports and exports to total imports and exports in India.
2. Discuss the major commodities imported and their share in the total agricultural imports in India.
3. Explain the major commodities exported, destinations and their share in the total agricultural exports of India.

References

Acharya.S.S. and N.L.Agarwal.2004. Agricultural Marketing in India (Fourth Edition), New Delhi: Oxford & IBH Publishing Company Pvt. Ltd.

Gandhi.G.P.2007. Export Prospects of Spices from India, 10(4): 16-20.

Gupta.G.P.2007. Export Prospects of Spices from India, Processed Food Industry,10(4):16-20.

Kumar.K.P. and Jayasheela.2008. Export Floricultural Products: Opportunities & Strategies, Southern Economist, 47(8):19-22.

Kumar.K.P., Jayasheela and V. Basti Hana.2007.Commercial Floriculture in India: Opportunities for Cut Flower Development, Southern Economist, 46(11):18- 22.

Manoharan.S. Agricultural Trade in India, Southern Economist, 47(6):38-40.

Sultan.Z.A.2008. Trade Reforms and India's Exports: An Analysis, Southern Economist, 47(7): 41-45.

Usha.K.R.2007. Export-Import and Logistics Management, New Delhi: Prentice-Hall of India Pvt. Ltd.

Further Reading Materials

www.apeda.com

www.eximbank.com

www.indianspices .com

www.mpeda.com

Chapter **17**

RETAILING AND SUPPLY CHAIN MANAGEMENT IN AGRICULTURE

Organized retailing is spreading and making its presence felt in different parts of the country. The share of organized retailing in the total retail sector is set to increase from about 2 % to 8 -10 % by 2010. The retail sector generates 6 % of total employment in India. The reasons behind the increase in growth of retailing is changing life styles of Indian consumers. The key factors that drive the growth of organized retailing are:

- Rising urbanization
- Growing economy
- Higher disposable incomes
- Growing consumerism
- Entry of national/international business houses into retailing
- Increasing nuclear families
- Changing number of educated and employed women population
- Media proliferation and rising awareness level
- Brand proliferation

- Traveling by the working groups of the society
- Popularity within working and studying bachelors for convenience food.

The largest category of retail businesses are specialized retailers selling food, and beverages from fixed retail outlets. The major formats of retailing are furnished in Table17.1.

Table 17.1 : Major formats of retailing

Format	Description	The Value Proposition
Branded stores	Exclusive showrooms either owned or franchised out by a manufacturer	Complete range available for a given brand, certified product quality
Specialty Stores	Focus on a specific consumer need, carry most of the brands available.	Greater choice to the consumer, comparison between brands is possible
Department Stores	Large stores having a wide variety of products, organized into different departments such as clothing, house wares, furniture, appliances, toys etc.	One stop shop catering to varied / consumer needs
Supermarkets	Extremely large self-service retail outlets.	One stop shop catering to va consumer needs
Discount Stores	Stores offering discounts on the retail price through selling high volumes and reaping economies of scale	Low prices
Hyper-mart	Larger than a supermarket, sometimes with a warehouse appearance, generally located in quieter parts of the city	Low prices, vast choice available including services such as cafeterias.
Convenience stores	Small self - service formats located in crowded urban areas.	Convenient location and extended operating hours.
Shopping Malls	An enclosure having different formats of in-store retailers, all under one roof.	Variety of shops available to each other.

Table 17.2 : Privately owned retail outlets in India

Retail name / outlet Type	Currency Name	Ownership	No. of clusters	Locations
Hypermarket	Giant	Local Joint Venture with RPG group (Hongkong)	9	Mumbai, Hyderabad, Vizag
Hypermarket	Choupal Sagar	Local ITC	1	Sehore, Mdhya Pradesh
Hypermarket	Metro Cash & Carry	Foeign (Metro AG, Germany)	2	Bangalore
Hypermarket / Supermarket	Big Bazaar /Food Bazaar	Local (Pantaloon Group)	17	Mumbai, Bangalore, Gugaon, Hyderabad and Kolkata
Supermarket	Food world	Local Joint Venture with RPG group (Hongkong)	93	Major cities in South India and Pune
Supermarket	Nilgiris	Local (Nilgiris Franchise)	30	Major cities in Tamil Nadu, Andhra Pradesh, Pondicherry and Pune
Supermarket	Trinethra	Local, Trinethra group	68	Major cities in Andhra Pradesh
Supermarket	Vitan	Local (Vitan DSI Ltd)	13	Chennai, Bangalore
Supermarket	Adani Raoji	Local (Family owned)	6	Ahmedabad
Supermarket	Fabmail	Local (Fabmail India Pvt. Ltd.)	10	Bangalore
Discount Grocery Chain	Margin Free	Local Cooperative (Consumer protection and Guidance Society	350	Major cities in Kerala, Tamil Nadu and Karnataka
Discount Grocery Chain	Subhiksha	Local Viswapriya Groups)	143	Major cities in Tamil Nadu and Pondicherry & expanding to other cities
Discount Grocery Chain	Sabka Bazaar	Local (Home Stores Pvt. Ltd)	25	Delhi and Adjoining Areas

Source: Singh.2004., Mukherji and Patel.2005.

Emerging Organized Retailing Formats

Departmental Stores

It is the commercial retail business which carries a wide range of merchandize that is organized into departments like apparel for men, women, children, home furnishing etc. The focus is on customer service. They stock multiple brands across product categories, though some of them focus on their own labels (e.g., Marks & Spencers, St.Michael). Several local departmental store chains have opened shops in India in the past five years (Shopper's Shop, Westside and Ebony).

Supermarkets / Hypermarkets

Supermarkets are self-service stores that satisfy regular shopping needs of consumers, including food and non-food items with an area of 500 to 2000 sq. m. where as Hypermarkets are large (> 5000 sq.m.) self-service stores that combine the features of a supermarket and departmental store carrying a large range of products at discounted prices. Supermarkets tend to be located in key residential markets tend to be located in key residential markets and malls, and offer competitive prices due to economies of scale in logistics and purchasing. This format is new to India with a few noticeable players such as Food World, Nilgiris and Subhiksha.

Speciality Chains

These retail outlets focus on a particular brand or product category, usually non-food items, and are located in high streets and in shopping malls. While most specialty chains compete on service, a segment called 'category killers' offers price as an advantage. This format has been the highest levels of adoption in India, with several chains establishing a strong presence, typically through franchising.

Reliance Fresh

Reliance Fresh is the retail chain division of Reliance Industries of India. The store is selling food, fresh produce, groceries and staples. Reliance entered into this segment by opening new retail stores at Hyderabad on 3rd November, 2006. The Rs. 25,000 crore retail venture is planning to introduce global brands in India to invest Rs.25,000 crore in next 4 years in the retail division and plans to begin retail stores in the top 70 cities within the next two years and target sales of US$ 250 crore by 2011 (Farooq, 20060. So far 220 super markets have been opened in 20 cities. Recently Reliance opened its first Hypermarket at Ahmedabad.

Retailing in Food Sector

Penetration of organized retailing in food sector is relatively low in India, 4 % against 70-80 % in UK, US & France, 13 % in China, 20 % in Kenya and about 50 % in countries like Thailand, South Korea, and Philippines.

Technology Trends

A successful retailer's winning edge will come from sourcing - how best it can leverage its scale to drive merchandise costs reduced, increase stock turns and get better credit terms from its vendors. There are obvious and hidden areas where costs can be pruned and the benefits of this lower cost of retailing can be passed on to customers, which in turn would fuel demand. One way of trimming costs is to use latest technologies in supply chain, inventory management and use of IT tools to track the consumption pattern and the changing habits of the consumers. Retailing is a 'technology-intensive' industry. Successful retailers today work closely with their vendors to predict consumer demand, shorten lead times, reduce inventory holding and there by save cost. Wal-Mart pioneered the concept of building a competitive advantage through distribution and information systems in the retailing industry.

With the help of 'database retailing', information on existing and potential customers is tracked. Besides knowing who purchased what, during which time of the year, festive seasons shopping pattern, all these information are compiled, analyzed and future shelf planning, discount offer or season sales planning is made.

Supplier Retailer Relationships

With technology replacing the supply chain and improving distribution and logistics chain, the role of conventional middlemen slowly fade away. There will be direct manufacturer retail chain combine to offer.

Innovations in Transportation Logistics

As retail chains begin to focus more and more on the retail end, the logistics support would begin to get outsourced. The cold chain involving nationwide cold storages, refrigerated vans to transport food articles and specialized logistics companies offering the fleet for these services to organized sector big retails is now a reality in India.

Social Trends

Changing social trends in India fuel the growth of food retailing in a coutry. The ICT revolutions, double income families where husband and wife both are working and more and more Indian women are now moving into education and jobs, packaged food, ready to cook and shopping convenience in organized retail ambience under one roof would be the increasing replacing the traditional grocery shop shopping. Increased income levels and more women willing to make use of their education by joining work has increasingly affected shopping pattern.

Foreign Direct Investment (FDI) in Retailing

FDI is important for the organized retail sector to improve service and upgrade capabilities. Although 100 %

FDI in Retailing is not allowed, foreign retailers can operate in India through joint ventures, where the Indian partner is an export house, franchising / local manufacturing / sourcing small-scale sector, or cash and carry operations. The McKinsey report states that FDI will help the retail businesses to grow from the present $ 200 billion to $ 460-470 billion by 2010. There are several benefits of FDI: it will improve competition, develop market, increase level of exports due to involvement of major players, raise investments in food processing sector, improve lifestyle, provide more product choice, and new product categories and increase the purchasing capacity of consumers.

Conclusion

In a fast changing global scenario traditional agriculture is to give way to modern precision agriculture in all dimensions. When the thrust is to increase incomes, production for the markets led by market demand, consumer preference duly ensuring quality and food safety becomes paramount. Foray of large organized retail players both domestic and international in food retailing make agriculture no more *a mandy business but a business that would meet the expectations of growing consuming public that is increasingly becoming quality and health conscious.* Building human capacity through formal and non-formal education and facilitation processes, to organize growers and link them with the various stakeholders to establish and manage efficient supply chains will become the order of the day to capitalize the dynamic and fast changing global scenario to benefit farmers, the ultimate consumers and all others in the Value Chain.

Supply Chain Management in Agriculture

"Supply-chain management straddles the concepts of operational effectiveness and strategy, both of which are critical to business success" (Elizabeth Woods, 2003). Interest in supply-chain management (SCM) in the agribusiness sector emerged as recently as the 1990s, but has grown rapidly as a result of a number of internal and external pressures, and is now a key area of research and commercial activity in the sector. A primary driver of the growing focus of agribusinesses on SCM is the changing competitive environment. Competition for consumer expenditure is taking place in an environment where consumers have a rapidly expanding range of choices and rising disposable incomes. It used to be that farmers grew one or other of a restricted range of products and presented it to market on the assumption that if the price was right, it would be purchased by consumers. There is no longer any such warranty that simply to supply a product without concern for the consumers' requirements or the existence of a market for the product will ensure a continuance in business.

Supply chain management (SCM) represents the management of the entire set of production, manufacturing/ transformations, distribution and marketing activities by which a consumer is supplied with a desired product. Folkerts and Kohorst (1998) defined supply chain as a set of interdependent companies that work closely together to manage the flow of goods and services along the value added to agricultural and food products in order to realize superior customer value at the lowest possible costs. Some call this as demand chain focusing on consumer requirements. The term value chain highlights the contribution of functional parts of the chain to the development of customer value across the chain. The practice of SCM encompasses the disciplines of economics, marketing, logistics and organizational behaviour to study how supply chains are organized and how institutional arrangements influence industry efficiency, competitions and profitability. One can also include the production practices in the field, which is important from the point of view of food safety and traceability.

SCM thus, provides a means to conceptualize management of the changes required in the system to efficiently respond to consumer needs based on integration and co-ordination of the efforts of all the business units involved in the production and delivery processes.

Two broad principal explanations can be advanced for the increasing interest in agricultural SCM: (i) the industrialization of agriculture, and (ii) the uncertainty associated with variations in product quality and safety. The high variability in quality and magnitude that is characteristic of the agricultural environment (both production, handling and processing) and basic food raw materials creates uncertainty in the ability of the industry to assure a consistent supply of good quality and safe products to the consumer. The ever-increasing adoption of SCM principles in agribusiness is perhaps one of the profound and long-term developments in business management relevant to agricultural traceability. Agriculture is inherently a fragmented industry, involving a diverse range of distinct enterprises (farmers, processors, marketers and distributors), and relies on inputs from various sources, often at distinct geographical locations. With respect to grains and fresh fruit and vegetables, most marketers and processors obtain their supply from diverse sources (farmers, whole-sale, retailers, brokers) in order to meet marketing targets. From the marketing and processing perspectives, SCM is an essential tool for integrating the activities of the various suppliers within the company's operations in order to assure the consistent delivery of quality-assured products and services to the consumer. For the consumer and other stakeholders, SCM focuses on improving the performance of the supply chain through the delivery of guaranteed safe, desirable and good quality food in a cost-effective manner. The increasing transaction costs of intensive agriculture and the need to reduce these costs, lies at the heart of interest in agricultural SCM.

Thus, managing supply chains requires an integral approach in which chain partners jointly plan and control the flow of goods, information, technology and capital from 'farm to fork' and *vice versa.* In order to react effectively and faster to consumer's demand, supply chain management needs to be consumer-oriented. It aims at coordination of production processes. Because of the many activities and aspects involved, it demands a multidisciplinary approach and sustainable trade relations. Ultimately, supply chain management should result in lower transaction costs and increased margins. For this, supply chain partnerships should be based on interdependence, trust, and transparency and mutual benefits. When these are ensured, the advantages of the supply chain management approach would be numerous.

Food Safety Concerns

Food safety concerns have led to the development of 'integral chain-care' tools such as social accountability, good agricultural practice (GAP), total quality management, and HACCP (hazard analysis and critical control points). Implementation of such tools throughout a supply chain enables chain partners to ensure the quality and safety of their products and guarantees acceptable social chain performance. Implementing such standards and systems impacts not only the organization of supply chains, but also financial aspects of chain cooperation. These standards and systems are now being used in the agricultural sector globally, but are largely absent in India. The need of the hour is therefore, facilitating all these in the context of the complexity and cost involved. Suitable organization arrangement with active support of government can improve the environment

Traceability in Food and Agribusiness

The term 'traceability' has become so widely used in recent times in various industries particularly in agriculture and food. Agricultural traceability simply refers to the collection, documentation, maintenance, and application of information related to all processes in the supply chain in a manner that provides guarantee to the consumer and other stakeholders on the origin, location and life history of a product as well as assisting in crises management in the event of a safety and quality breach.

With respect to a food product, traceability represents the ability to identify the farm where it was grown and sources of input materials, as well as the ability to conduct full backward and forward tracking to determine the specific location and life history in the supply chain by means of records. It contributes to the demonstration of the transparency of the supply chain through the use of verifiable records and labeling. Traceability adds value to the overall quality management system by providing the communication linkage for identifying, verifying and isolating sources of non-compliance to agreed standards and customer expectations.

Benefits of Supply Chain

Supply chain development not only benefits the private sector but also creates spin-offs that stimulate social, economical and environmental sustainable development in the region (employment generation, added value, minimization of product losses, etc.). The specific gains are;

- Reduction of product losses in transportation and storage.
- Increasing of sales
- Dissemination of technology, advanced techniques, capital and knowledge among the

- Chain partners.
- Better information about the flow of products, markets and technologies.
- Transparency of the supply chain.
- Tracking & tracing to the source.
- Better control of product safety and quality.
- Large investments and risks are shared among partners in the chain.

Public Support and Public Private Partnership

Public support (e.g. development of the institutional infrastructure) plays an important role to create an enabling environment for private sector development. Public support might take the form of a publicprivate partnership in a supply chain to share experiences, risks and bottlenecks. Public-private partnerships aim at win-win situations and are thus beneficial for the society at large. In developing countries and emerging economies, however, supply chain development is often hampered due to lack of governmental support. International organizations can assist these governments to upgrade cross-border trade and to link national and international partners to jointly tackle cross-border trade obstacles. Institution building, raising awareness, pilot chain projects and the development of a toolkit are important activities to foster supply chain development

The public research institutes might contribute by developing and testing new technologies, tools, models, and instruments to improve the performance of the supply chain. Government's role in public-private partnerships can be as co-financier of supply chain projects as in the case of Australia, Canada, the Netherlands, Thailand and South Africa, as creator of an enabling environment (e.g., through provision of research and physical infrastructure) and as mediator in trade negotiations.

SCM and Developing Countries

The main opportunities for developing a country's agribusiness would seem to lie in the expanding total population and increasing urban populations, and hence a growing consuming class. The other strong incentives for developing country agribusiness to improve its operational effectiveness will be growing export market and pressure of competition from imported commodities in the increasingly globalised marketplace for agricultural and food products. A corollary of this is the need for agribusiness to adopt global standards.

Supply-chain management provides one conceptual approach to build the capacity of domestic producers to match the products that exporting countries will be aiming to put into world markets. Most farmers in developing countries are smallholders. They are also information-poor. Consequently, they are usually viewed as being the least powerful in the marketplace. Traders, who are generally information-rich, are usually seen as wielding much of the power and of doing so at the expense of farmers. But this is not always the case and, indeed, there are instances of traders acting as "supply chain champions". As number of supply chains rise in developing countries, traders will have an important role to play in their management.

The Case of India

The demand for food products is increasing at the rate of eight per cent annually in India. The food expenditure accounts for about 53 percent of the private consumption expenditure. Increasing working population, rising disposable income and greater International exposure have all made the fast growing Indian market to witness a paradigm shift in the nature and quality of produce/

products demanded. The consumption basket is undergoing a change in favour of perishables like, fruits, vegetables, milk, meat, etc., besides other healthy, hygienic products. While this is the National scenario, the International scenario unfolds with the process of liberalization and globalization unleashing a large set of opportunities with consumers around the world particularly in the western hemisphere showing larger appetite for the tropical & sub-tropical fruits and vegetables. Catering to this section of population, besides the people of the emerging markets particularly in Asia, the super market chains that have their base either in North America or Europe are showing enormous interest in sourcing produce/ commodities around the world. The catch however is that the produce should meet the consumer preferences and the stringent private quality standards that the super market chains have evolved and established. The standards like "EUREP GAP" require a whole range of infrastructure, procedures and processes to be in place if at all we intent to capitalize on the opportunities unfolding in-terms of larger markets for these produce.

India has a diverse climate with potential to produce a range of tropical and subtropical fruits and vegetables that the whole world yearns to consume. The current annual production of fruits and vegetables in the country is around 160 million tonnes. It accounts for 10 per cent of what is produced around the world and stands second only to Brazil and China respectively, in fruits and vegetable production. But, the post harvest loss is estimated to be around 35 per cent in India. Only two percent of fruits and vegetables are processed as against 70-80 per cent in developed countries and 40 to 80 per cent in many Asian countries. The value addition in India is only seven per cent while it is much higher ranging between 23 and 188 per cent in China and U.K. This only highlights the enormous untapped potential available in India and the widening market that continuously throws open opportunities to increase incomes of farmers and others in the supply chain.

With productivities stagnating for the first time since the Green Revolution era in the first decade of the 21st century, only the precision agriculture, the GAP, the post harvest handling and processing; all meeting the International standards will open the reservoir of benefits. But, this is not an easy process. The supply chain that will have to make this a reality comprises a whole range of actors starting from the farmer ending with the retailer, in the process ensuring all quality and food safety norms besides 'in-time' delivery.

Relevance of Farm Varsities as Facilitators of Supply Chain and Agri-Business Promoters

The Universities have so far been serving as temples of learning. However, in the changing scenario of knowledge intensive production, marketing, trade & manufacturing activities, Universities besides being Temples of Learning should evolve into vehicles for development - Tier-1, which the Development Departments may ordinarily find difficult to do. Particularly, the Farm Varsities, in an Era of stagnating or declining productivities, have an added responsibility to contribute to farm incomes in such a scenario through promoting agri-business.

University-Development Interface-Global Experience

The Michigan State University in USA is a standing example of promoting agri-business, particularly in developing countries of South America and Africa on a considerable scale through it's programme namely, Partnership for Food Industry Development (PFID). It had initiated its activities in India through its Mango Market Development Project using it's PFID arm. Under this model, the MSU serves as an active facilitator, ultimately, helping growers to find markets and respond to markets. It has established linkage between;

- Government/Policy Makers/Regulators
- Certifying Agencies
- Traders/Exporters
- Processors/Manufacturing firms; and
- Farmers/Commodity Growers Association/ Federation

It works closely with the farmers and the users to ensure adherence to GAP specifications.

Case Studies

Case Study I : Supply Chain of Fruits and Vegetables - Singapore

One hundred and seventy types of vegetables from 39 countries and 87 types of fresh fruits from 46 countries were imported. They come in by land, sea or air. The bulk is unloaded at Pasir Panjang Wholesale Centre for distribution. Imported fruits and vegetables are sol through auction or private arrangement to retailers or distributors who in turn supply the produce to similar retailers.

Vegetables from 71 local farms are harvested in late afternoon. They are trimmed, sorted, washed and packed in returnable plastic container for delivery to wholesalers. A few farms pack their produce in consumer packs for direct supply to supermarkets. There is an increasing tendency for supermarkets and even restaurants to import or buy directly from growers or exporters. Demand for retail ready packs is on the rise.

Malaysia is the major supplier of leafy vegetables to Singapore. Leafy vegetables are bulk packed in a variety of containers such as bamboo baskets, recycled cartons, nylon sacks and more recently HDPE returnable containers and

Styrofoam boxes. Cameron Highland growers tend to overstuff the baskets resulting in damage and spoilage in the produce. Almost all fruit and vegetables from Malaysia are transported in open trucks under ambient temperature. Recently, a few importers have started to use reefer trucks to transport their vegetables. There is also an increasing use of HDPE returnable containers. Imports from other countries arrive in reefer containers. Temperate fruit and vegetables from Australia, USA and Europe are usually graded and neatly packed in cartons or Styrofoam boxes with proper labeling, brand names and bar-codes. There will be an increasing use of returnable containers and reefer containers in the distribution of fruit and vegetables.

Case Study II : Agricultural Marketing and Supply Chain Management in Tanzania

The agricultural products in Tanzania are sold mainly at the local market (cassava) or the national market (paddy) whereas other products (cashew nuts, cocoa, coffee, tea, cotton, tobacco, sisal) are mainly targeted for export. Due to the clear segregation of the consumer base the supply of exported goods is not merely an extension of the national supply chain but it is operated through a separate marketing channel run by different actors. Here the supply chain for cashew nuts is analyzed as an example of an export crop that has practically no domestic market and is thus purely cultivated for exports.

The Supply Chain of Cashew Nuts from the Producer to the World Markets

The major impediments for supply chain in Tanzania have been categorized into three groups: 1) Physical infrastructure, 2) know-how and capital, and 3) institutional framework. Insufficient physical infrastructure in terms of roads increases the cost of transportation, works as an informal market barrier, forms a wedge between the supplier price and consumer price, and increases the loss of perishable products. Lack of know-how shows in poor market orientation and business skills, and leads to difficulties in managing and obtaining loans. Furthermore, the current institutional framework is unable to support the formation of strong traders and producers' associations and other representative bodies to enhance capacity building and to bargain for fair terms of trade. In addition, the lack of market information and the weak legal framework lead to difficulties in negotiating trade agreements and enforcing the existing contracts.

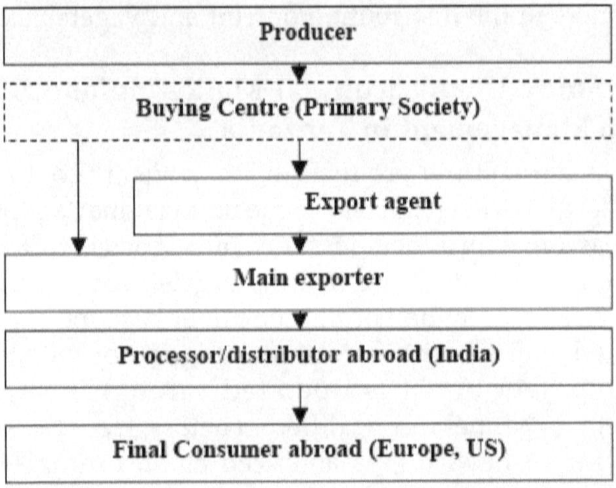

Source: Own illustration based on interviews with the relevant market participants.

Currently the necessary institutional framework has been substituted for by long supply chains of middlemen, and relying on personal relationships between producers, traders and brokers. In order to realize the full potential of agricultural trade as a tool in the fight against poverty, the suggested policy interventions are to prioritize and increase funding for physical infrastructure both from national and international sources; place emphasis on rural non-farm employment and intra-regional trade development (horizontal integration); promote large-scale capacity building in business skills and market orientation; improve equitable access to credit and improve the management of the current schemes; enforce the existing laws and support formalization of contracts to diminish risks of trading; and finally improve dissemination of market information to allow markets to work efficiently.

Case Study III - Supply Chain Management - Bhutan

Agricultural Marketing Services within the Ministry of Agriculture undertook a trial shipment of summer vegetables and fruits from Bhutan to Dhaka in Bangladesh in July 2004. From that exercise a number of valuable lessons were learned. The fund for the project was provided through the Rural Enterprise Development Program. This program is jointly funded by the United Nations Development Program and SNV, the Netherlands Development Corporation.

Summary

A total of 17 vegetables and fruit were taken to Dhaka:

Vegetables : asparagus, beans - French, beans - flat, brinjal, cabbage, cauliflower, chillies - Bhutanese style, chillies - round type, cucumber, ginger, pea, potato, pumpkin, radish, tomato, turnip, zucchini & *Fruit* : plums and passionfruit.

From initial harvest to the end of three days in the store in Dhaka it took eight days.

The route existed Bhutan at Phuentsholing, through West Bengal to Burimari on the India - Bangladesh border, then essentially paralleling the Tista and Jamuna Rivers to Dhaka. The journey took 22 hours of actual travel (Thimphu to Dhaka). Out-turn of the product varied. At the high end, products such as asparagus and tomato had losses as high as 60 percent. A comforting number of products had losses in 20 - 30 percent range. An encouraging number of products, including brinjal, beans, passionfruit, peas, and ginger, had an encouragingly low outturn of less than 10 percent. Nine products were considered to be able to physically withstand the length of time involved. The products were compared with that available on the market place at that time of the year. This reduced the number of likely products to six.

The six products were subjected to a detailed financial analysis to assess their economic viability. Keys to the assessment were: material costs to the farmer; packaging costs; labour costs including cleaning, grading, packing, and loading / unloading at eight points; transport costs; storage costs; documentation; taxes. From this analysis it was determined; that five of the products would be economically viable under current conditions.

Key Terms

Retailing, Retailing formats, Departmental Stores, Super markets, Hyper markets, Specialty chains, Supply Chain Management (SCM), Good Agricultural Practices (GAP), and traceability.

Chapter Summary

- The share of organized retailing is set to form 2 percent at present level to 8-10 percent in 2010.
- Rising urbanization, growing economy, high disposable income, growing consumerism, etc are the key factors that facilitate the growth of organized retailing.
- Branded stores, specialty stores, departmental stores, super markets, discount stores, hyper markets, convenience stores and shopping markets are some of the retail formats being operated in India.

- Retailing in food sector is influenced by factors such as technology trends, supplier - retailer relationship, innovations in transportation logistics, social trends and foreign direct investments.
- Supply Chain Management (SCM) represents the management of the entire set of production, manufacturing, transportations, distribution and marketing activities by which a consumer is supplied with a desired product.
- There is a growing interest in agricultural SCM due to i) industrialization of agriculture and ii) the uncertainty associated with variations in product quality and safety.
- Reduction of product losses in transportation and storage, dissemination of technology, advanced techniques, capital and knowledge among the chain partners, tracking and tracing to the source, better control of product safety and quality, etc are some of the benefits of SCM.

Chapter Highlights

In this chapter, importance of organized retailing, factors influencing organized retailing, features of emerging organized retailing formats like departmental stores, super markets, hyper markets, specialty chains and factors influencing retail food sector like technology trends, supplier - retailer relationship, innovation in transportation logistics, social trends and Foreign Direct Investment (FDI) in retailing have been detailed.

As regards, Supply Chain Management (SCM) in agriculture, its meaning, principles and benefits have been indicated. Further, relevance of farm varsities as facilitators of SCM and case studies of supply chain of fruits and vegetables and cashewnut have been highlighted in this chapter.

Review Questions

1. How organized retailing is contributing to Indian economy?
2. What are the key factors that drive the growth of organized retailing in India?
3. Explain the significant features of major retailing formats like a) branded stores, b) specialty stores, c) department stores, d) super markets, e) discount stores, f) hyper markets, g) convenience stores and h) shopping malls.
4. Explain the factors influencing organized food retailing in India.
5. Explain the concept of Supply Chain Management (SCM) and its relevance to agriculture.
6. Discuss the reasons for expansion of SCM in India.
7. Explain traceability in food and agri business, quality and safety of the agricultural products in SCM ?
8. What are the tools used to ensure the quality and safety of the agricultural products in SCM ?
9. What are the benefits of SCM ?
10. How public - private partnership could support SCM?
11. What are the roles of farm varsities as facilitators of supply chain and agri business management.
12. Explain the SCM being undertaken in a) India, b) Singapore and c) Tanzania.

References

Gupta.K. 2007.Food Retailing & Branding in India, Processed Food Industry, 11(1):29-33.

Paty.B.K. and B. Swati.2007. Organized Food Retailing in India – A Stock Taking, Southern Economist, 46(3): 17-20.

Swati.S..T. Alam and G.K. Goyal.2007. Modern Food Retailing in India, Indian Food Industry, 26(5):39-44.

Further Reading Material

Altekar.R.V.2005. Supply Chain Management: Concepts and Cases, New Delhi: Prentice - Hall of India Pvt. Ltd.

Battacharya.S.K.2000.Logistics Management: Definition, Dimension, and Functional Application, New Delhi. S.Chand & Company Ltd.

Burt.D.N., D.W. Duber and S.L. Starling.2003. World Class Supply Chain Management (Seventh Edition), Boston: Irwin McGraw Hill Higher Education.

Chapter 18

GETTING STARTED

For the prospective small business owner who possesses the necessary personal qualities, managerial ability, and capital , and who is not inheriting a family enterprise, there are two ways to get the business started: buy out an existing establishment or start from scratch with a new firm.

Buying an Existing Business

There are both advantages and disadvantages in buying an existing business. If the small business entrepreneur decides to buy an existing business, there are many things (s)he must investigate and analyze the business if (s) he is to make a good purchase decision.

Factors to Investigate and Analyze

To arrive at a wise purchase decision, the small business entrepreneur must investigate various aspects of the existing business. The entrepreneur must analyze and evaluate:

- Why the owner wants to sell ?
- The physical conditions of the business
- The market in which the business exists

- The financial conditions of the business
- Legal aspects of the purchase in order to arrive at true value of the business.

Advantages of Buying an Existing Business

There are several factors that may make an existing business an attractive purchase.

- It is a proven business, which reduces the risk and often makes it easier to finance
- The business often has well - established customer goodwill.
- Lines of supply and credit have already been established.
- Employees have already been hired and trained.
- The physical facilities are sometimes available for rent rather than purchase, which reduces the amount of capital necessary to buy the business.
- Sometimes it is difficult to find potential buyers for business firms because of lack of skills, lack of interest, or lack of capital. Consequently, one may find an existing business that is being sold at a very low price relative to the value of the business. This is often true of manufacturing firms, which are sometimes sold far below the replacement value of building, machinery and equipment.
- Equipment and machinery are already in hand. There is no need to find vendors and purchase.
- Usually, the methods and systems of operation have already been created, the "bugs" are worked out, and they are running.

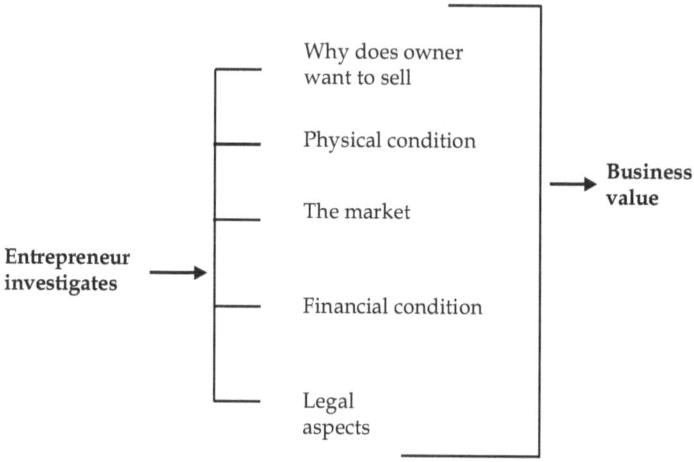

Factors to investigate when buying an existing firm

Disadvantages of Buying an Existing Business

There are also factors that may make an existing business unattractive as a purchase.

- The business may be offered for sale because it is losing money. The buyer of an existing business must be very careful to determine the truth of why the business is being sold. The reason the seller gives may not be the real reason.
- Customer, supplier, and creditor ill will, rather than good will, may have been established and may carry over to the new owner.
- The employees working in the firm may not be desirable employees, and it may be difficult to get rid of them because of unionization or other reasons. Also, firing undesirable employees often has an adverse effect on the morale of good employees in situations where they don't know what to expect when a new owner takes over the business.
- It may not be the best location for the business.

- The facilities may not be completely suited to the needs of the business. If remodeling is required, the cost may be excessive.
- Innovations in the business may be difficult owing to present facilities. For example, the size of the building may prevent the addition of new lines of products that would help sales.
- There may not be a business for sale of the type you are looking for in a given market, or it may cost an excessive amount of money to purchase.
- The equipment and inventory may be old, outdated, or in need of repair.

Starting a New Business

Starting a new business also has advantages and disadvantages. Starting a new business also requires extensive investigation and analysis if the business is to have the best chance of success.

Advantages of Starting a New Business

Factors that may make it attractive to start a new business rather than purchase an existing business are :

- Location is many times one of the most critical decisions for a business firm. It can be the difference between success and failure in many businesses. Often the only way to obtain the best location is to start a new business.
- Physical facilities can be constructed to conform to the most efficient use for the business planned. Existing buildings seldom can be arranged to provide the most efficient work flow possible, particularly in manufacturing firms, without having wasted space.
- Innovating in a new business is much easier than in an existing one because of physical limitations of the existing business.

- All phases of the new business can be established by the owner without having to change something as when buying an existing business.
- Existing business sometimes have ill will of some customers, suppliers, creditors, and employees. The existing business may also have an image (such as a price image that the new owner does not want. Starting anew business allows the entrepreneur to establish whatever image is desired.
- In many cases, there may not any business of the type that fit the capabilities of an entrepreneur. Consequently, the only alternative left is to start one.
- When purchasing an existing business. The buyer usually pays for the profitability of the firm. Sometimes a new firm can be established for less money and still realize the same profit.

Disadvantages of Starting a New Business

Factors that are understandable to start a new business rather than buy an existing business are

- There is a higher risk factor in starting a new business.
- It often takes considerable time and expenditures of for a new business to build its customer patronage.
- Funds are usually harder to obtain to start a new business to than buy an existing, successful firm.
- It usually takes time to work out the "bug" in a new business, both in facilities and procedures.
- Lines of credit and supply must be established.
- An existing business has sales, expenditures, and profit records to help project future profit. These must be estimated when starting a new business. This makes them much less accurate and dependable.

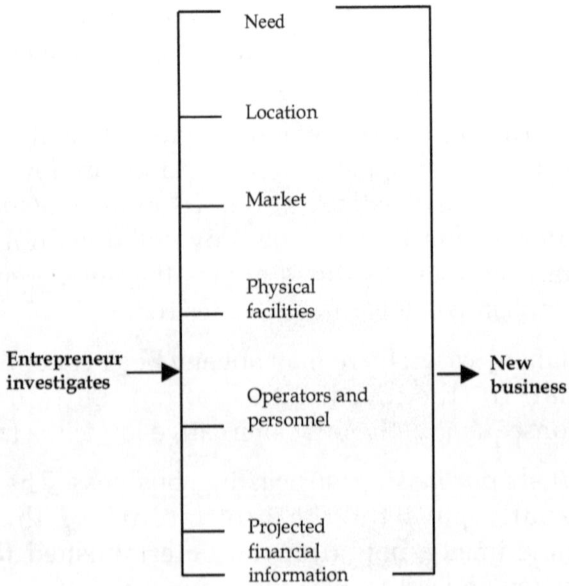

Factors to Investigate when starting a New Business

Project Investment Analysis

'Investment' refers to the addition of durable assets to a business. 'Financing' refers to the means of acquiring the control of assets by cash purchase, borrowing, leasing or custom hiring. Clearly, an investment can be financed in several ways and each may affect its profitability and risk.

Investments have Four Characteristics

- Point input and point output case e.g. inputs - production investment for crop
- Point input and continuous output case e.g. digging a well, land reclamation, land development
- Continuous input and point output case e.g. casuarina, eucalyptus, sheep, goat pig rearing
- Continuous input and continuous output case e.g. plantation crops, orchard crops, perennial crops

Steps in Investment Analysis

Investment or capital budgeting involves several steps:

- A search for profitable investment opportunities
- Determining the amount of capital required for each investment alternative
- A method of computing the cost of capital which takes into account the availability of funds
- A method of recognizing future cash flows and the time value of money
- Determining the criteria or methods to select the most profitable investment(s)

A Search for Profitable Investment Opportunities

Searching for profitable investment alternatives is an important and on going function of the farm manager. Some investment opportunities, such as the need to replace a tractor or a farm equipment item are obvious and require little search effort. Other investment opportunities may be less obvious, such as adopting new forms of technology. Farm investment opportunities generally include one of the following categories.

- Maintenance and replacement of depreciated capital items
- Adoption of cost reducing technology
- Expansion of output in existing enterprises, and
- Expansion in output through the addition of new enterprises

Determining the Capital Requirement

The cost of initial investment, operation and maintenance cost over economic life of capital constitute the capital requirement.

Computation of Cost of Capital

In capital budgeting analysis, using the income capitalization method, a discount rate which is the cost of capital, is selected. This discount rate is the farmer's required rate of return on investments. As such discount rate is the farmer's opportunity cost. That is, the cost of capital for any investment alternative is the rate that such capital can earn in its next best alternative use. Usually for convenience the interest rate offered by credit institutions (12%) is taken as discount rate.

Method for Recognizing Future Cash Flows and Time Value of Money

Concept Time Value of Money : Interest rate serves as the pricing mechanism for the time value of money. The rate of interest is considered as an exchange price between the present and future rupees. Thus rupee 1 today exchanges for (1 + i) rupees at the end of period one in future. Or alternatively a Rupee 1 payment made at the end of one period in the future exchanges for 1/(1 + i) rupees now.

Compounding is the process of finding future value of present amount.

Future value = PV x $(1 + \text{interest rate})^{\text{no. of conversion periods}}$

V_n = $V_0\,(1+i)^n$

PV = Present Value

$(1+i)^n$ = is the compounding factor (interest rate)

n = No.of years

The term $(1+i)^n$ can always be computed. However, the procedure becomes tedious for higher values of n. Fortunately, numerical results of such equations have been tabulated for wide ranging values of i and n.

Discounting is the process of finding the present value of future account.

$$\text{Present value} = \frac{\text{Future amount}}{(1 + \text{interest rate})^{\text{no of conversion periods}}}$$

$$V_O = \frac{V_n}{(1+i)^n} = V_n / (1+i)^{-n}$$

i = Interest rate (discount factor)

n = No.of years

The Effects of Time and Interest on Present and Future Values

The important variables determining present and future values of payments are:

- The number of conversion periods and
- The size of interest rate per compounding period.

Discounted Measures

In undiscounted measures of investment analysis, the time value of money is ignored but they are very important in ranking and choosing the alternate investments. In discounted measures of investment analysis the time value of money is taken care of.

- Net Present Worth or Value (NPV or NPW)
- Benefit Cost Ratio (BCR)
- Internal Rate of Return (IRR)

Discounting Factor

In calculation of net present worth or benefit cost ratio, discounting factor must be chosen prior to investment analysis. Usually the discounting factor used is the opportunity cost of capital. The bank rate given on long term deposit (12%) is usually chosen as the discount rate. The farmer instead of investing in the proposed investment can deposit in a bank and earn 12% of interest i.e., the proposed investment should earn more than bank interest rate.

Net Present Worth

$$NPW = \sum_{t=1}^{N} \left(\frac{B_t}{(1+i)^t} \right) - \sum_{t=1}^{n} \left(\frac{C_t}{(1+i)^t} \right)$$

This is simply the present worth of incremental net benefit or incremental cash flow stream. It is interpreted as the present worth of the income stream generated by an investment.

B_t = Benefit in year 't'   i = Discount factor

C_t = Cost in year 't'   N = No. of years

Selection Criterion

Accept all independent projects with a zero or greater net present worth when discounted at opportunity cost of capital. Ranking of acceptable alternate independent project is not possible with net present worth criterion because it is an absolute and not a relative measure. It is also the preferred selection criterion to choose among mutually exclusive projects.

Benefit Cost Ratio

This is the ratio of present worth of benefit stream to present worth of cost stream.

$$BCR = \frac{\sum_{t=1}^{N} \left(B_t (1+i)^{-1} \right)}{\sum_{t=1}^{N} \left(C_t (1+i)^{-1} \right)}$$

Selection criterion : Accept all independent projects with a benefit cost ratio of 1 or greater when the cost and benefit streams are discounted at opportunity cost of capital.

Internal Rate of Return

In NPW and BC ratio, market rate of interest is chosen. It differs from place to place. Internal rate of return is that discount rate that makes the net present worth of incremental net benefit equal to zero. In other words it is the maximum interest that an investment could pay for the resources used.

Selection criterion : Accept all independent projects having an internal rate of return equal to or greater than the opportunity cost of capital.

$$IRR \quad \sum_{t=1}^{N} \left(\frac{B_t}{(1+i)^t} \right) - \sum_{t=1}^{n} \left(\frac{C_t}{(1+i)^t} \right) = 0$$

<table>
<tr><td rowspan="2">LDR+ Difference between the two discount rates

X

IRR =</td><td>Present worth of incremental net benefit stream (cash flow) at lower discount rate</td></tr>
<tr><td>Absolute sum of the present value of cash flow at two discount rates(signs ignored)</td></tr>
</table>

IRR = Internal rate of return

LDR = Lower discount rate

Entrepreneurial Opportunities in Modern Agriculture

Farming (on Farm)	Product Marketing	Inputs Marketing	Processing	Facilitative
1. Crop	1.Wholesale	1.Ferilizer	1.Milk	1.Research and Development
2.Dairy/Poutry/Goat	2.Commission Agent	2.Agrl. Chemicals	2.Fruits	2.Marketing Informations
3.Fish	3.Retail	3.Seeds	3.vegetables	3.Quality control
4.Rabbit	4. Transport	4. Machineries	4.Paddy	4.Insurance
5.vegetables	5. Export	5.Animal feed	5.Sugarcane	5.Energy
6.Flowers	6.Finance	6.Poultry hatchery	6.Cashew	
7.Ornamental plants	7.Storage	7.Veterinary Medicines	7.Coir	
8.Palmrosa	8.Consultancy	8.Landscaping	8.Poutry	
9.Fodder		9.Agrl.credit	9.Cattle	
10.Sericultue		10.Custom service	10.Tannery	
11. Agro-forestry		11.Bio-control units	11.Brewery	
12. Beekeeping		12.Bio-tech units	12.Paper board	
13.Mushroom				

A Business Plan is a document where you plan your business to have an organized and effective response to a situation which may arise in future. Business plan is not just for a start up company but also for those which are growing. It is not only used to establish realistic goals or targets to achieve but also to determine the current position. A workable business plan is detailed below.

- Determine where the company needs to go
- Forewarn of possible roadblocks along the way
- Formulate responses to contingencies
- Keep the business on track to reach its planned goals

Start a business plan with describing your business and product or services. Tell about the market you are targeting and the stage of development your company is in. If you get stuck up on a particular part of the plan-leave it for time being-and come back later and finish it . You can not make a perfect first draft- so just get some thoughts down to start the process and you can always come back and change it or polish it up later. While making a business plan, keep the following points in mind.

i) Keep Target Audience in Your Mind

While writing your business plan, keep in mind the intended audience and why you are writing the plan. For example, if you are trying to get debt financing, emphasis should not be on the huge profit potential - but on the certainty that the debt can be repaid. If you are writing a plan to help you run the business better, you may start with general background information on the company and the industry, and focus on the areas of your plan that are currently most important to you.

ii) Strategy - Core of Your Business Plan

Basically, the first part of the business plan should be geared towards helping develop and support solid business strategy. The plan should explain the market, the industry, target customers and competitors. Write about customer needs and the benefits of current products and services. Evaluate the strengths and weaknesses of each competing firm and draw out the opportunities for your product or service in the market place. All of these steps largely aim to help you in creating a strategy for your business. The second half of the business plan should explain how to execute your selected business strategy. Your products and services, your marketing and operations should all closely tie in with your strategy. Have a strategy that will set the course for your business rather than having a smart-sounding strategy for your plan.

iii) Think Competitively Throughout Your Business Plan

In present competitive market, you would probably be facing some serious competition sooner or later no matter how unique your business idea is. You need to think competitively throughout your business plan. As an entrepreneur, you need to identify where you will do things in similar manner as your competitors, where you will do things differently, what will be your real strengths and real weaknesses, where will you create your niche. Focus your plan on being different than your competitors and compete with existing players less directly. Find a particular market niche to focus on. Think over these points. Can you find a unique strategy? Can you position your products differently? Can you use different sales or marketing vehicles? Your business plan should be able to answer these questions.

iv) Be Realistic with Your Business Plan

Lots of business plans sound, good on paper, but do not work in the real world market place. It is difficult to attract people to a new product or service, just because it is better. People or companies have established buying patterns and are currently doing business with someone else. To do business with you, it takes more than attracting them to your business. You have got to steal your customers from someone else's business and create your own base of loyal customers. It is possible that your competitors may launch new products or services or cut their prices to counter your entry in the current market. For a new start up company, it is easy to over estimate sales projections as it is easy to underestimate costs. There are always going to be some unseen expenditure, hefty amount of cost overruns, expensive problems, and items that you simply overlooked. So, forecast conservatively and try to have an extra cushion of cash tucked in reserve.

Tips on Creating Business Plans

People

In seeking fund from banks, venture capitalists or other outside investors, you will increase your chances of success if you get someone committed to your management team who at least has a recognizable name.

Alternately, you can include as exhibits to your plan any positive media clippings you can find, such as items from trade publications, about members of your management team. If you do not have any clippings, try contacting relevant publications to get media coverage-perhaps about your start-up business proposal.

Keep Your Business Plan Factual and Succinct

Try to keep the plan factual, do not use hyperbole or generalizations to describe the potential of your business plan. Use more factual information you present to reach their own conclusions. Keep it succinct. Don't put too much detail when creating plans. If a business plan is too long, it might be skimmed and focus on what is really important might be lost.

Involve Everyone

Involve / use expert opinion or key employees to create business plan. Then work with them until you are satisfied. Have key people get together to get the plan in synchronized fashion and to get any disagreements out in the open. The more input people have in creating the plan, the more responsibility they will feel toward it.

Key Terms

Business plan, target customers, strategy investment, capital requirement, cost of capital, time value of money, future value, discounting, present value, compounding, discount rate, net present value, benefit cost ratio, internal rate of return.

Chapter Summary

- A business plan is used to determine where the company need to so, fore warn of possible road blocks along the way, formulate responses to contingencies and keep the business in track to reach its planned goals.
- While preparing a business plan, the following points are to be considered; the intended audience to whom the plan is being prepared may be considered ; the business plan should be geared develop and support soild business strategy in the business plan, should be designed such that the entrepreneur overcomes the competition and business rivalry; and above all, the business plan should be workable and realistic.
- There are two ways to get the business started: a) buying an existing establishment and b) starting from scratch with a new firm. There are advantages and disadvantages in both the ways.
- Investment refers to the addition of durable assets to a business.

- Financing refers to the means of acquiring the control of assets by cash purchase, borrowing, leasing or custom hiring.
- Searching for profitable investment alternatives is an important and on going function of the farm manager.
- Compounding and discounting techniques are used investment analysis.
- Under discounted measures of investment analysis, Net Present Value (NPV), Benefits Cost Ratio (BCR) and Internal Rate of Return (IRR) are the three tools used to measure the financial feasibility of the projects.

Chapter Highlights

Meaning of business plan, points to be considered while making a business plan, tips on creating business plan, points to be considered while purchasing existing business, advantages and disadvantages to buying an existing business, advantages and disadvantages of starting new business, different types of investment, steps involved in project analysis, compounding and discounting techniques and entrepreneurial opportunities in modern agriculture have been discussed in this chapter.

Review Questions

1. Define Business plan.
2. What are the uses of a Business plan
3. Discuss the points to be kept in mind while preparing a Business plan
4. Explain the two ways for starting a business. What are the advantages and disadvantages of those two ways?
5. Define a) Investment b) Financing
6. What are the four different characteristics of investment?

7. What are the steps involved in investment analysis?
8. What are different categories of farm investment opportunities?
9. Explain the concept of time value of money
10. Explain the following discounting techniques used in investment analysis.
    a. Net Present Value (NPV)
    b. Benefit Cost Ratio (BCR)
    c. Internal Rate of Return (IRR)

    How the project cab be chosen based on the results of the above analysis ?
11. Explain the entrepreneurial opportunities available in modern agriculture.

References

Pickle.H.B. and R.L. Abrahamson.1990. Small Business Management (Fifth Edition), New York: John Wiley & Sons

REFERENCES

Baumback C.M. and K. Lawyer 1979 *How to Organize and Operate A Small Business,* New Jersey: Prentice hall, Inc.

Heller R. and T. Hindle 2000 *Essential Manager's Manual,* China: Colour library Direct Ltd.

Halles W.D. and R.T. Hubbard 1977 *Small Business Management: Planning and Operation,* New York: Van Nostrand Reinhold Company.

Justis R.T. 1981 *Managing Your Small Business,* New Jersey: Prentice Hall, Inc.

Jayaraman. R.1991. *Reading material for Entrepreneurship Development Programme for Women,* Prepared by Centre for Entrepreneur Development, Department of Entrepreneurship Studies (Faculty of Business Administration) Madurai Kamaraj Univerisity.

Lokanadhan.K.1996. Agricultural Business Management (Madurai: Department of Agricultural Economics, Agricultural College and Research Institute)

Lokanadhan. K. K. Mani. A. Pouchepparadjou and K.Chandran 1998. Agricultural Management: An introduction (Madurai: Department of Agricultural Economics, Agricultural College and Research Institute)

Murali.B.P, M. Doddamane and V.S. Sukumaran 2002, *Reading Material prepared for Faculty Development Programme in Entrepreneurship,* sponsored by National Science and Technology Entrepreneurship Development Board, Department of Science and Technology, Government of India and held at Entrepreneurship Development Institute of India, Bangalore from December 30th, 2002 to January 11th, 2003.

Pandberg.D.I. C.Ritson and L.M. Albisu (ed) 1997.Gro-food Marketing, New York: CAB International.

Branson. R.E. and D. G. Norvell.1983 Introduction to Agricultural Marketing, New York: McGraw-Hill Book Company.

Pickle.H.B. and R.L. Abrahamson 1990. *Small Business Management,* New York: John Wiley & Sons.

Philip Kotler 2003 *Marketing Management (Eleventh Edition),* New Delhi: Prentice Hall of India.

Raveendaran.N., S.D. Sivakumar, N.Ajjan, K.B. Chandran and K.Selvakumar 2002 *Reading material for Training on Establishing Agriclinics and Agribusiness Centres,* Department of Agricultural and Rural Management, Centre for Agricultural And Rural Development Studies, Tamil Nadu agricultural University, Coimbatore.

Rawlins. N.O. 1980 *Introduction to Agribusiness,* New Jersey: Prentice Hall, Inc.

Singh.N.2000 *Principles of Management: Theory, Practices and Techniques,* New Delhi: Deep & Deep Publications Pvt. Ltd.

Arora.K.C. 1998. *TQM and ISO 14000,* Delhi: S. K. Kataria & Sons: Publishers & Distributors.

www.nic.in

www.promarinternational.com/studiesforsale.html

SUBJECT INDEX

D

E

F

G

H

I

N

O

P

Q

R

S

T

FSC
www.fsc.org
MIX
Papier | Fördert
gute Waldnutzung
FSC® C083411

Kolibri 360 GmbH
Ferdinand-Jühlke-Straße 7
99095 Erfurt, Deutschland
produktsicherheit@kolibri360.de